The Half-Remembered Reality

The Half-Remembered Reality

An Exploration of Synchronicity and Parapsychology

Barbara Cook Loy

Entelechy Press publishes books devoted to the fulfillment of the Self. Coined by Aristotle, the term *entelechy* has come to mean a force propelling one to self-fulfillment. The soul, the world, the divine, each participates in the effort of actualization.
entelechypress.com

Cover and book design by Patrice Morris

ISBN 978-0-98223060-2

Library of Congress Control Number: 2009931729

Published in San Rafael, California, USA

Everything in the world is alive and animated. . . . But we can see mind only in forms analogous to ours. The most important thing is that we have no reason to consider our mind as the only and highest form existing in the universe.

The question stands thus: How can we learn about the existence of mind of other sections of the world, if they exist? By two methods: through communication . . . and by means of conclusions by analogy.

For the first . . . a change of our form of perception and representation is required.

The second may result from a gradual expansion of the faculty of drawing analogies. . . . In trying to look at things and ourselves from a new angle . . . in trying to liberate our thinking from the customary partitions of time and space, we gradually begin to notice analogies between things, where previously we had seen nothing at all. Our mind grows, and with it grows the capacity of drawing analogies. . . . And then . . . we suddenly notice around us a mental life the existence of which we never suspected before. And we understand why we could not see it before. It lies on another plane, not on the plane on which our mental life had previously existed. In this way precisely this capacity of drawing new analogies is the beginning of changes which lead us to another plane of being.

—P. D. Ouspensky, *Tertium Organum*

CONTENTS

FOREWORD

Though we ordinarily believe that we experience the world objectively, we may sometimes witness events that challenge our preconceptions and call us to a deeper examination of ourselves and our right relation to the world. Consider these examples:

- A mother awakens at dawn from a dream that her son is coming to visit. Stirred from her bed, she goes to her front door and is astonished to see his car cresting toward her over a distant hill.

- On a whim, a welder travels half an hour across town in rush-hour traffic to visit to a friend's job site, only to discover the friend half dead, buried up to his ankles in a ditch beneath a caved-in mountain of earth. After the friend is revived, the welder is surprised to learn that his friend's last thought—about half an hour before—was of him.

- A woman resting in a peaceful, open area on a mountainside is suddenly overcome with mortal terror. Finding no danger but unable to calm herself, she leaves the area. A week later, she is shocked to read in the newspaper that an airplane has just crashed near that spot.

- One afternoon, a young woman suddenly feels drawn to retrieve old letters from a long-lost love from her attic. As she begins to read them, his figure appears before her, pleading for forgiveness, which she grants. The next day she is startled to see his obituary in the newspaper and to learn that he had died the day before.

The events described in these stories might seem like miracles. But Barbara Cook Loy says, "It is not that God intervenes in miraculous ways to upset the natural order, but rather that the natural order reveals itself as far richer and more mysterious than we have allowed ourselves to think." In *The Half-Remembered Reality,* Cook Loy helps us to a much more meaningful way of thinking about such mysteries.

The parapsychological phenomena illustrated in these stories are scientifically inconvenient, to say the least, given their anecdotal nature and apparent violations of causality. Because of this inconvenience, parapsychology has remained a subject on the fringes of science. However, Socrates' dictum "Know thyself" makes no exception for explanatory inconvenience. Such phenomena have been reported in many cultures around the world at least since biblical times, and reports continue in the modern era. If such things physically occur, should we not strive to understand them? And even if they are limited to our imagination, should we not still seek to understand better the nature of the human mind that can conceive of such remarkable things? There are no good reasons to ignore them, only bad ones, such as dogmatic aversion.

But if we deign to consider parapsychological phenomena at all, we are most likely to resort to naïve fictions to explain them. We rely on many such fictions on a daily basis. For example, we still allow ourselves to use locutions like "sunrise" because, to our eyes, the sun appears to move while the earth does not, even though, thanks to Copernicus, we now know that this is but an illusion. Similarly, efforts to "explain" the parapsychological phenomena in these stories by reducing them to strictly physical forms—such as some kind of resonance, transmission, or signaling systems—lead to the same kinds of contradictions as did our naïve concepts of "sunrise" and "sunset," because they marginalize what is most central to these phenomena: the psyche. Just as it is easier for us to conceive of "sunset" than to think in terms of the earth's rotation, so it is easier for us to imagine purely physical explanations for what are clearly not simply physical phenomena. What is needed to rectify this unsatisfactory situation is the equivalent of a Copernican revolution for parapsychology.

It was into this explanatory vacuum that Carl Jung introduced his concept of synchronicity as a way to frame the intersection of objective events and their subjective meaning. Jung referred to synchronicity as the "acausal orderedness" that underlies the relationship between events and their significance or meaning to an observer. Barbara Cook Loy's major premise is that synchronicity can usefully guide and inform an exploration of parapsychology.

Jung himself applied his concept of synchronicity to astrology, to the oracular Chinese text the I Ching, and to parapsychology, among other subjects. In astrology, he treated synchronicity as the coincidence of planetary alignments with their significance to human history and individual character. In 1950, in the foreword to the Wilhelm-Baynes translation of the I Ching, Jung treated synchronicity as the coincidence of a random coin toss with a particular oracular reading from the I Ching text. Jung's seminal work has been taken up by subsequent generations of researchers. For example, Stanislav Grof, a pioneer in the field of transpersonal psychology, has applied synchronicity to the study of non-ordinary realities. Jung's work on synchronicity as it relates to astrology has been further developed by Richard Tarnas. In *The Half-Remembered Reality,* Barbara Cook Loy extends Jung's study of synchronicity as it relates to parapsychology, achieving a new synthesis of his ideas.

In essence Cook Loy asks, What are the parameters implied by synchronicity that govern the relation of physical events to their associated meaning? What are the boundaries of this relation, and how can these boundaries be used to understand parapsychological phenomena? Because the synchronistic relation between meaning and physical event is acausal by definition, there are no causal restrictions on these relations. Thus, she says, synchronicity provides an appropriate framework for the study of parapsychological phenomena such as clairvoyance and telekinesis because it compactly supports all the necessary degrees of freedom presented to our experience by these phenomena.

Using the framework of synchronicity, Cook Loy presents a reasoned and fearless investigation into the structure of our deepest subjective landscape, proposing a model of mind and consciousness that amplifies Jung's concept of synchronicity to encompass parapsychology. Completed in her ninetieth year, after a labor of a quarter century, drawing on a lifetime of experience as a psychotherapist, this book represents the culmination of her life's work as a healer and scholar of the soul.

Working from antecedents such as Leibniz's preestablished harmony, the Perennial Philosophy of Aldous Huxley, the epistemology of Alfred North

Whitehead, Kant's a priori categories, and the psychology of C. G. Jung, Cook Loy shows how the mind can encompass and envision logic and reason, as well as dreams, clairvoyance, telepathy, precognition, and other parapsychological phenomena. Her treatment of the paranormal aspects of the psyche is especially notable for taking a nonpathological view. Her perspective honors and reveals the true breadth of the psyche.

Cook Loy's patient and careful development of synchronicity is itself worth the price of the book. Synchronicity theory is a slippery subject, conditioned as we are to viewing everything in causal terms. But just as mathematics achieved a new level of expressive power and integration with the invention of complex numbers—by coupling a real and an imaginary number—so we gain expressive advantage through synchronicity theory because of the way it couples outer events and their inner significance. Just as the real and imaginary parts of a complex number must be joined but kept distinct, so too the physical events and the associated meanings of a synchronicity must be joined but kept distinct. In this way, synchronicity theory establishes a "meaning field" containing both physical and psychic dimensions.

The concept of a meaning field harkens back to the correspondence theory of the ancients, Aristotle's entelechy, the noumenal realm of Kant, the geographical parallelism proposed by Schopenhauer, and Jung's psychoid archetype. From these antecedents, Cook Loy develops the notion of the meaning field as a matrix from which synchronicities arise, unifying psychic and physical realities. From this perspective, we can better understand the shock felt by the people in the stories told above: their synchronistic experiences revealed to them powerful and personal evidence of the deep interconnectedness of the psychic and physical realms. Cook Loy says, "There are happenings in our visible world that fall outside the categories of space, time, and causality, but that, having meaning, . . . seem to call for rational explanation and to be attributable to a quality of 'mindfulness' in the universe itself. Though approached through our subjectivity, the meaning has its own being, its own objectivity. It works through us, but not by us."

Her decades as a psychotherapist and her extensive training at the Jung Institute in Los Angeles have grounded Cook Loy in the theory and practice of depth psychology. Like other sciences, depth psychology strives to adapt the agenda of the Enlightenment—to extend rationality ever more deeply into nature—to reveal a more comprehensive understanding of the psyche and its proper relation to the world. With its marriage of human passion and critical inquiry, depth psychology seeks to advance our knowledge of the underpinnings of consciousness. But there have been some notable instances in history where the Enlightenment agenda has paradoxically resulted in the discovery of the limits of epistemology. For example, in physics, Henri Poincaré dashed our hopes of ever being able to predict with a probability better than chance the future of such simple dynamical systems as the interaction of three gravitational bodies, even if we know the initial conditions of the system to an infinite degree of precision. In logic, Kurt Gödel demonstrated that even trivial representational systems such as arithmetic contain fundamental contradictions.

Similarly, psychologists found that the very psychic structures they studied were, like the Labyrinth of the Minotaur, recursive and unbounded, and that some important fields of study—myth, dreams, creativity, psychopathology, parapsychology, and so forth—would overthrow the very Enlightenment perspective from which they were to be examined. While Jung's concept of synchronicity indicated a promising way forward, it did not pave the way because it implied that the Enlightenment perspective—with its sharply distinguished notions of subject and object—was itself an obstacle. Likewise, quantum physicist David Bohm's concept of implicate order denies the tenability of decoupling thought from reality. The thread connecting the ideas of Jung and Bohm is that consciousness and matter share a common ground. Building on their work, Cook Loy follows synchronicity much as Theseus followed Ariadne's thread—wherever it leads.

Her exploration can be unsettling at times, as when she discusses cases of precognition, apparitions, and out-of-body experiences. She reminds us that a phenomenon may appear to be paranormal only with respect to our theories, not with respect to reality itself, which remains the ultimate arbiter of what may exist. Her primary concern is understanding the nature of mind and cosmos that can support the existence of these phenomena. She takes the broadest perspective in her quest to understand and identify how mind stands in relation to world. This means she also grapples with spirituality and examines the beliefs held in different cultures about spirits, those "powers or intelligent energies in the universe that stand over and above our ego position and yet understand and are involved with our personal concerns."

If in places the reader senses an uncritical flavor in her treatment of parapsychology, Cook Loy is unapologetic, insisting, "We must let go of some of the categories of the conscious mind in order to free ourselves to apprehend a deeper reality." Of this deeper reality she says, "Our own psychic depths could be assumed to derive from them, forming a concentrate of them as a fish forms a concentrate of the potencies of the sea." She concludes one chapter this way: "In synchronicities we discover a mysterious kind of activity in the world that happens at the very margins of our consciousness, like a strange sound in the night that stops as we come to wakefulness. What was that? we want to say. Does it suggest the presence of something unknown that we almost recognize from out of the past? Some half-remembered reality?"

This important work comes as the philosophy of science is grappling with the role of the observer and the limits of objectivity in scientific research. Likewise, modern religions are gradually awakening to the necessity of a common understanding of the terrain of the soul. In addressing these questions, Cook Loy's original and insightful exploration of parapsychology and synchronicity amply demonstrates that both the world and the psyche are indeed "far richer and more mysterious than we have allowed ourselves to think."

—Gareth Loy

PROLOGUE

Synchronicity and depth psychology have always had a very long common border. At the beginning of the twentieth century, when depth psychology was just emerging through work with dreams, and synchronicity was still unknown, that border was not well defined, and there were frequent forays back and forth from either side. Parapsychology was still known as the "occult," and psychologists were concerned to distance themselves from it to ensure that their image was not contaminated by notions and experiments inspired by that side. Nearly all parapsychologists were still doing "psychic research" and trying very hard to be scientifically acceptable. Unfortunately, no matter how hard they tried, they were still branded with the hot iron of the occult.

That Jung was risking his reputation is implied in a letter to him from Freud written in May 1911, when Freud was still taking the role of the indulgent father toward his younger colleague:

> I know that your deepest inclinations are impelling you toward a study of the occult, and do not doubt that you will return home with a rich cargo. There is no stopping that, and it is always right for a person to follow the biddings of his own impulses. The reputation you have won with your *Dementia* will stand against the charge of "mystic" for quite a while. Only don't stay too long away from us in those lush tropical colonies; it is necessary to govern at home.[1]

Actually Jung took a very cautious approach. Although Freud thought him strongly impelled toward the occult in 1911, Jung did not publish on the subject until 1952 in an essay on synchronicity.[2] And he was careful to publish this groundbreaking work alongside an essay by Professor Wolfgang Pauli, whose credentials as a physicist were of the highest order. In this way, Jung wrapped himself in the mantle of science as he ventured across the border to write of the occult. Jung has always been given credit (rightly) for having an open mind on the occult, which he mentions frequently in his writing, but he was well aware of its ill repute in many quarters.

Meanwhile, a number of prominent physicists had associated themselves with the revival of interest in the paranormal that occurred with the founding of the Society for Psychical Research in London in 1882. This early interest gradually narrowed to a select few and never developed strongly in the United States. The rift between scientists who were open and those who were opposed to psychical research was reminiscent of one that had developed in the time of Galileo some three hundred years before. By directing his telescope at Jupiter, Galileo had discovered four of the planet's twelve moons, a discovery that threatened the cosmology of many churchmen of the time. A number of them had refused even to look through Galileo's telescope, an act of willful omission that scientists have never forgotten nor forgiven. Now the shoe was on the other foot. Would the scientists look at the accumulated evidence showing that paranormal events actually happen and in fact have happened for thousands of years?

Today this rift has weakened, and there is much interest in parapsychology and synchronicity, particularly among the younger physicists. Jung in his essay on synchronicity seems to take the view that all parapsychological events are synchronistic, hence acausal. If true, this would solve a great many problems by moving these phenomena outside the embrace of physics, which generally insists upon a causal approach. It is not certain, however, that Jung was right and that all parapsychological events can be described as synchronistic. The discussion continues on a new level. This book is a contribution to the discussion from the side of depth psychology.

CHAPTER I

The Analogy as a Key to the Mystery of Healing

Reflections on a Theme of C. G. Jung

O Nature, and O soul of man! How far beyond all utterances are your linked analogies! Not the smallest atom stirs or lives on matter, but has its cunning duplicate in mind!

—Ahab, in Melville's *Moby Dick*

My patient, a bright but stubborn young woman of twenty-eight, had reached a stalemate. Sitting across from me with pursed lips, she eyed me resentfully and refused to utter a single word. The total amount of her verbal participation that day had been to say that she would not have come at all except that a friend had told her that when you are angry at your therapist, you should come in and have it out.

She had lost her job some four months before and had fallen into a severe regression, which looked to me like an uncontrollable retreat into the embryonic state. Throughout the summer, she had been in a passive-aggressive condition, refusing to get a job, rejecting every suggestion I made, and blaming me for her depression. But I noted to myself that, in spite of her passive-aggressive stance, she had heeded her friend's advice and had shown up for our session, indicating, perhaps, a silent plea for help. With matters at the crisis point, I decided to risk a deeper intervention, and I resorted to the following analogy.

I told her that I would try to describe her situation with the aid of a story, for I saw her caught in the archetype shown in the myth of Achilles. I then related in great detail the story of Achilles stubbornly sitting in his tent, refusing to join the battle during the Trojan War after King Agamemnon took his woman, Briseis, away from him. I described how the war was being lost and how his dearest friend Patroclus borrowed Achilles' armor to try to stop the Trojan advance. Only when they brought back the body of his friend, killed on the battlefield, was Achilles stung into action. I explained to my patient that I saw her following this same pattern, and I wondered whether she, like Achilles, would wait for something like a disaster to jar her out of her inactivity, or whether she would get into action earlier, realizing that there could be no payoff in her present attitude.

Although initially still defensive, my patient began to respond and within two weeks had made significant progress. She moved from a phase of pre-therapy into serious work.

The use of the mythological analogy made it possible to convert the crisis into a positive experience and brought an added increment of consciousness to the patient. By using analogy, I avoided direct confrontation, which probably would have brought down more angry libido on my head. The myth indirectly but unmistakably showed the nature of the pattern at work and the probable outcome, and placed it in a universal context as a trait that could grip heroes as well as resentful young women. From this position, the patient's energies, previously focused on blaming me, could move into new channels.

Later I saw that I had applied the time-honored method of mythological amplification not to the patient's dream imagery but to her whole condition as she presented herself. That condition called forth—indeed, demanded—a response from me. That I responded by the use of an analogy was not surprising, given our regular use of mythological analogies to provide the archetypal context of dreams. But as I considered the encounter from the standpoint of the analogy, I found myself giving renewed thought to what Jung calls the "overwhelming importance of the little word *like*," the basic principle of homeopathic medicine.

It occurred to me that I might be able to make far more conscious and discriminating use of the analogy than I had previously done. In this way I would be able to walk round and round a given aspect of the process of inner change, never fully comprehending, but always turning up different facets in a kind of appreciative and growing intimacy.

Unraveling the Nature of the Analogy

A close reading of Jung's *Collected Works* reveals numerous references to the analogy, many of them made in passing while other issues are pursued. Taken together, these references throw an interesting light on the development of thought in the history of culture as well as in the process of personal growth and healing. It is not too much to say that some of the deepest secrets of the art of psychological healing are hinted at in these paragraphs. Consider the following, from one of Jung's earlier works:

> A positively overwhelming importance attaches to the little word 'like' in the history of human thought. One can easily imagine that the canalization of libido into analogy-making was responsible for some of the most important discoveries ever made by primitive man.[1]

And, in truth, not merely primitive man. Modern man, too, turns to the analogy for advances beyond his present ways of thought. New fields of exploration have been opened and new possibilities of relationship suggested through analogical reasoning. One whole branch of psychology, behaviorism, drew its understanding of the scientific method by analogy with the objective, experimentally verifiable approach of nineteenth-century physics. Similar applications of analogical reasoning have occurred in connection with many other scientific discoveries. For example, the new science of political economy was led to consider the circulation of money through the economy by analogy with Harvey's discovery of the circulation of the blood. In physics, Niels Bohr's early description of the interior of the atom was made by analogy with the solar system: the electrons orbited around the nucleus of the atom as the planets orbited around the sun.

Folk wisdom frequently uses this method. A locomotive was originally an "iron horse"; an automobile was a "horseless carriage." Radio was at first a "wireless," and one who flies is still an aviator, from the Latin *avis,* meaning bird. People liken the new technological marvel to the old, and so familiarize themselves with it. The analogy enables us to move stepwise from the old to the new with reduced anxiety and uncertainty. It is an invaluable tool for integrating new insights.

Originally derived from the realm of mathematics, the analogy expresses an equality of ratio or proportion. Already in Plato the idea of proportion was extended to relationship generally; the word expresses an equivalency or likeness of relations with regard to some circumstance or effect. Analogies are often expressed in the form of a proportion, as when it is said, "Knowledge is to the mind what light is to the eye." Analogical reasoning assumes that the same law that operates in one case will operate in another when there is a certain resemblance between the things compared. Correct use of the analogy means that the differences as well as the likenesses of the things compared must be brought out; only in this way can the worth of the analogy be tested.

An analogy is not an example. If we say, "Like all carnivores, the lion is aggressive and dangerous," we have not made an analogy, for the lion is merely a subclass of the larger class of carnivorous animals, all having the same general characteristics. Nor is the simile an analogy; "Like the desert wind at sundown, the lion leaps on its prey." It is precisely the virtue of the analogy to unite the same and the different. (Sameness is comforting, but difference gives life its smack and bite.)

Analogy and Proportion

An analogy uses symbols to convey that the relation of A to B is the same as the relation of C to D. The formula for the analogy is the same as the formula for a proportion. Analogies can be varied and expanded in many interesting ways. The expression "A is to B as C is to D" can also be written

2 : 4 :: 3 : 6.

It can become

A : C :: B : D (Alternation)

or

B : A :: D : C (Inversion)

or

BC = AD and A/B = C/D

or

A : B : C : D :: E : F : G : H (Expansion)

or

A : B :: C : D :: E : F :: G : H.

By the time we have expanded the analogy in the ways shown, we have a matrix or arrangement in which the terms are analogically related to each other:

A	B	C	D
E	F	G	H

From this we can move on to a conceptual matrix, and it becomes clear how analogy, metaphor, and simile are linked:

Tree	Soil
Tribe	Tradition
Tolstoy	Russia

The analogies are obvious in both the rows and the columns: A tree is to its soil as a tribe is to its tradition, and as Tolstoy was to Russia.

Tree : Tribe : Tolstoy :: Soil : Tradition : Russia.

If we say that "Tolstoy was a tree," our metaphor will be neither convincing nor expressive. But if we embroider it a bit and say, "Tolstoy was the great old oak of Russia," we will convey something significant about the man. We may accordingly revise our matrix, substituting "oak" for "tree." The symbolic approach allows for this, where the oak can stand or substitute for all trees. We can then shift easily to a simile: "Tolstoy stands like a great old oak upon the soil of Russia." Other imagery flows out of the same matrix: a tribe removed from its ancient traditions is like an oak uprooted from its native soil.

It is undoubtedly in this poetic spirit of shared likeness that we can understand the dawn-age names of tribe and clan: the members of the bear clan participated in the ways of life of the bear; its members could say truthfully, "We are bears." The members of a modern football team say the same thing.

Such linguistic devices bring forward a processual perspective that focuses on the changing nature of things, how they flow and melt and merge into each other, how they interact in relation to each other. Because it is a perspective that removes us from the thing-oriented ways of thinking that our language tends to foster, it tends toward wholeness rather than division. It restores imagination to the thinking faculty and brings out the likeness between apparently disparate elements.

The analogy moves toward imaginative and associative thinking processes as well as proportional, mathematical, and logical ways of thought. Analogy in the service of psychology could become the bridge connecting two modes of discourse that have become so estranged—the literary and the scientific. Analogy by its very nature links or relates realms of experience that tend to be separated by the divisive nature of strictly analytical or deductive modes of thought. If certain writers are correct, it may be a way of thinking more congenial to the feminine nature, which tends toward relatedness rather than discrimination and fragmentation.[2]

The word *healing*—whole-making—is used to include an entire range of psychological growth processes. Sometimes healing is represented by the achievement of a new and higher level of consciousness, sometimes to a change of behavior in the direction of finer adaptation. For many, especially the young, it may require the breaking through of an impasse that has blocked growth and the assumption of the responsibilities that go with increasing maturity. What is to be emphasized is that healing refers to a *set of processes* and not to a completed state. Disease is a process going on in the body, not a thing or an entity. As a process—a flowing, changing, repetitive movement—its course can be altered. A change that brings about a renewal of harmony is what we know as healing. A disease process may be cured (altered) by another process that is similar (analogically related), though not identical. We will pursue this in the next chapter.

We are involved, then, at the interface between the realm of words and the realm of lived experience, where our words must speak truth or be congruent with reality, lest we lose our reason, our health, our good spirits and zest for life. We are journeying between philosophy (particularly epistemology, the theory of the method and grounds of knowledge) and depth psychology, which aims to restore mental health as well as to develop the higher mental faculties. At these in-between areas, we reach to the fundaments of our knowledge, and, if well guided, arrive at new insights.

Our immediate concern, however, will be with the analogical aspect of dreams, since it is through attention to dreams that we (following Jung) hope to reach toward higher consciousness.

The Analogical Nature of Dreams

Jung's views on the analogical nature of dreams are given in his early writing where he discusses the handling of dreams involving sexuality, and particularly the motif of incest. As an example he offers the dream of a young man:

> I was going up a flight of stairs with my mother and sister. When we reached the top I was told that my sister was going to have a baby.[3]

Freud would interpret this dream as a repressed wish for incestuous activity. The stairs are well known as a veiled reference to the sexual act on account of the rhythmic climbing, while the baby the sister is expecting would have to be the logical outcome of the incest. Jung offers a quite different view.

The patient was a young man who had recently completed his university degree but had not been able to choose a career. Instead, he gave up and became neurotic. His associations to the dream suggested that it dealt with this issue. To *mother,* he associated something long neglected: "My work," he confessed with embarrassment. To *sister,* he associated the idea of love of a woman, the meaning of which he had come to recognize as he kissed her goodbye. To *stairs,* he associated climbing—getting to the top. To *baby,* he associated newborn—becoming a new man. Clearly then, the dream had to do with the patient's discomfort at having neglected his responsibility to choose a profession, climb toward success, and claim the right to a new birth and the love of a woman. It was an analogical depiction of the real-life problem confronting him, and had nothing to do with incest.

The Prospective Function of the Analogy

Jung understands the analogical nature of dreams as they arise out of the unconscious to be similar to the activity of consciousness as it confronts the issues of life. "We try to grasp the unknown future on the model of our experience in the past. . . . Whenever we wish to assimilate something unknown, we do so by means of analogy. This is the way we always recognize things, and it is also the essential reason for the existence of symbolism; it is a process of comprehension by means of analogy."[4] The dream is a subliminal process of comprehension by analogy. Seen in this way, the dream has an exploratory or prospective function, enabling the dreamer to mobilize past experiences to aid in the advance toward the future.

The unconscious, Jung is saying, makes use of the same techniques as consciousness to find answers to life problems whose solutions are, by definition, unknown. The whole psyche, conscious and unconscious, gathers itself and coalesces around the questions, the conflicts, and the challenges that confront the individual as she moves through life. The psyche is not merely reactive, but brings its own unique attributes to bear on the questions of life. One sign of increased self-knowledge is seen when the individual recognizes a new problem as being *like* one she has confronted before; this means that she has begun to become aware of the patterns that govern her life and can now take more responsibility for them.

The importance of the prospective function of the analogy and the way this may lead to a redirection of the life energies is shown by Jung in his *Two Essays on Analytical Psychology*,[5] where he describes the case of a young homosexual man whose analysis begins with two significant dreams in which he finds himself in a great cathedral. Jung notices that the young man's problem derives from a strong tie to the mother, and that even in childhood he was fascinated by the image of Cologne Cathedral and aspired to be a priest in such a great church. Since the life task requires that the growing boy eventually break the tie to the mother, "the developing personality naturally veers away from such an unconscious infantile bond. . . . Instinct seizes on the first opportunity to replace the mother by another object. If it is to be a real mother-substitute, this object must be, in some sense, an analogy of her. . . ." The church provided such an analogy for the young boy, because the church, says Jung, is in the fullest sense a mother.

> The intensity with which his childish fantasy seized upon the symbol of Cologne Cathedral corresponds to the strength of his unconscious need to find a substitute for the mother. . . . We naturally think that a man must have known this meaning consciously before it could get to work in his fantasy, and that an unknowing child could not possibly be affected by such significations. Such analogies certainly do not work by way of the conscious mind, but in quite another manner.[6]

Here it is as if instinct itself has the power to use the analogical method: consciously the growing boy was powerfully drawn to the image of the cathedral, but at a level far deeper than his conscious awareness, a path was being opened by which he might eventually move beyond the "life-crippling tie to the mother." It is the patient's attraction to the analogical substitute for the mother that enables his life energies to move forward. Jung speaks of a "libido analogue . . . an idea that can give equivalent expression to the libido and canalize it into a form different from the original one."[7]

The patient's dream reveals the hidden groping of the life force, using the analogical stepping stone of the church, toward a new level of life. Or, to use a more organic image, it is as though the image of the cathedral offers a support for the budding tendrils of the creative life urge, tendrils that would otherwise sweep out sightlessly into the emptiness of space. The life force unconsciously reconnoiters by way of the analogy—or perhaps we should say that the flowing of the life force becomes visible to us through the lens of symbol and analogy as revealed over time in dreams. The libido seldom makes a leap out toward the wholly new or strange but moves stepwise along a path whose antecedents can be traced among earlier life patterns.

Analogy as Gradient

The above is so important to the issue of growth and healing that I wish to emphasize it. The *libido requires a gradient,* and not just any gradient will do. Jung says, "Psychic energy is a very fastidious thing which insists on fulfillment of its own conditions. However much energy may be present, we cannot make it serviceable until we have succeeded in finding the right gradient."[8] The right channel has to be one toward which some inner tendency of the organism is attracted, otherwise there will be no movement—which is the reason why the "good suggestions" of friends and therapists seldom work. It is also the reason why the image of the cathedral is valuable in Jung's case. The right gradient will often be represented by a goal analogically related to the earlier life tendency—the same and yet different.

Certain bodily reparative processes are possible only at the embryological level of complex organisms or among very primitive organisms, before cell differentiation has progressed very far. It is as if, when organisms pass a certain threshold of complexity and cell differentiation is quite advanced, the spontaneous reparative process is sacrificed in favor of other life possibilities. In the same way we find that certain reparative processes of a psychic nature can occur only at very primitive levels, requiring a deep and intensely painful regression on the part of the patient. One who has taken a wrong turn may be required to go back to the crossroads to find the right way. Such a crisis of growth is a humbling experience that can lead to new life, provided the individual perseveres at the required life task.

The dream process can offer new understandings of developmental processes on all levels. The growth of the human organism, even at the embryological state, may be accompanied by the flickering of a dreamlike inner process in which further goals are symbolically anticipated. Certain dreams, particularly in childhood, contain echoes of this goal-oriented activity, with mind and body working in concert throughout the life trajectory.

The continuity of the biological and the behavioral, the physical and the psychic, is suggested here. What is significant at both levels is the strength of the impulse that presses toward health and wholeness as opposed to sickness and deformity. Even in cases where the life urge seems utterly lost and the patient is in a suicidal state, one may regularly see in dreams the slow mobilizing of the forces needed to overcome the hiatus. If such indicators are not present, the prognosis is poor. All healing techniques, whether of mind or body, depend upon this innate drive for healing and wholeness. The healer's task at either level is clearly one of cooperating with the patient's own drive toward growth and development.

The Orientating Function of Analogy

The life force is characterized by an inner dynamism—it explores, compares, and imaginatively tests out possible lines of conduct. All the methods by which consciousness orients itself, makes choices, and pursues its goals are found at unconscious levels, and it may be assumed that the conscious methods are derived from these hidden roots. Two things can be said about this. One is that as long as the therapist is aware of a creative striving of the patient's libido as pictured by the dreams, the healing process can proceed along the gradient opened up in the dreams, cooperating with the subterranean movement already proceeding in the unconscious. The dream offers a window into the unfolding of that process, both in its universal and particular aspects.

The second point to be made here is that the function of *orientation* is a fundamental life process—indeed, it is not too much to speak of it as the very hallmark of sanity. We speak of the patient threatened with psychosis as, first of all, *dis*oriented. That a function so basic goes on at a deeper level than the conscious should not surprise us. That orientation can be achieved by way of analogy-making may be seen even in the case of panic-stricken patients who feel themselves overwhelmed by mental states utterly foreign to anything in their previous experience. At such a time the terrorized application of a destructive analogy can lead to further disorganization, while a healing analogy may lead to renewed stability.

It is necessary to add here, however, that the analogy thrown up by the unconscious may be so far from the patient's conscious standpoint that it can serve to orient only the therapist and not the patient, until the latter has gone through a difficult process of self-recognition. Sometimes the clearing of an analogical path has already proceeded a long way in the unconscious of the patient before it comes to consciousness. The conscious recognition of the pathway is accompanied by a sense of joy and release: "Now, at last, I know where I'm going!" These feelings, of course, do not guarantee that the path chosen will be in the best interests of the patient in the long run, but only that the stasis of life has been broken through. An impulsive person may be drawn into premature action; in some dismay, the therapist may observe the patient heading out with all sails flying into an affair that can only end in disaster. Marriage on the rebound is an example, where the new partner is clearly an analogical substitute for the lost love. If the patient has not yet come to understand the unconscious demands and expectations he places on the woman in his life, his solution may be premature. However, in cases where the necessary gain in consciousness has been made, a person may be carried over a lifelong barrier by a powerful thrust of energy. It becomes clear that within the apparent blockage of life was a slow gathering of forces destined to carry the individual to a new level. Sometimes quite surprising avenues of life involvement are discovered, and the patient, his sense of orientation restored, moves toward self-direction at higher levels of consciousness.

Dream Truths

Because dreams are often so fantastic and confusing, it is appropriate to ask to what extent the analogies appearing in dreams can be relied upon. This query will lead to an examination of some of the basic assumptions with which we approach the dream level of reality. Jung makes the reasonable suggestion that the unconscious cannot lie; it is simply nature speaking. The dream as it presents itself is a fact of nature like a tree, a rock, or a mountain stream. It is nature in her elemental symbolizing mode, nature mirroring nature. If we pause to contemplate it, we are bound to find it a remarkable thing, not explained by any current scientific theories, that nature not only acts, but in living creatures accompanies her activity with an intelligible pictorial record. The question of truth arises only when we try to comprehend and interpret the dream's meaning. Our particular preconceptions will determine what we take to be the meaning of the dream, but if approached with no reference points at all, it will probably be unintelligible.

Jung compares his method of dream interpretation to the ancient practice of hermeneutics, as applied to sacred texts.

> The essence of hermeneutics, an art widely practiced in former times, consists in adding further analogies to the one already supplied by the symbol: in the first place subjective analogies produced at random by the patient, then objective analogies provided by the analyst out of his general knowledge. This procedure widens and enriches the initial symbol, and the final outcome is an infinitely complex and variegated picture. . . .[9]

If the dream offers an encapsulated analogical commentary on the dreamer's life situation, and if we come to its meaning by a reverse process of analogical hermeneutics, it might be said that we unravel by our art what was previously raveled by nature herself. For if the dream is nature speaking, then by our unraveling we are, as it were, decoding the secret language of nature, a language of mysterious beauty and evocative power. Dreams are frequently revelatory, which is why the same technique that is used on scripture may be applied to the dream. A volume (rather than a note) of caution, however, must be advised. In no other arena of life do we have to be more aware of the effect of our presuppositions in limiting and directing what we can learn.

To what extent is the dream process influenced by consciousness and, particularly, by the accumulation of insight? Clearly there is such an influence; dreams that come after months of therapeutic work differ radically from those arising at the beginning of therapy. Insofar as insights affect the dream process over a period of time, it can no longer be said that nature is speaking in utter spontaneity, for it is now nature subjected to conscious influences. As fear of the unconscious diminishes, consciousness becomes open to the dreams, and influences move in both directions. What we seem to see is a dialogic relationship developing between the two levels, each in turn modified by the encounter.

On the question of rightness, Jung states:

> There is no science on earth by which these lines [of psychological development] could be proved "right"; on the contrary, rationalism could very easily prove that they are wrong. Their validity is proved by their intense value for life. And that is what matters in practical treatment: that human beings should get a hold on their own lives, not that the principles by which they live should be proved rationally to be "right."[10]

Jung's pragmatic test of truth, while immensely convincing to both therapist and patient, may not convince the philosophically minded critic. The test of truth is generally taken, even by highly evolved persons, to be that which fits into their prior preconceptions, from a rational standpoint. Truth is always established within a preexisting matrix of meaning or belief system. When working with dreams, however, the issue is not whether the dream's message fits our earlier presuppositions but the reverse: Do our preconceptions and worldview need to be enlarged to accommodate the dream? Many a dream may challenge not only our lifestyle but our basic assumptions about reality. Indeed, in dreams we frequently seem to hear the intonations of a great voice containing wisdom far beyond anything available to the conscious mind. Such a voice is capable of offering an unexpected challenge to the complacency of the ego. Jung calls this the compensatory function of the unconscious.

Analogy in Science and Metaphysics

The creative outreach of analogical thinking appears not only in dreams, but in the development of thought in science and metaphysics as well. In some cases the use of a promising analogy has helped resolve intractable scientific problems. Here we need to distinguish between an analogy used as a teaching device to illustrate something already known, and one that arises at the dawn moment of inspiration to light up a region hitherto dark to our understanding. In the latter case, the analogy appears as a spontaneous act of creation or even as a revelation. Jung mentions, for example, Kekulé's discovery of the benzene ring, a key development in the field of chemistry that came to the chemist at a time of intense concentration on his chosen problem. He had a vision of couples dancing together, which Jung recognized from his studies of alchemy as an image of the *coniunctio,* the union of opposites in the "divine marriage."[11]

What struck Jung was that precisely this analogy had preoccupied the alchemists for some seventeen centuries before modern chemistry was born. They were fascinated by the question of chemical combination, having noted that some substances repel each other, while others readily unite. Seeing the substances as living matter, they interpreted this attraction as affinity, amorous desire, love. And being less inhibited than we, they called the substances by the name of mating couples—dog and bitch, or cock and hen. Their analogies readily conveyed the idea that some substances would freely unite, while others would not. The alchemists were applying to the chemical substances the same intuitive method and the same language of analogy and symbol that Jung later applied to dreams.

From the perspective of modern chemistry, it would appear that the alchemists remained stuck in an unpromising analogy for seventeen hundred years, but Jung took the view that their analogies, by holding their fascination with the question of chemical combination, kept them hard at work until the secrets of modern chemistry were gradually revealed. In the meantime, with their attention focused on a problem insoluble at the time, they gained the ability to make the creative analogies that led them toward higher forms of consciousness.

Just as in the healing realm the unconscious may throw up analogies that the conscious mind of the patient can grasp only after a long period of work, so in the realm of science the analogy can make leaping connections that only the hard work of many thinkers can integrate into a consciously systematized worldview. At this the practical scientist draws back in dismay, while the intuitive and the dreamer feels his or her soul kindled; here is the golden thread of Ariadne that gives anticipatory guidance to the daily work. There is an obvious analogy between the effort of the patient to move out of a stuck place into an unknown future—and her timorous and often stubborn hesitation before the task—and the effort of the scientist to abandon preconceptions and move into the unknown of the material universe.

Similarly, in the healing art we need to affirm the spontaneous creative efforts of the psyche no less than the reductive explanations that frequently lack forward-moving power. A clear appreciation of the creative power of the analogical mode of thought tends to correct this imbalance. It opens us to the fluidity of the psyche and establishes us within a many-layered reality, some of which may be wholly alien to the preconceptions of consciousness. As in creative scientific work, so in therapy: A difficult process may be sustained by the intuitive understanding kindled by a promising analogy. One is reminded of the not-infrequent dreams showing a light at the end of a tunnel.

Whatever its value for science, the analogy has a long and honorable history among Hermetists, Kabbalists, and Gnostics. The Sufis, too, make use of analogies in their famous teaching stories for the purpose of raising consciousness. Use of the analogical method by the Hermetic philosophers was based on the fundamental teaching attributed to Hermes Trismegistus known as the Doctrine of Correspondence: "As above, so below," or "The visible world is in all its parts a manifestation of the invisible." The world of multiplicity was understood to have developed by emanation from the higher spheres, each one more encompassing than those below.

Another statement of the same principle was "the microcosm mirrors the macrocosm." For the Hermetists, the analogy became the primary means of conveying metaphysical truths. They gave careful thought to the correct use of the analogy, understanding that metaphysical principles cannot be verified by the appeal to empirical evidence; therefore, the correctness of the reasoning must itself stand as the guarantor of validity. They finally concluded that reason alone is not adequate for the perception of ultimate truths, yet they did not give up the search for such truths, for it became their goal to develop a higher intuitive faculty capable of reaching from the empirical world to the realms beyond. They saw that it would be possible to explore the ways of the higher realms by analogy with the lower, and, if desired, to influence and manipulate those processes through the natural sympathy between the levels. This was magic; the Hermetists were magicians. Their analogies worked because of the likeness of processes at the visible and the invisible levels.

The thinking of the Hermetists derived from the Platonic worldview, a synthesis of profound ancient wisdom. It is believed that Plato's scientific and mathematical knowledge came from the East through Pythagoras and had its origins from within the sphere of music.[12] The proportions involved in musical harmonies were known in ancient times—not only the basic ratio of 1:2 that defines the octave with its tonal similarity on higher or lower levels, but the other ratios defining the degrees of the musical scale. This knowledge gave rise to a whole spiritual and symbolic worldview in which sound, rhythm, and harmony formed the connecting link between the numbered aspect of the world and the spiritual and imaginal. Seen objectively, music is defined by numbers, ratios, and proportions; experienced subjectively, it evokes an emotional response. By its emotional power and its appeal to memory and imagination, it speaks to the inner world of humans; by reason of its mathematical structure, it relates to the ordered nature of the universe, including the orderly movements of the seasons and the planets. Because of this extraordinary range, music became for the ancients the key to the unitary nature of the world. No wonder, then, that Plato wrote in the *Timaeus* that the structure of all things is based on numerical proportions.

In past epochs, the natural sciences aimed to explain not only how the physical world works but also how to live the good life. The scientific enterprise was not divorced from the spiritual. The good life was one lived in accord with the great harmonies of nature, and since men and women were a part of nature, the study of the natural world offered guidance in the search for human salvation. At the same time, the inner development of the human being could lead to a broader understanding of nature's way.

If analogical thinking declined in importance in the modern era, it was less because its worth had been exaggerated than because it was a way of experiencing the world that was receding into the past—a way more symbolic than literal, more inward than outward, more intuitive than thinking, more unifying than dividing, more feminine than masculine. It was a way that gave more emphasis to the subjective world than the objective, and that took metaphysical truths seriously. As these ancient ways begin to come into use once again in newly modified forms as a corrective for the fragmentation of the current worldview, we may suppose that the value of the dream and the analogy will once again be more widely recognized. Indeed, we seem to see this in some of the latest developments in modern science, where we can discern the outline of a whole new level of integration.

The Analogical Path to the Self

Wholeness reveals itself through dreams, words, scientific breakthroughs, and embryonic pathways. Yet are not these all expressions of the one thing—the life force in its fastidious choice-making? In this way we see the life process as having a central formative core around which it revolves. As I think of this, the image forms in my mind of a merry-go-round, with the animals and the children circling and the music playing, all revolving about the governing mechanism at the center, which reminds me of one of my favorite quotations from Jung:

> We can hardly escape the feeling that the unconscious process moves spiral-wise round a centre, gradually getting closer, while the characteristics of the centre grow more and more distinct. Or perhaps we could put it the other way round and say that the centre—itself virtually unknowable—acts like a magnet on the disparate materials and processes of the unconscious and gradually captures them as in a crystal lattice. For this reason the centre is (in other cases) often pictured as a spider in its web, especially when the conscious attitude is still dominated by fear of unconscious processes. But if the process is allowed to take its course, as it was in our case, then the central symbol, constantly renewing itself,

> will steadily and consistently force its way through the apparent chaos of the personal psyche and its dramatic entanglements. . . . Accordingly we often find spiral representations of the centre, as for instance the serpent coiled round the creative point, the egg.
>
> Indeed, it seems as if all the personal entanglements and dramatic changes of fortune that go to make up the intensity of life were nothing but hesitations, timid shrinkings, almost like petty complications and meticulous excuses manufactured to avoid facing the finality of this strange or uncanny process of crystallization. Often one has the impression that the personal psyche is running round this central point like a shy animal, at once fascinated and frightened, always in flight, and yet steadily drawing nearer.[13]

These poetic words of Jung pick up all the incidents of ordinary life and make them whirl like a carousel around a powerful center. Our life, he tells us, is not chance, not random, not subject to go this way or that if we only willed it; rather, it has its own right patterning, contains its own inner guidance, its structural defining center—the self.

By looking at this process from the perspective of the analogy, we get a sense of how the merry-go-round is drawn up into a spiral, moving upward through the planes of existence, yet remaining true to its own inner necessity. The healer becomes a facilitator of the life process, respecting its inner integrity and helping to discover a path over the hurdles that would inhibit its dynamism. The study of the analogy therefore leads to this central symbol, the inner knower, the self.

And if we generalize this centered process of growth and come to understand, with the ancient philosophers, that the life process of the individual mirrors the world process itself, since the microcosm mirrors the macrocosm, then we approach an intuitive sense of a meaning, purpose, or orderedness at work in the universe that transforms our world from a chaos into a cosmos. That would be a vision that speaks to the deepest need of the human soul in a time of doubt and confusion. It would tend to replace the atomization and isolation of our world by a strongly unifying tendency, and this is undoubtedly the most urgent problem facing each of us—and humanity as a whole—today. It is the purpose of this book to seek out some of the steps by which such a vision again becomes possible.

CHAPTER 2

Analogy and Magic in Healing

Analogy is the final word of science and the first word of faith. . . . Reason and faith, by their nature, mutually exclude one another, but they unite by analogy. Analogy is the sole possible mediator between finite and infinite. . . . Analogy is the key of all the secrets of nature and the sole fundamental reason of all revelation. . . .

—Abbé Constant Fouard

Magic is the teacher of the physician.

—Jung, quoting Paracelsus

Consider . . . that each part of the universe is a kind of analogy to the whole and is therefore structurally related to the whole.

—David Bohm and F. David Peat,
Science, Order, and Creativity

We have seen how analogy, by juxtaposing the strange and unknown to what is already known and familiar, can expand horizons, redirect the libido, and ease the transition to what is new and strange: The new road is likened to the old road and so opened for exploration. The analogy allows us to move into the future while holding to a thread of the past.

Perhaps the most important function of the analogy, however, is sympathetic magic, or magic by analogy, which has to do with health and healing. Dating back to prehistory, the connection between healing and magic formed part of the life of every human culture. In those times, the two functions were the province of the same person, the tribal shaman. Surprisingly enough, magic by analogy is still alive today, as we will see, for it is an eternal process, reappearing again and again in history when conditions are right.

Healing by Analogy

Let us examine an example of magic by analogy provided by Claude Lévi-Strauss.[1] He describes how a shaman treats a case of difficult childbirth in a Cuna Indian woman of the Republic of Panama. The cure consists in the telling of a long, repetitive tale or chant. After describing in fairly mundane terms the events leading to his appearance on the scene, the shaman goes on in increasingly mythological language to relate his healing journey. Accompanied by the *nuchu,* or protective spirits, whom he has been able to enlist, he travels to the home of the female spirit Muu, who has exceeded her authority and so brought on the crisis. His journey is a symbolic parallel to the physical sensations of the patient and provides a mythological bridge to her actual experience.

The abode of Muu is the vagina and uterus of the afflicted woman; the shaman makes a hazardous journey along Muu's way, past such dangerous beasts as an alligator, an octopus, and a tiger, all of which must be overcome and tied with iron chains, "the tongue hanging down, the tongue hanging out, saliva dripping, saliva foaming, with flourishing tail, the claws coming out and tearing things all like blood, all red."[2] By finally penetrating to the very center of the disorder, the shaman is able to release the woman's *purba*, or soul, and bring about a resumption of labor. He retreats with his spiritual helpers, taking care to raise a cloud of dust behind him so as to obscure his path and ensure that Muu will not try to follow. His retreat is accompanied by the dilation of the woman's uterus to allow the birth of the child.

Lévi-Strauss suggests that all the elements of the shaman's story, with its magical animals and malevolent spirits, form part of a "coherent system on which the native conception of the universe is founded."[3] The sick woman never questions these foundations. The shaman's tale helps integrate the sufferings of a difficult delivery into the larger universal structure in a meaningful way. In the language we have been using, it links the physical level of reality to the mythological to form a unified whole. The woman's pain, bleeding, and terror become a meaningful aspect of the Cuna mythological world picture. With this intuitive understanding, she relaxes, and the birthing proceeds.

Lévi-Strauss points out that once the sick woman comes to understand, she does not merely resign herself; she gets well. "No such thing happens to our sick when the causes of their diseases are explained to them in terms of secretions, germs and viruses." In modern medicine, he suggests,

> the relationship between germ and disease is external to the mind of the patient, for it is a cause-and-effect relationship, whereas the relationship between monster and disease is internal to his mind, whether conscious or unconscious; it is a relationship between symbol and thing symbolized, or . . . between sign and meaning.[4]

The mythological relationship speaks directly to the unconscious.

In essence the whole episode sounds so like a piece of dream work in the Jungian mode that one reads it with astonishment. The duel focus by which the images echo on two levels at once—the personal and the transpersonal or magical—might be borrowed from a modern therapy session. Like a tuning fork that allows all strings tuned to C on a piano to resonate together, the shaman's chant brings the different levels of mind and body into accord. Lévi-Strauss himself compares the shamanic cure to modern psychoanalysis. He takes note of manipulations that "must be carried out through symbols, that is, through meaningful equivalents of things meant which belong to *another order of reality.*"[5] He shows that the representations offered by the shaman bring about a relaxation in the woman, which in turn allows for the natural functioning of her organs in childbirth.

> Labor is impeded at the beginning of the song, the delivery takes place at the end, and the progress of the childbirth is reflected in successive stages of the myth. . . . It is the effectiveness of symbols which guarantees the harmonious parallel development of myth and action. . . . The effectiveness of symbols would consist precisely in this "inductive property," by which formally homologous structures, built out of *different* materials at different levels of life—organic processes, unconscious mind, rational thought—are related to one another.[6]

This example of healing resembles my use of the story of Achilles to help a patient over an episode of passive-aggressive behavior. Both stories derive their effectiveness from the "little word *like*." Both are examples of magic by analogy, or sympathetic magic, and both bring understanding. Naturally it did not occur to me when I told the story of Achilles that I was practicing magic—a very old kind of magic. The vast cultural differences tend to obscure the resemblance, but the power of the analogy to light up a situation and make it transparent is evident in both cases. It turns out that we are making use today of one of the oldest cultural acquisitions of humanity. This may stand as evidence of the validity of the method.

As another example of magical healing, Jung mentions the Latin text of the Mass, which makes frequent use of "the famous *sicut*" (meaning "as" or "like"): "this [word] always introduces an analogy by means of which a change is to be produced."[7] This theme is elaborated in Jung's masterful essay "*Transformation Symbolism in the Mass*," where he describes the Mass as a reenactment of the passion, crucifixion, and resurrection of Christ, and says that without the participation of the divine element in the Mass, as held by church dogma, the rite would be "no different from common magic."[8] That is, it would be seen as the magical reenactment of a mythological parallel linking the human level to the divine level, thereby bringing about the healing (whole-making) of the participants. However, in the Mass the analogical enactment is significant because of its meaning—it is the "revelation of something existing in eternity, a rending of the veil of temporal and spatial limitations which separates the human spirit from the sight of the eternal."[9] It is the showing forth of an eternal mystery. Here again we have a glimpse of something divine at work in the healing process and of the need to form a living connection to a level of reality that transcends space and time. In this essay, Jung rejects the effort to understand the divine action, saying that when we try to comprehend it intellectually, "the bird is flown." Instead, he approaches it mythologically, holding to the mode of expression of the deep psyche. Yet, although he does not say so, the Mass is precisely magical; parts of it come out of some of the most ancient strata of human culture, long before the Christian era, and that is what gives it its extraordinary power.

Sympathetic magic is an outer way of imitating (enacting or dramatizing; making visible) the inner unconscious process (or nature's process) of producing an analogical parallel. Churchly rites of confirmation or baptism are imitations of nature's ways of dying to the old to be born to the new, as are the initiation rites of primal people. Sympathetic magic is another such rite. The priestly healer or shaman enacts a dramatic story or intones a prayer that parallels the situation to be influenced. The shaman acts in lieu of the patient's own unconscious and reinforces its intent, assuming that its intention is to heal. The shamanistic enactment may take the form of a ritual or be spoken as a prayer, incantation, or invocation, but whatever its particular venue, it would be surrounded by all the mystery and paraphernalia of magic and accompanied by strong emotions of awe and anticipation that link the person to another level of reality. It would have the effect of rechanneling or converting the energies previously flowing into pathways inimical to life and growth (unless, of course, we are dealing with black magic).

Jung illustrates the magical action by recounting how the ancient Egyptian priests cured cases of snake bite. Their method was to intone a hymn in which the goddess Isis wounds the god Ra by putting a coiled serpent in his path and later cures him. This ritual action is not easy for us to comprehend. The ancient priest clearly assumes that the gods are involved whenever a human is bitten by a snake. What to us is an accident is, to the ancient priest, a god-inspired event. Snake bites, after all, can kill. And if the gods are present in the wounding, it follows that they must also be present in the healing. By his ritual action, the priest invokes the powers of the goddess Isis, because she is the real wounder and healer. To be bitten by a snake is to participate in an eternal, mythological occurrence; and to be healed has the same significance. The snake bite rings on two levels at once—the divine and the human. Long ago in prehistory, Isis wounded Ra and cured him; that was the primordial act of which all later snake bites are an imitation. The priest addresses his patient under the aspect of eternity, for the gods are eternal.

Further exploration of the analogy will be concerned less with the pathway than with the life energy itself—the life force or libido—the dynamic element that strives toward realization. This energy is evident in magical practices, which will cast further light on growth and healing.

The Healing Function of Analogy

In his essay "The Structure of the Psyche"[10] Jung speaks of the case of a twenty-seven-year-old officer who had come to treatment with painful physical symptoms, including severe attacks of pain in the region of the heart, a choking sensation in the throat, and piercing pains in the left heel. No physical damage was evident in any of these areas. The attacks had begun two months earlier, and the patient had no idea of the cause. Though he had been jilted by his girlfriend at the time his symptoms appeared, he saw no connection between the two occurrences, since, as he said, a man could always get another girl.

Here the unconscious has produced a number of healing analogies. The pain in the patient's heart represented his repressed heartache, which can be seen as an analogical substitute for his psychic pain—*he* did not ache, but his heart ached for him. His pain in the throat represented his unshed tears. Both of these symptoms, says Jung, must be seen in light of the fundamental principle that the symptomatology of an illness is at the same time a natural attempt at healing. The symptoms, of course, are only one stage in a healing process. The young patient's inability to allow himself his own pain and sorrow stopped the natural movement of his inner life; he could not respond to the trauma as a whole person. To have consciously felt the emotion of pain (and, quite possibly, anger) would have been a truer and more holistic reaction, for emotion involves both mind and body. As it was, his body flashed a set of warning signals by its pain—a kind of fragmented response. "My heart aches, and I need to weep."

Whether the statement is made on the psychic or the physical level, it must be *expressed* if life is to go on. The grief energy demands to come to consciousness and to somehow get out; some power forces the issue from within toward a completion of the gestalt, as if the whole being were now caught up in the griefwork. When the more conscious emotional outlet is blocked, the grief energy forces its will on the yielding stuff of the flesh, and a symptom is born. There appears to be a substitution of the bodily for the emotional outlet. The symptom appears as a substitute reaction, occurring quite outside the conscious will, or even knowledge, of the young patient.

However, the symptom does not represent a blind retreat—what is noteworthy is its *precision*. It speaks in somatic language exactly what was not recognized at the level of consciousness. The heart aches, and the throat is convulsed with unshed tears. There is evidently a rightness, or a meaningful connection, between the organs chosen and the message to be expressed. Both pains stopped when the patient was able to experience his grief consciously.

When Jung says that a symptom is a natural attempt at healing, then what is meant is that the psychic energy finds an expression, albeit a circuitous one, and is not totally blocked. A blockage may bring about a deeper and more painful regression as the libido retreats to ever lower (more unconscious) levels seeking an outlet. The symptom can be regarded as healing in the sense that it draws attention to a failure of adaptation that calls for self-examination and renewed striving. It can be interpreted as a message demanding to be heard, one that may be decoded by a symbolic reading. At that point, the symptom is transformed into a symbol having healing power.

How can a symbol—a mental image or picture—bring about a healing change in a bodily organ? If we are convinced that mind and body, or consciousness and the material world, form two separate and distinct realms, and that the material is the more basic of the two, we will be at a loss to account for such an influence. By separating mind and body, we have created a problem for ourselves. How can we get them back together?

A God Is Involved

The ancients did not have this problem. For them, the force that demands an outlet was symbolized by Asklepios, the god who had the power to wound as well as to heal. Of the intertwined serpents on the staff of Asklepios, one represents the regressive movement, toward symptom formation, while the other represents the progressive movement, toward *symbol* formation. The symbol is psychic, the symptom bodily, but together they form a unified process—they are manifestations of the same god.

Asklepios stands at the intersection where mind and body meet, far from the knowledge or control of the conscious mind. To the god, the levels of being, mind and body, so different to our perceptions, are one; if we could see through the divine eye, we would experience a unified awareness where we now experience division. The action of the god becomes at once psychic (meaning-laden, symbolic) and physical (bodily, symptomatic). The god appears in his wounding mode via the symptom and in his healing mode via the symbol. He is a creature of two worlds.

From this perspective, the heart can be seen as having a symbolic or metaphoric function, as when the lover says, "My heart is in your hands," or the poet says, "My heart leaps up." In the symbolic realm, the heart is the organ of love, courage, and the joy of love and life. This metaphoric function is as real as the purely physical function of the heart as a pumping device—real, that is, in the sense of producing physical effects in the form of symptoms. Similarly the throat is the channel through which nourishment is taken in and creative self-expression emerges. Lacking an intuitive and processual view, we will see a heart attack only as the breakdown of a pumping mechanism, when it may also be the result of a long-term deprivation of love. The ancients, taking seriously the metaphoric aspect of the world, said that each organ of the body stands at the base of a symbolic edifice that reaches up to the gods, for they saw within the symptom a hidden intentionality that could only be called by the name of a god.

This ancient way of interpreting the patient's symptoms has implications that reach out in many directions. It enables us to understand, for example, why Jung remarked that in modern times the gods have become diseases. He was suggesting that if we, as modern persons, see the gods as mere remnants of a bygone era, then the symbol-forming process is blocked, and we are left with only symptom formation for the release of psychic energies not compatible with our conscious attitude. Treatment would surely involve the restoration of the symbol-making capacity, permitting life to flow on into new channels. These implications have the effect not only of revising our view of the healing process but, at the same time, of altering the modern materialistic worldview by opening up the symbolic (metaphoric) aspect of bodily processes.[11]

It is a growing practice among psychotherapists to urge the patient to discover the symbol hidden in his or her bodily pain in order to bring relief. Thus we are moving toward a view of disease that parallels the ancient understanding, though we will undoubtedly coin a new and more "modern" language to clothe our insights. Perhaps we will begin to think of consciousness as somehow permeating the body as light permeates the atmosphere. Or perhaps we will think of each atom of the body as being ultimately psychic in its nature. We will then have a clear understanding that when we address the psychic aspect of the body by way of visualizations, we are trying to make contact with another level of consciousness that is closer to the dream level and does not think as we do in our normal waking states.

A possible alternative to this view would be to say not that the heart has a level of consciousness of its own, but that *we project mind and purpose into the heart* from our own consciousness. This is a particularly acute question in Jungian psychology, where projection plays a major role in the individual's life, both inner and outer. We will deal with this in the next chapter, but in the meantime we may recall Ouspensky's claim that mind, in all probability, exists in many segments of the universe, but that we can perceive it "only in forms analogous to our own."[12] We have no reason to conclude, he says, that our minds are the only ones in the universe.

By adopting this new—and very old—perspective, we open ourselves to the meaning of the heart not only as a pumping device, but as the organ of expression of the divine energies. Apparently these energies are neither blind nor dumb, but relate with precision to the human condition. They show evidence of a mind or awareness superior to our human waking consciousness, justifying the description *godlike*. Then the gods begin to stir to life once more, healing the collective neuroses and physical ills that accompany their death. They are seen as eternal processes—functions, not entities—which do not act causally but proceed synchronistically to their goal. The wounding and healing are *synchronistic accompaniments* of the presence of the god, not effects.

The Serpent Symbol and the Duplicity of the Archetype

To return to Jung's case of the jilted officer: The clinical picture presented is a confusing one, because we are looking simultaneously at symptoms coming from different levels of the psyche, though this seems clear only in retrospect. The pain in the patient's heart and the strange sensations in the throat related to his unhappy love affair and had recent antecedents, but the pain in the heel was of a different kind and did not yield in the same way.

Seen symbolically, the heel represents either vulnerability or its opposite, aggressive might. The heel is the vulnerable part of otherwise invulnerable figures such as Achilles or Krishna. The expressions "under the heel of the tyrant" and "to grind under the heel" point to the power to oppress or kill, while "to turn up one's heels" means to be defeated. The patient has been hit at a most vulnerable point, one that may also be his strength. Indeed, the patient's problem might be described by saying that he attempts to make himself invulnerable and to stand above the experience of anguish. But since anguish is what he must deal with, there can be no escape.

If we view this pain from the same perspective we have taken with regard to the other symptoms—that is, as a symbolic effort of the life force to find expression—then we can speculate that it indicates a wound to his manly virility—or his notion of virility. Though he wishes to believe that he is not hurt by the fickleness of a mere girl, the truth is that he is deeply hurt, as evident in a dream he relates to Jung in a later session. He dreams that he is walking in an open field. He steps on a snake and gets bitten on the heel. Feeling poisoned, he wakes up, frightened.

Both the dream and the pain, like his other symptoms, can be seen as an effort at healing, but this time healing at a deeper level of the psyche. At this deeper level we may expect dream images of a more mysterious and universal kind to appear. Hence the image of the snake that bites his heel. Jung points out that the dream image of the snake parallels the event that precipitated the patient's illness; when the girl jilted him, she inflicted a wound that paralyzed him and made him ill. For this patient, girl and snake are related to each other by their power to lame, the unconscious linking these experiences by analogy.

One might predict that in the absence of introspection and insight, a new relationship with a woman would have the same wounding effect on this young man—that this pattern is the repetitive, analogical drama that will continue to play itself out in his life, given his inner programming. He will perhaps continue to expose himself to the experiences of rejection that will trigger feelings of unworthiness and loss, or, more likely, will defend himself by not committing to a relationship and so exposing his vulnerability. He is an unwitting actor in a script he did not consciously write and from which he cannot easily bow out. Here the single life experience is seen to be linked to a long-range life pattern of which the young patient is wholly unconscious. The possibilities of a given archetypal pattern tend to unfold in analogous life dramas. (In more conventional Jungian terminology, we would say that this is the way the mother archetype will continue to be actualized in his life.)

As long as the patient remains unconscious of the archetypal patterns at work in his life, so that they work themselves out without his conscious understanding, his whole fate will depend upon whether the archetype has a positive or negative influence. His conscious choices and preferences will have very little to do with it; again and again he will be caught in the net of the negative mother. In such cases, one sees the person reenacting the same destructive behavior over and over, all the while remaining oblivious of what is happening. These repetitive entanglements tend to have a certain analogical similarity as the life energies continue to be pulled into the same channels. A channel is the lived experience of following a particular pattern or life drama, with all the joy or pain that belongs to that pattern. The individual needs to ask, What am I doing? Or, using other language, What god am I serving?

That is why Jung advised that alcoholics, when they begin the effort of turning their lives around, must say, "I have no power over alcohol. Alcohol rules my life." Addictive personalities are ruled by a god they have not consciously chosen and do not understand. Their god is a disease. If they are to change their life pattern, they must discover another god more powerful than alcohol: their own higher power.

Now, in the present case, Jung sees the snake dream as "an attempt at healing by an activation of the collective unconscious and the raising of the symptom to the level of a mythological event. We are evidently dealing here with that same old serpent who had been the special friend of Eve."[13] Just as Eve gained new consciousness through consorting with the viper, so the unconscious of the patient gropes toward new consciousness by throwing up the snake image, the mythological parallel to his personal plight. It is as though the dream is saying to him, "You have been wounded as many before you were wounded, by the bite of the healing serpent who demands consciousness." This would be an effort to heal aimed at the profound level of the psyche where the original wound occurred; it would be another case of like curing like. That which is translated into the picture language of the unconscious becomes depersonalized and appears to the dreamer *sub specie aeternitatis:* "Not as my sorrow, but as the sorrow of the world; not a personal isolating pain, but a pain without bitterness that unites all humanity. The healing effect of this needs no proof."[14] What Jung describes here is a purging effect—catharsis—not unlike the effect of Greek tragedy as described by Aristotle. Such a purgation may well be another stage in a process of healing, as the personal problem is seen to be the unfolding of a universal drama. The person is lifted beyond bitterness to the profound experience of the pain of all humanity. He no longer bewails his personal misfortune, but allows it to open him to the pain that humanity has always known.[15]

In some cases, the patient understands fully the mythological background of his problem but is still left in bitterness and despair, his life energy blocked. Though consciousness is touched by the mythological parallel, the deeper levels of the unconscious remain unmoved. If that is not to happen in the present case, it will be because this young man will have undergone an initiatory experience designed to bring him a new sense of his own masculine power, and with it a new and better relationship to the feminine. Only then will the patient experience true healing. Otherwise we might have a man with deep a philosophical attitude who still is unable to relate to women. But what Jung says is that, in this case, we are dealing with the psychological phenomenon that lies at the root of magic by analogy, or sympathetic magic. Why does Jung speak of magic by analogy instead of initiation? This question leads to further exploration of the healing process.

If the same living energy is expressing itself in both the wounding and the healing, then the healer may be able to bring about a change by directly addressing that reality rather than the channel (or symptom) by which it expresses itself. He may do this not only with words, but with ritual, dance, music, chanting, mythological utterance, or some other means of connecting to the higher (or deeper) reality. It is the connecting to, or evoking of, that reality—Asklepios—that is central to the practice of sympathetic magic (or psychic healing), and it is here that the modern worldview is challenged.

The best way we have today of describing this is to say that the magical enactment works directly on the unconscious to produce bodily healing. But what exactly do we mean by this? Presumably we mean something not too different from what the ancient priest-shaman intended, that is, to touch the deep layers of the unconscious, where we connect to the eternal images of myth and scripture. However, the gods of today, if they have any existence at all, have become symbols, existing within the "collective unconscious." The ancient priest and his patient lived far closer to the gods than we do. I suspect that what is unconscious to us was not at all unconscious to the Egyptian priest, who could talk directly to his god and expect an answer, as did Moses in the Old Testament. We are confronted here by a structure of consciousness different from any known to us, one involving a quite different metaphysics from our own.

A fine example of sympathetic magic is shown in the Old Testament, where Yahweh sends a plague of serpents to bite and kill many of the Israelites journeying through the desert. When the people come to Moses for help, he consults Yahweh, who tells him to make a fiery serpent and set it on a pole; he promises that all those bitten by the serpents will be healed by looking upon this image. In obedience to this command, Moses makes a serpent of brass, which has the desired healing effect. Here we have not only the familiar theme that like cures like, but even more: Yahweh takes the role of Asklepios as both wounder and healer! (Yahweh also took this role when he introduced the serpent into paradise.) Note the similarity of the brazen serpent on the pole to the staff of Asklepios. The same living energies are involved in both the wounding and the healing. The Israelites understood this clearly, because for them the god-image combined both good and evil; for us, such understanding is difficult, since the god-image has been divided, and the evil or wounding side ascribed to the devil. It is not surprising that the Israelites were later found burning incense to the brazen serpent, whereupon it had to be destroyed as an idol. Perhaps this was an indication that the people had fallen away from their original intuitive understanding of the meaning of the symbol, and had taken to worshipping the symbol itself instead of perceiving the presence to which it pointed, and allowing that presence to vibrate within them.

Sympathetic magic was commonly practiced in biblical times. When Moses came down from the mountain, he found the people worshipping a golden calf. Exodus 32:20 says, "And he took the calf which they had made, and burnt it in the fire and ground it to powder and strewed it upon the water, and made the children of Israel drink of it." This might be seen as a symbolic integration of the meaning of the people's transgression by literally ingesting what they had done. It can also be interpreted as a kind of magical prophylaxis: by drinking some of the gold-stuff, they are vaccinated against the worship of false gods—a form of homeopathic medicine practiced to ward off a spiritual rather than a physical ailment. Indeed, sympathetic magic is also known as "homeopathic magic."

As I worked on this material, a dream of similar theme was brought to my attention. In it the dreamer is vaccinated by a priest who breaks some incense in a chalice containing a doughy substance. He eats some of the substance himself and then vaccinates the patient by laying open the skin on the back of his hand and placing some of the substance under the skin. The dreamer, in his associations, called this substance the "hair of the dog that bit him," this being a tendency to let things "get under his skin" in a way that was detrimental to his personal relationships. The vaccination is designed to prevent this from continuing. Again, we have like curing like. That the priest eats some of the healing substance suggests that he included himself as well as his patient in the healing process that is happening within the dream. Note Jung's mention of the unity of the redeemer and that which is to be redeemed.[16]

The priest represents a higher faculty of the psyche that knows what is to be done for the healing of the patient. If we see this dream ritual as a means of bringing together the priestly and personal levels of the psyche, then we would speak of an analogical relationship rather than a unity between priest and patient. They are the same and yet different, but both must change. This suggests a linking factor between the redeemer and the redeemed: We can call it simply "energy" or better, "energetic process," and we might equally speak of a symbolic resonance between the two levels. We would not be wrong to call it the energy of love, for it is love that brings unity out of separateness.

It is surely of interest that a healing activity that was once carried on by an entire community acting in concert with its priests now occurs only in the secrecy of the therapeutic session. That something of timeless import is involved cannot be denied, and I cannot but think that we are groping now toward an understanding of what was once the worldview of most humans. Hopefully we will reach this understanding in a way that embraces both our present knowledge and the metaphysical insights of the past. Let us consider some more examples of magical healing.

Frazer, in *The Golden Bough*, gives a number of examples of the use of homeopathic magic by primal peoples.[17] A shaman, deciding to work evil on someone, makes a little wooden image of his enemy and then runs a needle into its head or heart. Healers in ancient India cure jaundice by banishing the patient's yellow color into a creature to which it more properly belongs, such as a yellow parrot. A Dyak medicine man, called to treat an illness, lies down and pretends to be dead. His fellow medicine men then bind him up and treat him as a corpse. After a while, they revive him, and his recovery leads to the recovery of the sick person.

Sympathetic magic is an ancient, worldwide phenomenon and is by no means extinct in the modern world. Jung tells us,

> The first achievement wrested by primitive man from instinctual energy, through analogy-building, is magic. A ceremony is magical so long as it does not result in effective work, but preserves the state of expectancy. In that case the energy is canalized into a new object and produces a new dynamism, which in turn remains magical so long as it does not create effective work.[18]

A great deal of meaning is here condensed in a few words: When the energies are converted into effective work (i.e., when they result in a physical action in the world), they are reduced to another level to be used by the conscious mind for conscious purposes. By remaining on the symbolic level, they retain their effortless, godlike quality.

In the same way that a lightning rod rechannels the raw energy of lightning into safe pathways, or that a millrace rechannels a stream to make the flowing water turn a mill wheel, sympathetic magic converts chaotic and unfocused but powerful energies into more directed forms through the rechanneling effect of an analogical ritual. The energies thus become usable for human purposes. All energy-converting devices can be viewed in this same way. They are analogical counterparts of nature's own way. This appears as a development of the tiny, almost invisible, seed phenomenon in which an analogy is cast up from the human psyche to create what Jung called a "libido analogue," which has the effect of rechanneling the energy into a different, though analogous, pathway. Recall the case mentioned in the previous chapter, in which a young patient's dreams of a cathedral drew his energies into a more mature, though analogous, pattern.

So long as magic is understood as analogous to energy-converting devices, our worldview is not challenged. Energy conversion is everywhere in the modern world, and we do not see anything sacred about these devices or the energy conversions they accomplish. But while lightning rods or steam engines involve energies that are not alive (or so we believe), sympathetic magic is very different, for the energies involved have a living, godlike quality, a *meaning-responsive* aspect, although they have a limited number of pathways or channels that they can take. Jung notes, "The old custom of the 'bridal bed' in the field, to make the field fruitful, expresses the analogy in the clearest possible way; as I make this woman fruitful, so I make the earth fruitful. The symbol canalizes the libido into cultivating and fructifying the earth."[19]

Here Jung is seeing the analogy as useful in a practical way in that it led the man to give his energy to plowing and tilling the soil; that is, it mobilized and rechanneled his libido. Jung is suggesting that the magical enactment works upon the performer of the magic; in this case, the energies would move down toward the performance of work rather than remaining at the magical level. However, what we are interested in pursuing here is the possibility that the magical enactment does, in fact, promote the growth of the crops. That would seem far more magical to our way of thinking. Jung left out of this discussion what he was careful to include in his study of the Mass, namely, the participation of the divinity—whether it be called the vegetation numen, the corn spirit, the goddess of agriculture, or the God of the higher religions—whose activity is essential to the growth of things. Without this mysterious canalizing action, no amount of sweat and muscle applied to the field will have any effect.

If there is a magical evocation of the divinity (the higher reality) through the analogical act of coitus—the fertilization of the woman is like the fertilization of the earth—it is as though the sexual union becomes a kind of prayer or supplication, calling forth the divine procreative energy into the field where the act is performed. To the primal mind, presumably, it is the same divine energy that expresses itself in the act of conception and in the germination of the seed. An action that is senseless without the participation of the deity takes on meaning when seen in this light. But even if we grant that there are divine energies at work in sympathetic magic, we are still left with a puzzle: *How* is it to be understood?

Perhaps we should say here that the primal mind did not make the many distinctions that enable the modern person to think with great precision (though this capacity can sometimes cause us to get lost in the wealth of ideas). For this reason, ancient peoples used "the little word *like*" far more commonly than we do. Their acts of "magical causation" depended on this mode of perception, with the differences left in the unconscious or never known. They failed to see the distinctions that are so apparent to us. Theirs was a kind of "seeing in the dark," or intuition. Only when we come to a totally new situation are we obliged to use intuition just as they did.

In the examples given by Frazer, it is as if the enactment of an analogical *process* has some special effectiveness; by acting upon the wooden image of a person, that person is made ill. By enacting a process of getting well, the patient is made well. Homeopathic magic depends for its effectiveness upon a certain relatedness or similarity—an analogy—between the event enacted and the process or event to be influenced, leading to the conversion of energies into new pathways. But as has been shown, something more is needed than mere imitation. Frazer thinks that in such occurrences, things are assumed to act on each other at a distance through a secret sympathy, the impulse being transmitted by means of what may be conceived as a kind of invisible ether. Here again we have a hint of something mysterious or divine at work as a transmitting or connecting agent.

Searching for the Secret Link of Effectiveness

M. L. von Franz discusses the problem of how to explain sympathetic magic, alluding to synchronicity, or the more-or-less simultaneous occurrence of inner and outer events linked by meaning, not by linear causation.

> What Jung decided to term *synchronicity* (thus freeing it from this blurred idea of a magical causality) was conceived of in the past, before it was completely discarded at the end of the 17th century, as a correspondence; the teaching of the *correspondentia* of microcosm and macrocosm. That, in a way, is the archaic basis of all the magical performances of mankind. For instance, everything has its analogy, and an analogy is not only what we would now call a parallelism of form, but it has also a secret link of effectiveness. In African rain magic, the most frequent way of making rain is to pour out a calabash of water while certain incantations and prayers are said, accompanied by certain dances. Then the rain starts.

> Eighty-five percent of all magical activities are the repetition on a small scale of something which at the same time happens on the cosmic big scale. If this is done with the right psychological attitude then there is a parallelism between what the microcosm (man) does, and what happens in the macrocosm, in the whole surrounding universe. Rain and fertility charms and all such things are always based on this idea. . . .[20]

What is the "secret link of effectiveness" that is involved here? And what is the "right psychological attitude"? We may pursue these questions by further consideration of Jung's case of the young officer. We have said that the snake dream appears as a compensatory effort to heal the patient's wound. Now it makes a great deal of difference whether we think the healing image arises from within the ego, or whether we think it comes from a deeper realm outside the ego and beyond its control, though experienced introspectively. If the former, then we heal ourselves; if the latter, then we are aided in our healing efforts by a power beyond our own knowledge and control. Jung insists on the latter alternative when he describes the healing factor as an "activation of the collective unconscious." We might equally call it the unconscious personified by the god of healing, Asklepios, and we might speak of the snake dream as a gift of the god. Jung says,

> This part of the unconscious (i.e., the collective unconscious) evidently likes to express itself mythologically, because this way of expression is in keeping with its nature. But to what kind of mentality does the symbolical or metaphorical way of expression correspond? It corresponds to the mentality of the primitive, whose language possesses no abstractions, but only natural and "unnatural" analogies.[21]

Jung is saying that aboriginal peoples lived closer to the collective unconscious than we do. He goes on to explain the origin of the collective unconscious in the age-long effort of human beings to adapt and endure within their world. Their experiences are recorded in the primordial images or mythological motifs that embody not a photographic record of sights and sounds, but the emotionally charged living experience itself. Thus night is filled with hobgoblins and ghosts who pursue the tossing sleeper on the bed, while myth and story convey the glorious sense of deliverance that comes with the rising of the sun, the birth of the hero, the apotheosis of the god. Myth, then, is not an explanation but a celebration, a joyous reliving of the experience of the dawn or a fearful calling up of the terrors of the night. It is the emotionally charged imagery that arises by immersion in these happenings and can be seen as their psychic counterpart. It is very close to the dream. Both the sun-hero myths and the fantastic night tales are the natural and unnatural analogies of the living experience, reverberating with echoes of a heightened sense of reality. Such images make clear the original unity prevailing between our primal ancestors and their world, where "what happens outside also happens in [them], and what happens in [them] also happens outside."[22] This unity, forged in the white heat of lived experience, transcends all theoretical assumptions.

When the sun rises, it is the sun god Apollo driving his fiery chariot across the heavens, or it is a herd of golden horses with flying manes and tails racing into the morning sky. How otherwise can one capture a moment of awe and surprise when the whole being awakens to glory? How, except in image, metaphor, poem, or song? This is the very birthing of myth. It is as if the great images of myth and fable are stored in a definite "place" that may be called the collective unconscious—the modern Olympus—for they reappear again and again in dreams, even in societies where the myths are no longer recited and the members have no conscious knowledge of mythology. The images give form to the underlying energies eternally at work. Through the images, the lived experience of the race becomes available to the individual, particularly in times of crisis not resolvable by conscious understanding, and a whole new mode of intuitive perception awakens. Such a return of the half-remembered reality is a numinous experience still having the power to ignite the imagination. The energies of wounding are converted (rechanneled) into the energies of healing.

In Jung's later work, an alternative view of the collective unconscious appears. Instead of arising in the course of human experience, he suggests, the archetypal patterns stand prior to all experience and are, in fact, the source of all life dramas. Out of this Source, particular forms arise and then fade in the course of history, but the Source itself is eternal, prior to the emergence of any particular form and independent of human experience. Every life-form then becomes a manifestation of the divine, and the whole living world is ensouled.

One sees the divine shining through every unique individual; that is the reason why human life and all living forms are sacred and need to be preserved. This is a very great shift of emphasis regarding the role of humanity in the larger cosmic drama. Are the "gods" really transcendent, dwelling prior to and beyond humanity, or are they human creations? Do humans make their gods by projecting the healing and redemptive roles into a heavenly realm?

The mythological mode of understanding continues today, for it is an eternal aspect of the world. To the lover, marriage with the woman of his choice represents salvation, and her loss equals utter desolation. Similar bonding may occur in the therapeutic situation, where the patient sometimes clings to the therapist as to a savior. Death is still identified with the clutches of a monster; the renewal of health brings a sense of joy and release. Such experiences call up the memory of similar ones that have occurred over the millennia of life on earth; thus the collective unconscious, says Jung, is the living deposit of ancestral experience. It is not a museum of long-banished stuff but a living reservoir of attitudes and reactions ready to spring into life when the conditions are right. Its power and influence are shown by the high emotional charge involved in the reliving of experiences long since shaped into typical behavior patterns with their accompanying archetypal imagery.

Jung's later view of the collective unconscious re-creates a sense of the primordial state of unity within which magic by analogy may occur. This is not a matter of belief or conviction involving the gathering of evidence. It is instead an intensely lived experience, a state of being. Human and world constitute a unitary field; the myth is the awakening of that field into image and analogy. It is *inspiration*—to inspire means to breathe in. The myth is world breathed in. In the act of myth-making, the formless energies of the world are given form and meaning. From this we may say that different psychic states correspond with different world-states—the theory of correspondence again—and that these correspondences are not so much made by the psyche as discovered in relation to the world. In these correspondences, we sense the secret link of effectiveness of which von Franz speaks.

The Theory of Correspondence

When we work with dream imagery, we are working with the analogues of instincts, presuming that the movement of these analogical representations corresponds with the movement of the instincts themselves, and that if the analogical substitute is set right, the instinct, too, will tend to be set right. We assume that a resolution occurring on the symbolic level lays the groundwork for a resolution on the material level. This helps to make clear why it is preferable to work with dream imagery arising from the person's own psyche, rather than with imagery prescribed by a set of "exercises" having no necessary relation to the individual's unique psychic condition. However, without the element of numinosity there will be no decisive effect on the patient's life. We need the fiery chariot of the god, or the emotional force of the racing golden horses to move us out of merely habitual ways.

In contrast to our own timid use of the principle of correspondence stands the attitude of the Renaissance magus, who did not hesitate to try to connect to the powers of the stars themselves through his astrological knowledge. He understood that the planets perform their mighty roundelay in concert with the lesser rhythms of human life. The old philosophers developed tables of correspondence along both the horizontal and the vertical planes. All scales or series of related phenomena could be set side by side—natural numbers, letters of the alphabet, musical notes, colors, signs of the zodiac, planetary gods, metals, precious stones, plants, animals, parts of the body—and natural correspondences found to connect these series along horizontal lines. At the same time, each item in a series could be connected to a corresponding one in another series by natural pulses moving in the vertical direction.

Thus the metal of Venus was copper, her color was turquoise, and she ruled over the throat, kidneys, thymus, and ovaries. The color red belonged to Mars, god of war, whose metal was iron, whose animal was the wolf, and whose stone was the ruby. There was not complete agreement among the philosophers as to these correspondences, but it was on the basis of such assumptions that talismans and amulets could be made having the power to connect the higher with the lower levels or draw upon the powers of the gods. By making his talisman at the astrologically determined time when the power of Venus was on the ascendant, or at a time pervaded by the Venus power, and by bringing his own mind into a corresponding spiritual state, the magus might expect that it would embody some of the essence or power of Venus. His understanding would be that a talisman is a visible embodiment or representative on the material plane of the subtle powers deriving from the planetary level. Thus his work would be an imitation of nature's own way, an intervention in the streams or rays of power descending from the planetary spheres.

Our own lives are not without echoes of this long-forgotten worldview. Thus we think that candlelight, soft music, a little wine, and exotic scents are conducive to the atmosphere of love. It no longer occurs to us to connect this with the subtle influence of the love goddess, though there may be those who would carry a good-luck charm in an affair of the heart. Yet even today, cut off though we are from the planetary powers, the beloved and loving person will feel a swelling of the heart and a turning toward some higher power with tears of joy and gratitude. According to the old philosophers, it was just this lift of the heart, this participation in the divine energies, that linked the worlds together in sympathy and love and led to healing.

The movements of birthing, growing, fading and dying, of systole and diastole, are eternal movements, forever proceeding on all levels of the universe. But since all the universe is a set of processes (some so slow in relation to our own life cycle that we think of them as things), then things or images are likened to each other by the similarity of the processes in which they participate. Such similarities are not invented by the conscious mind but are recognized within the deep psyche, itself a part of the world process, in the same way that archetypal forms were recognized in the first place—in the effort and intensity of lived experience, where person and world come to constitute a unitary field. By the use of analogies, we gain awareness of the similarity of these processes on all levels and highlight the relationships of correspondence that bring together outer world and inner, lived experience and image pattern.

The right psychological attitude, then, seems to consist in either a deeply *intuitive* awareness of the oneness of the universe or a highly *emotional* experience of this unity. These two states, so different in our subjective experience, have in common one element—the setting aside of the ego with its ready-made interpretive structures. This allows an opening to the profound experience of union. Man and woman become one with the "bridal bed" of the field, and the divine action experienced in the sexual act is also seen in the generative process in the field. Or, in the case of the Israelites, the same God at work in the biting serpents is also at work in the healing serpent of brass, for wounding and healing form a unitary process involving the same energies.

It is worth repeating that we do not make the magical process "work" simply by our sincere belief. There is a vast difference between belief and total involvement of the whole being. What is effective is the action that grows out of the living encounter between person and world and the symbols forged within that encounter. If we humans in our wholeness are self-regulating systems with the potential for healing within our own depths, and if each individual is a microcosm that mirrors the macrocosm, is not the universe itself also such a self-regulating system, having within itself the power to heal whatever is one-sided and unbalanced in any of its parts? Why not, then, conceive the possibility that the profound need of the human being or of the human race for healing may be answered by the healing forces within the world process, of which we, after all, are a part? This would be a modern way of understanding the significance of prayer.

We have seen that the unifying process can emerge forcefully and involuntarily through symptoms. Thus the young man jilted by his girl was attacked by pains in the heart and a choking sensation in the throat. The unifying process can also manifest through compulsivity—that is, the ego has nothing to say in the matter, and the patient is taken over by something more powerful than ego. Using the standpoint of the ancients, we could say that when stricken by grief, the young officer participated in a world process of eternal significance. By consciously rejecting that experience, he was forced to undergo it within his body. Healing could not come in the form of denial, but only in the conscious acceptance of the measure of pain that belonged to his life.

Since wounding and healing constitute a unified process—are ruled by the same god, Asklepios—it is quite possible that we can, by our imitative art, reverse the wounding tendency by voluntary and intentional effort. We can set up a lightning rod, so to speak, to divert the energies of disease, thereby intervening consciously in a process that happens outside our control in other instances. We might also say that in such rituals, correspondences are rediscovered that were there all along but that we have lost in attaining our present form of consciousness.

In our discussion, we have taken our guidance from the dream, as though the dream is a symbolic effort of the life force to express itself—or as though the wound itself is allowed to speak. The dream does not merely describe the situation ("I feel terrible!"). It goes to the heart of the disease by describing its etiology in symbolic terms. The young man is stricken at a vulnerable point, the heel. The snake symbol rings on many levels, as though something very wise is speaking, and this in turn suggests that something central in this young man is touched. We get a glimpse not only of the wound, but of its whole history and its possible healing, as though we are permitted to eavesdrop on an eternal process. The wounded organ tells its story in the dream, and mind and body are unified.

Out of this analysis Lévi-Strauss draws conclusions about the etiology of certain neuroses. The traumatizing power of certain situations, he indicates, resides in the fact that

> the subject experiences them immediately as living myth. By this we mean that the traumatizing power of any situation cannot result from its intrinsic features but must, rather, result from the capacity of certain events, appearing within an appropriate psychological, historical, and social context, to induce an emotional crystallization which is molded by a pre-existing structure. . . . These structures as an aggregate form what we call the unconscious . . . The unconscious ceases to be the ultimate haven of individual peculiarities—the repository of a unique history which makes each of us an irreplaceable being. It is reducible to a function—the symbolic function, which no doubt is specifically human, and which is carried out according to the same laws among all men, and actually corresponds to the aggregate of these laws.[23]

This sounds remarkably like Jung's conception of the collective unconscious with its archetypal structures, although Lévi-Strauss specifically denies the "so-called archetypes."[24]

The example recounted and analyzed by Lévi-Strauss brings to mind an experience Jung mentions in an essay entitled "The Psychological Foundations of Belief in Spirits." His essay was written in 1919, but the tale of sympathetic magic was appended in a footnote written many years later. Here is Jung's account:

> When I was on an expedition to Mount Elgon (Africa) in 1925–26, one of our water-bearers, a young woman who lived in a

> neighbouring kraal, fell ill with what looked like a septic abortion with high fever. We were unable to treat her from our meager medical supplies, so her relatives immediately sent for a *nganga*, a medicine-man. When he arrived, the medicine-man walked round and round the hut in ever-widening circles, snuffing the air. Suddenly he came to a halt on a track that led down from the mountain, and explained that the sick girl was the only daughter of parents who had died young and were now in the bamboo forest. Every night they came down to make their daughter ill so that she should die and keep them company. On the instructions of the medicine-man a ghost-trap was then built on the mountain path, in the form of a little hut, and a clay figure of the sick girl was placed inside it together with some food. During the night the ghosts went in there, thinking to be with their daughter. To our boundless astonishment the girl recovered within two days. Was our diagnosis wrong? The puzzle remained unsolved.[25]

The puzzle, of course, is still unsolved. But using the language suggested here, we might say that the "ghost-trap" stands as a representative on the visible and material plane of the higher powers that are able to control the activity of ghosts. It is essentially a symbol. The little drama enacted within the trap when the ghosts come to visit their daughter's effigy is again an analogical representation of that action by which the ghostly powers are made to submit. Using the concept of the levels of being, we must assume that the *nganga* was able to enter into a higher psychic state that enabled him to defeat the ghosts by acting on them from a superior level of power, whether they lived up on the mountainside or within the mind and body of the young woman, or, indeed, had no spatial location. The *nganga's* trapping of the ghosts resembles the chanting Cuna shaman's chaining of the wicked animals, whose thrashing about had made for a difficult birth. In both cases, the healer aids the regenerative forces within the patient and restrains the destructive ones by way of a symbolic ritual. Today we would probably conceptualize the ghostly parents as a negative parental complex—negative, that is, in the sense that it saps the patient's ability to live on the human level. We may question indeed whether the ghosts have a spatial form of existence, but the shaman's activity gives them a "local habitation and a name" (to borrow from Shakespeare), linking them to the world of space and time.[26] To attain the higher (or deeper) state with its special powers was the essence of the shaman's training, and it retains a quality of mystery today, though it is not entirely mysterious.

In this case described by Jung, as in that recounted by Lévi-Strauss, the healing is accomplished by the telling of a story or myth that is compatible with the patient's worldview and serves to explain—and heal—her symptoms. This is not so very different from many modern psychotherapies in which the healing consists in the telling of a story or myth. The modern patient may be encouraged to construct her own narrative, whereas in earlier times the shaman supplied it, but in either case the story is satisfying to the patient and brings meaning to her suffering and a resolution of conflict. Like the methods of the shaman, our methods are culture-bound and tend to reflect the belief systems of the time; however, I do not wish to say that the cure, in either perspective, works in an entirely rational way—that is, a way compatible with modern belief systems and cosmologies.

Modern Analogical Magic

Our discussion so far has highlighted the necessity of forming a connection between the phenomenal world and the archetypal realm, or between the individual ego and the divine, as well as the numinous effect of this contact. Through this connection, what was senseless and chaotic suffering becomes part of a world order; a new sense of hope and purpose arises within the patient, whose latent powers of healing can now be mobilized. One sees this in modern psychotherapy, when the patient suddenly becomes alert and begins to lay hold of his or her situation with an awakened sense of meaning and power.

The dream of a forty-four-year-old patient shows that magic by analogy is alive and well today. At the time of the dream, the woman was in great pain over the threatened loss of her lover:

> *My old friend Alan holds me still with my mouth open, and holds a large female spider over me, and squeezes it until the juice from it drops into my mouth and runs down my throat. This horrifies me, but somehow it seems that it is meant to help me. I awaken from the dream with a start; my throat hurts and*

> *feels as though it might be swelling. I know I have had a powerful dream. Later, in the morning, I am awakened by a spider running across my face.*

The spider is a spinner of fate; indeed, the word *spider* comes from the Old English *spinnen,* to spin. The etymology reveals the ancient intuitive wisdom that saw an analogy or correspondence between the patient, time-bound work of the spider and the weaving of human destiny. As the spider spins the web-stuff from its own body, it brings the invisible into concrete manifestation in the same way that human destiny comes over the threshold of nonbeing. It is the prerogative of females to weave human fate—the Fates were women, since in ancient times spinning was women's work. (Note that in the dream, the spider was female. On a cosmic scale, the creation or weaving of form out of formless energies is the work of the Yin, or feminine principle.) Not infrequently, the spider in mythology has a beneficial relationship to humankind.

Both Mohammed and King David were saved from their enemies by spiders spinning a fresh web over the mouth of the caves where they were hidden. Robert Bruce, the Scottish king and patriot, was encouraged to persevere in his war against the English when he saw a spider finally throw its thread across the mouth of his cave after seven failures. Both images—of spinning and of caves as places of safety or renewal—suggest the looming presence of the Great Mother. Indeed, in Native American lore, Spider Woman is a helpful spirit who imparts saving knowledge and protects human beings. Spiders once played a part in folk medicine, sometimes by being carried around like an amulet, sometimes by being eaten.

We may view the spider, then, as an arachnid form of the Great Mother in her role as spinner of fate. From the viewpoint of the spider, there is a sacrifice involved—the spider's life is squeezed out for the healing of the dreamer. This strange and archaic idea is related to the imagery of the Crucifixion. Edward Edinger, in his book *Ego and Archetype,* shows a fifteenth-century woodcut picturing Christ being crushed or squeezed like a grape for the nourishment of the human realm.[27] In this analogy, Christ, like the grape, is crushed in order that his life-giving blood, like the wine, may inspirit humanity.

It is precisely a sacrifice that the dreamer is called upon to make in the loss of her lover; she must swallow the pain of loneliness and estrangement. It is the throat that is wounded and the throat that receives the strange magical treatment. Moreover, it is a helpful animus figure—Alan, a longtime friend devoted to the spiritual life—who applies the needed remedy. This man symbolizes her own devotion to the spiritual path, which comes to her aid at a time of personal distress; indeed, the image conveys the healing power of a spiritual attitude in the vicissitudes of life. Thus the spider can be seen as an image of the self, drawing the dreamer along the path of her ongoing life. She reports a sense of fatedness; something within her has always known that this passionate affair was not destined to endure.

In connection with the dream, a synchronistic event occurs when a spider crawls over the dreamer's face to awaken her—an awakening that is both symbolic and physical. This is a sure sign that the archetypal level of the psyche has been activated. We have here, then, all the elements of magic by analogy:

- a numinous connection to higher levels of reality
- a magical enactment on one level of reality that connects to another plane and brings healing
- a transformation of energies as the dreamer moves from states of rebellion and grief to acceptance

As in the snake dream of Jung's patient, the woman's spider dream depicts the inner counterpart of the outer magical processes that have been described. In the weaving back and forth between inner and outer planes, it is possible to gain a deepened sense of the correspondences that were central to the alchemical worldview. Indeed, the weaving has the effect of opening a vision of that dynamic wholeness that embraces both inner and outer, and is the ultimate source of healing. A quotation from Jung's previously mentioned essay, "Transformation Symbolism in the Mass," underscores the importance of the principle of correspondence.

> [The] rupture of the link with the unconscious and our submission to the tyranny of words have one great disadvantage; the conscious mind becomes more and more the victim of its own discriminating activity, the picture we have of the world gets broken down into countless particulars, and the original feeling of unity, which was integrally connected with the unity of the unconscious psyche, is lost. This feeling of unity, in the form of

> the correspondence theory and the sympathy of all things, dominated philosophy until well into the seventeenth century and is now, after a long period of oblivion, looming up again on the scientific horizon, thanks to the discoveries made by the psychology of the unconscious and by parapsychology.[28]

Hopefully, our discussion thus far has helped to show why the theory of correspondence is again looming on the scientific horizon, and why it may yet have healing power for us. We live in a time when a more encompassing worldview is urgently required, but it is a vision that can only grow out of deep understanding. It cannot be forced. Continuing with Jung:

> The manner in which the unconscious forcibly obtrudes upon the conscious by means of neurotic disturbances is not only reminiscent of contemporary political and social conditions, but even appears as an accompanying phenomenon. In both cases there is an analogous dissociation; in the one case a splitting of the world's consciousness by an "iron curtain," and in the other a splitting of the individual personality. This dissociation extends throughout the entire world, so that a psychological split runs through vast numbers of individuals who, in their totality, call forth the corresponding mass phenomena.[29]

Note the correspondence between the inner and outer realms shown by Jung in the life of the individual and in the fate of nations, as well as the consequences of a failure to work toward the recovery of wholeness. Nothing less than world destruction may hang in the balance. The new worldview now beginning to come into focus, with the aim of restoring this lost sense of wholeness, will surely hearken back to the alchemical view, whose principles embody an intuitive vision that the healing of the individual and the healing of the world are a single process.

Recall Lévi-Strauss' contention that the shaman's story forms part of a "coherent system on which the native conception of the universe is founded," thus revealing the patient's suffering and healing to be a meaningful part of the larger world order. The same sense of a unified world order (but a far more sophisticated one) underlay the healing rituals of the Asklepian temples in ancient Greece; the patients who engaged in these rituals had a sure sense that they were involved in actions having ultimate validity. Can we begin to envision a similar possibility regarding our own healing rituals by seeing them as belonging to a new world order emerging from modern science and depth psychology?

CHAPTER 3

Projection

To know and to understand conceptually are two different things, are often mutually exclusive and contrasted.

—Rudolph Otto

The difference must not be overlooked between the unity which was there before there is duality, and the unity that has to be won back in a new upsurge of the religious consciousness.

—Gershom Scholem

If object and self have disappeared, peace reigns the whole day.

—Zen proverb

A new phase of our journey begins as we take up projection. Thus far we have discussed wounding and healing as a unified process involving mind and body. We have come to see the meaningful nature of symptoms and the healing potential of symbols. Departing from our customary language and myths, we have begun to speak of gods and goddesses as well as shamans and magic. The healing god, Asklepios, has appeared as a unifying figure linking mind and body, wounding and healing. As we have watched the healing process play out at different levels, both in the individual and in society, healing has come to represent a kind of Rosetta Stone, connecting practices and knowledge that on the surface appear very different, but on further examination reveal a hidden similarity. The idea of unification has emerged as an important step toward achieving health. We will find that all these ideas relate to projection, which has more to do with mental health than physical.

The word *projection* comes from the Latin *projectus* and *proicere,* which in turn come from *pro,* meaning "before" or "in front of," and *jacere,* "to throw"—hence to cast forward. In general psychological terms, the term denotes externalizing or regarding subjective states as though they were objective, for example, attributing traits such as one's own emotions to another. Projection necessarily involves a polarized or two-sided view of reality, a subject and an object. It is related to an understanding of one's limits, to what is considered to be "in here" (self) as opposed to "out there" (other). Since the individuation process requires the reconciliation of opposites, including the fundamental opposites of "inner" and "outer," the concept of projection plays an enormous role in growth and healing.

As customarily formulated, projection means that one's own unacceptable or unwanted thoughts, desires, feelings, or motivations are unconsciously attributed to another person (or object), who offers a "hook" for the projection. For example, instead of realizing that I am often irresponsible, I discover, with a sense of indignation and outrage, that my neighbor is an irresponsible person. Although my neighbor may actually possess this trait to some degree (and hence provide an attractive target for my projection), my excessive and irresponsible amplification of this attribute of my neighbor reveals the projection, which binds me to my neighbor in a state of unconscious identification, or "archaic identity." This identification is strictly unconscious; at conscious levels, I feel nothing but wrath at the person's errant behavior. From the standpoint of the ego, the projection serves the useful purpose of allowing me to take no responsibility for my disowned trait. The more I resent my feckless neighbor, the less I will be able to take responsibility for my own fecklessness. The identification remains unconscious because I have not been able to recognize the hated quality in myself. Once I am able to do so, my indignation evaporates. I have successfully "withdrawn my projection," a process requiring no small moral effort.

Facets of Projection

Projection has a number of aspects, some that relate to the earlier phases of the inner journey when the patient is mainly concerned with personal issues, and some to the later stages when more universal and societal themes come to the fore. In general, projection has received rather bad press, for it is associated with unconsciousness. In an essay titled "Archaic Man," written in 1931, Jung says,

> Projection is one of the commonest psychic phenomena. It is the same as *participation mystique*, which Levy-Bruhl, to his great credit, emphasized as being an especially characteristic feature of primitive man. We merely give it another name, and as a rule deny that we are guilty of it. Everything that is unconscious in ourselves we discover in our neighbor, and we treat him accordingly.[1]

The term "participation mystique" was put forward by Lucien Lévy-Bruhl, a French philosopher and sociologist of the early years of the twentieth century. He also developed the hypothesis of a "prelogical mentality" among primal people, a theory that seemed to many to explain rituals and practices that do not make sense from our perspective. The idea of a prelogical mentality met with great success among a wide variety of readers, including philosophers and psychologists, but was never accepted by ethnologists.

Lévy-Bruhl himself later repudiated the concept of participation mystique. Jung deplored this change, for it seemed to him to explain many of the unconscious phenomena he observed in his patients.

Projection is the mechanism behind paranoia and the hatred—of other nations, classes, political factions, ethnicities, and religious groups—that leads to wars. Its great significance for the healing of individuals and, indeed, of whole societies is obvious in the savagery that fills the history books and the headlines. The universality of projection can hardly be denied; to the extent that we scatter our own disowned traits among uncounted others, we exist as fragmented persons. Our goal here will be to examine the processual aspects of projection with a view to recognizing, owning, and dissolving particular projections as they surface. Beyond that is the question of what role projections play in establishing our whole worldview.

Not only negative qualities are projected; one may also project good or creative qualities, thus failing to discover them within one's own being. All the admired qualities are then found in the hero, idol, or lover, who appears to be the very embodiment of one's ideals. It may be that such positive projections help account for the seeming lack of creativity among women during the patriarchal period from which we are only now emerging. In Jungian terminology, this would be described as the "projection of the animus," or the male component of the feminine personality, onto the male partner, who is seen as the empowered personality, able to take care of the woman. This allows the woman to remain in a state of childlike dependency, while the man's life may expand remarkably, feeding off her projections, as though carried by some invisible power.

Within a projection is a unit of energy that must be called psychic rather than physical, and that has definite effects on the environment. Negative projections of one or both parents can have terrible effects on children. One child may unconsciously be chosen to be the carrier of the shadow side of the family. Even in the absence of physical abuse, the child on whom the negative projections fall will suffer a sense of inferiority and "badness" that may stamp him for life. For the child to become healthy, the parent must become aware of these crippling attitudes and withdraw the negative projection.

Withdrawing the Projection

As one emerges from a stubborn projection, the whole affair begins to have a pathological feeling. One feels caught by it, stuck with it, drawn back into it often against one's own will. The projector perceives ill will here or a conspiracy there, even while knowing that both are partly illusory. Caught in contradiction, he or she remains depressingly entangled. We might speak of the person in the grip of a massive projection as "spellbound." The end of a romance commonly occasions the withdrawal of a projection. During the breakup stage of what seemed like an exciting love affair, the relationship may come to appear to the partners as misguided, if not downright sick, and the state of being in love becomes closely allied to symptom formation as a "falling together." Yet even the attempt to withdraw the projection, however faltering, represents a higher level of consciousness than the stage of being "caught" by it.

Here is a dream fragment from a man who was beginning to evaluate his attitudes toward money and to withdraw his projection on people who have money:

> *I have had dinner at an expensive restaurant. At the end of the meal I get in line to pay my check. As I go to pay at the window, a swarthy man, elegantly dressed, goes around me, pushes some paper at the two men behind the window, and lounges against the counter. I am annoyed. He asks what business I'm in. I say I am in the business of being elbowed out of my place in line. He looks startled, as if no one had ever told him anything like this before. He extends a warm handshake and mumbles something about a deal, and I shake hands.*

Later the dreamer associates the swarthy man with someone who was probably "in the rackets." "He would sell his soul for money—there was an arrogance about him just because he had money. He would be the part of me that gets inflated with money and admires anybody who has it." The dreamer speaks candidly to the shadow figure and, with the same honesty, accepts him as an aspect of his own nature. Perhaps for this reason, the inner racketeer does not become dangerous but learns something from the encounter. "Making a deal" with the shadow might be a way of living consciously with that dynamism rather than being pushed about unconsciously—a significant forward step for the dreamer.

Since we do not consciously "make" our projections, it is perhaps not accurate to say that we "withdraw" them either. Such wording might suggest that the ego, given a small increment of consciousness, could suddenly take charge where it has not been in charge before. Recall that projections "happen" to us; we do not make them happen. Perhaps we do not so much withdraw projections as discover, gradually, that the whole spell or field—the vision, the joy, the terror, the excitement—has disintegrated, and what we thought was the occasion of our fulfillment turns out to be something quite different, perhaps even a trapdoor. There is a notable resistance to withdrawing projections, not only because we do not care to recognize hateful qualities in ourselves, but equally because we do not care to recognize the degree to which they have clouded our judgment. In either case, we feel obscurely in the wrong, deflated, unable to assess our own reality, like a child called to account for something he never really "meant" to do. After all, the projection, being unconscious, arises outside the ego's domain. The humiliation of recognizing it as a projection of one's own unconscious has to be accepted in the course of therapy as the price of increased self-knowledge. In a sense, dealing with projections in therapy may be taken as a prototype of the therapeutic process in general.

M. L. von Franz attempted to bring some order into the process of breaking the hold of projections by dividing it into five stages:

1. Archaic identity of subject and object
2. Differentiation of self from object
3. Need for moral evaluation
4. Experience written off as illusion
5. Psychic experience taken seriously—recognition of psychic reality of the projection[2]

Strictly speaking, the withdrawal of projections begins at von Franz's second stage, when the growing person notices that his or her feelings are not the same as those of family members and friends, and begins to set independent goals for him- or herself while at the same time evaluating the attitudes of others to decide whether they have the ring of truth. There is a drawing apart at this stage that is often seen in the stormy relationships between parents and adolescent children. When the differentiation is more or less complete, one begins to feel like a "different person," as if one had formerly lived in a state of confusion or fogginess ("participation mystique"). Unfortunately one also feels more alone and isolated now—another reason why people hesitate to give up their projections.

Sometimes the struggle is between the individual and the values of a whole society, as with such issues as militarism or pollution of the environment. In these cases, what was formerly seen as admirable or perhaps even glorious comes to be seen in a different light as the projection is withdrawn. This is more than an attitude change. In the beginning there was an element of ego identification with the phenomenon; the glory of king or country redounds to the glory of the loyal citizen. Such powerful loyalties can scarcely be dealt with in moral terms alone; a spiritual orientation involving a higher loyalty is required. The issue of moral evaluation becomes even more wrenching as one's own feelings and attitudes come into question. Shadow elements of deception, laziness, self-indulgence, self-hatred, greed, manipulation, or a hundred other moral ills may come gradually, and often reluctantly, to the surface as projections are dissolved, and call for a massive effort of self-understanding.

Whether the projection can be properly described in retrospect as an "illusion," as von Franz contends, is a complex question that depends on the perspective from which it is viewed. Many people, including Jung himself, often do not go on to the fifth stage. Here is an example: Suppose that you know and admire someone whom you (and many others) believe to be a saint. Her wisdom and goodness even inspire you to develop many saintly qualities of your own. However, as you come to know her better, you realize that she has serious human faults. By the time you have reached the fourth stage, the "saint" has become a fallible human being. Shall you then decide that her saintly qualities were a sham and your inspired experience illusory? Or will you accept her as a flawed human being, recognizing that you made some gains of your own while in the grip of the projection? To the extent that the projection has been withdrawn, it has become a doorway leading to an improved perception of reality.

In a 1917 essay titled "General Aspects of Dream Psychology," Jung ascribes further importance to projection when he writes, "Primitive man has a minimum of self-awareness combined with a maximum of attachment to the object: hence the object can exercise a direct magical compulsion upon him. All primitive magic and religion are based on these magical attachments, which simply consist in the projection of unconscious contents into the object."[3] In accordance with this view, Jung describes the "bridal bed in the field" as designed to call up the energies of the farmer. At that time, he did not see these energies as belonging to the wholeness of that situation or as a field phenomenon, but rather as a projection emanating from the psyche of the farmer. What is psychic is seen as limited to the confines of the human body. If these early views of Jung are accepted, we might ask at what point (if there is such a point) magic and religion cease to be projections and become more than illusory.

It has been suggested that scientific theories are projections of the human psyche, and indeed that all creative products are projections. Here the word *projection* is being used to describe a disciplined, conscious effort, not a merely unconscious happening. It is true, of course, that our theories emerge from human beings and do not necessarily embody ultimate truths, but it is questionable whether *projection* is properly used in this way, especially if it is regarded as an unconscious mechanism to be largely overcome in the course of development. This use of the term calls for further examination.

Projection is a universal human phenomenon. Whatever is universal cannot be called pathological—at least in the personal sense of the word. It is simply the human condition. The tragic effects of mass projections stand as a backdrop to the whole blood-drenched history of humanity, yet they can be changed only as each of us directs attention toward the fact of our own unconscious. At that point, we become involved with the existential concerns of humanity in general and at the same time with the idea of individual therapy. Here we, by our personal work, help to relieve the suffering that has always been a part of human life, and our concern for the growth and healing of individuals takes on a larger meaning.

Projections as Doorways

The therapeutic setting is one place where projections invariably occur. A considerable literature has developed on the topics of transference and countertransference since Freud first called attention to them. Transference is usually described as a specific form of projection wherein a person unconsciously recapitulates in the present a relationship that was important in his childhood—for example, by projecting attributes of the original parental relationship onto the relationship with his therapist. The arising of transference in therapy is generally considered to be a good sign, as it indicates that the therapist can commence healing and repatterning the patient's parental relationship wounds in earnest. Countertransference is also a form of projection, but here a therapist projects her own unconscious thoughts and feelings onto the patient. Left unexamined, countertransferences can lead the therapy astray. But the alert therapist will monitor her inner state for these countertransferences during sessions and use them to understand what the patient is trying to elicit from her. The therapist, upon recognizing an active countertransference, can often employ this realization to significantly deepen the therapy and accelerate healing.

Jung brings an added dimension of understanding to transference by seeing it as more than projection:

> Accordingly I cannot regard the transference merely as a projection of infantile-erotic fantasies. No doubt that is what it is from one standpoint, but I also see in it, as I said in an earlier letter, a process of empathy and adaptation. From this standpoint, the infantile-erotic fantasies, in spite of their undeniable reality, appear rather as a means of comparison or as analogical images for something not yet understood than as independent wishes. This seems to me the real reason why they are unconscious. The patient, not knowing the right attitude, tries to grasp at the right relationship to the analyst by way of comparison and analogy with his infantile experiences. It is not surprising that he gropes back to just the most intimate relationships of his childhood in the attempt to discover the appropriate formula for his relationship to the analyst, for this relationship is very intimate too but differs from the sexual relationship as much as does that of a child to its parents.[4]

This view, that projections may point to an effort at comprehension and adaptation by reference to analogous experiences, applies in many other human situations as well. If we dismiss such efforts as "mere" projections, thereby implying that they are based on illusion and that they call into question the person's ability to assess reality, we place the patient in a bind from which he or she can be freed only with difficulty. It would be more therapeutic in many instances to see the response as a beginning effort at comprehension rather than a reversion to infantilism. The business of enlarging one's boundaries involves trial and error. Presumably the patient's interpretation of the therapeutic relationship will be corrected in the course of time as a part of the healing process. The example given by Jung illustrates the fact that what appears as a projection, insofar as it emerges as part of the patient's effort to cope with an unknown situation, and to the extent that it is dealt with responsibly, can become a doorway to an enlarged understanding and a new capacity for adaptation.

Projection involves both cognitive and emotional components. In practice these two are never entirely separate, but they may be taken separately for purposes of analysis. From the cognitive standpoint, projection is interpretation—that is, how we understand and draw meaning from our reality. "There is no difference in principle between interpretation and projection," Jung says in one of his letters.[5] To some extent, therapy can be seen as a process of making progressively clearer interpretations of reality.

The suggestion that the cognitive side of projection involves the application of analogical reasoning at an unconscious level—trying to orient oneself by turning to prior experiences of a like kind—is entirely valid. But the retrieval of these experiences also brings up the entire emotional context (psychic field) in which they were once embedded; consequently, the emotions that appear may be quite inappropriate to the new situation. This helps explain why projection can involve a great deal of "heat"; when our emotions are somewhat off the mark, we often cling to them all the more tenaciously as if to compensate for the lack of fit. However, the emotions involved in projections cannot always be considered invalid or ill-conceived. The emotional aspect of projection leads humanity into its greatest follies as well as its greatest heroism. The soldier who dies for his country, the woman who remains forever true to the lost love of her youth—these and a thousand other life dramas all can be seen from the standpoint of projection. Jung refers to this idea when he says that animus and anima (the archetypal templates of the contrasexual aspects of the personality) are the great projection-making factors, pulling us into the world drama around us. Is this drama based on illusion, or is it the very stuff of reality? Philosophers have never ceased to debate this enormous question; it can be viewed from either perspective. Let us simply admit that in ordinary life, we tend to see a partly illusory world, colored by projections of many kinds, and that our actions and life choices are partly based on illusion.

A beginning answer to these questions may be found in a suggestion made by Huston Smith in his book *Forgotten Truth*.[6] When one invests manifestly finite objects with infinite worth, he says, it is not so much that the lover projects infinity upon his beloved, as that he glimpses infinity *through* her. "She has, for the duration of his passion, become for him a symbol as (for Dante) was Beatrice: she in whom Heaven's glory walked the earth bodily." She is the aperture through which he glimpses the divine. He is, in a sense, seeing through her to some enchanted realm beyond. This explains the complaint of the beloved, "You don't see me at all," as well as the reluctance of the lover to withdraw the projection. Withdrawal would require him not only to revise his opinion of his lady, but also to sacrifice his window into eternity. The vision that is awakened in him, though perhaps not an accurate description of his lover, should not be denigrated; his resistance to "facing reality" has to be honored. If we do not stay stuck in blame, resentment, vengefulness, or regret, these very projections can be the stepping stones that lead us to new levels of consciousness.

By the process of withdrawal, we find our vital energies finally rising again, leading us to new life engagements. It will certainly appear to the person making this movement that he or she was formerly in the grip of an illusion. If it was a "negative" projection, and he has now succeeded in accepting the despised quality as his own, he will emerge contrite but relieved, in some deeper sense, by the accomplishment of a difficult moral task. But if it was a case of love, a "positive" projection, he will likely feel rather flat, recalling that in his previous state he was energized, felt wonderful, welcomed each day as it dawned—had, in fact, a whole new sense of the meaning and value of life. Was all that, too, an illusion? Or was it the awakening of a capacity for meaningful and joyous living such as he had not known in his ordinary state? Was he wrong to attribute all that to his lady, who has now become an "ex"? If this was illusion, wasn't it the grandest illusion of all? Or was his original mildly depressed state the illusory one?

It might be said that since the lover does not really know what eternity may be, he is still discovering only his own unconscious contents, albeit "through" his lady. But now the situation can be seen differently: instead of her being only a "hook" on which he "hangs" his projections (which, of course, are at least partly illusory), she is made to function in her symbolic capacity. Seen with a double vision, she is at once the physical woman and the metaphysical woman. In her presence, whatever of eternity he is permitted to experience—Beauty, Wisdom, Glory, Love—is awakened. All we know of heaven, it is said, is what shines through in just this way. The capacity for double vision—the poet's view of the universe, extolled by William Blake and other mystical poets—cannot be dismissed as delusional.

Here imagination and reality join hands; the mystery of the universe glows briefly before the eye, at once real and mysterious beyond knowing. At first we are left with the great surprise of having so nearly laid hold of it; then comes the need to write a song or a poem to recall the glory that overwhelmed us as we reached, half-frightened, toward it. In such experiences we approach the ineffable oneness of the universe, the plenum void, and it is from this source that the great sense of empowerment arises. That is why all the world loves a lover—like the moon he glows with the reflected light of glory. The great intensity that marks such experiences testifies to their value. Sadly, in our world they are seldom lasting.

The state of being "in love" is more than a flinging out of mutual projections. A flowering of empathy appears, as well as an opportunity for self-discovery. Our reactions to the beloved begin to throw light on our own potentialities, while at the same time we come to know the other in an experience that is creative of selfhood for both. In love, the deepest layers of our being awaken into tremulous life, wary as little animals venturing out of the nest; we find love to be as scary as war. Love stimulates the imagination; what we do not know about our beloved we discover as if by revelation; the atmosphere quivers with unbidden imagery. It is a time for sowing, with the harvesting to come later in the form of increased understanding of self and other. If the deepening self-knowledge of both partners has gone hand in hand with the development of mutual empathy, the relationship can move to new levels like a single stream gathering momentum as it flows down from the hills.

Psyche as a Container

The idea of projection is based on a particular analogy in which the psyche is seen as a container whose contents can be poured forth or cast out into what is presumably a different container. Such a view does not arise in another analogy in which the psyche is seen as a continuous flow, like a stream of water. In that image, two psyches might flow together like two streams. There would still be some turbulence at the boundary where the two merge, but the process of uniting would be seen in a different light, not as a casting out of mutual projections, but as a kind of interpenetration as each stream is permeated by the other. For each partner there is as much a taking in as a casting forth; what we are picturing is the unconscious growth of awareness that is the invisible counterpart of the outer comradeship.

The state of being "in love" opens the doorway to a unitary level of consciousness from the inside; it is an initiatory experience leading to a different quality of being. That is what makes it magical. If the lover will allow new capacities to grow within her in response to the openings that have come, she will be left with a permanent acquisition of sensitivity and power. The Sufis say that the seeker must be "capable of God"—and so it is with love. Like a spring that flows from the depths of the earth, love has its source in depths beyond our ordinary knowing.

I am attempting to describe a state in which "psyche" is not separate from world—it is world in the very act of experiencing itself. It is world come alive, intensified, and recognizing itself as world. A quality of magic spreads to the whole natural world, which becomes enchanted. This psychocosmic state is available at all times, but in ordinary consciousness will be seen as "unconscious."

Here the wise man or woman approaches the child; the simple clarity of the little child, refined and developed, becomes the clairvoyance of the sage. It is the faculty spoken of in scripture: "Unless ye become as little children . . ." (Matthew 18:3). The fact that some people never move out of the oceanic feeling of containment in the family or group, and never develop their own potentialities as unique persons, should not cause us to deny the value of the kind of "uniting with" that proceeds from the innermost reaches of the soul. The development of individuality also has its dangers when it involves the loss of "fellow feeling," or empathy. Without the capacity for "suffering with," a precious human attainment, all community would eventually break down.

Problems with the Concept of Projection

In the foreword to her previously cited book *Projection and Re-Collection in Jungian Psychology,* M. L. von Franz says that while the concept of projection does describe an easily demonstrated set of facts, at the same time it leads into certain borderline areas where there are unsolved problems, and where a clear consensus has not come into being. The time has now come to delve into some of these marginal areas.

Our modern consciousness divides the world into an "inner" and an "outer," a subject and an object, polarizing our view of reality into one of separate persons and objects. This division stands at the very root of our consciousness. We cannot become conscious of anything until we separate it off from all other things. In the book of Genesis, God began his Creation (which was also the creation of consciousness) with a series of acts of *division.* He separated the light from the darkness, the upper waters from the lower, giving to each its identity. Only in this way could the Creation come to know itself. This division continues today with every act of coming to consciousness. Within our world we stand alone, confronted by strangers. Distinction, separation, and division are the hallmarks of that world. It could be said that the more the ego is consolidated—the more it separates the categories of the world in the interest of acquiring consciousness—the more projection is needed to throw a bridge over the gap between subject and object. The effect of projection is to unite by an unconscious emotional tie that which would otherwise remain separated within our mental structure. One might think of projection, then, as an unconscious effort to overcome the dualism and separation of the conscious worldview.

Jung, as noted, equated projection with participation mystique, the mental structure of "archaic people." Early in his work, when he was casting about for a parallel to some of the problems he observed in his patients, he thought he had found it among "primitives," or primal people. From the perspective of our current consciousness, theirs appears to be inferior—but only as long as we remain unaware of their impressive knowledge and life patterns. Von Franz reveals the difficulties with this use of language at a point where she is trying to clarify Jung's terminology:

> But the archaic identity of subject and object still lives at the very bottom of our psyche, and it is only above that layer that relatively

> clearer, more distinct discriminations between subject and object are, in many degrees, built up. The lower or more primitive layer should, however, not be regarded as lesser in value: on the contrary, if we must form a value judgment, it is there that the real secret of all life-intensity and cultural creativity lies.[7]

Do we not create certain difficulties for ourselves when we suggest that the lower, or "archaic," level of consciousness is in fact the higher from another perspective? Which is "higher" and which is "lower"? Do such terms even apply?

To illustrate: The story is told of an anthropologist traveling through the African bush with his native companion who heard the sound of drumming from the region of a nearby tribe. The native fell on his face, saying, "Their chief is dead." The anthropologist, thinking his companion must have got the message from the beat of the drums, and wishing to probe the mystery of drum signals, insisted on being told what drum rhythm had given him this precise information. The native denied that he had got the idea in that way. What he said was that the drums told a different story—they told him to look within. He had done so, and immediately perceived the face of the dead chief. He had picked it up on his inner radar screen! Dr. John Layard, the British anthropologist who related this story, hypothesized that the communication took place through the sympathetic nervous system, as happens with insects.[8]

The native was practicing clairvoyance,[9] which has a certain resemblance to projection. In clairvoyance, an event occurring in the outside world (at least to our mode of understanding) is experienced inside, as when the native looked within. An outer event is transposed and becomes an inner one. In projection, a seeming reversal occurs; an inner happening or attitude is experienced as though in another person. In both cases there is a coming together of inner and outer; it is probable, then, that both projection and clairvoyance emerge from a level of the psyche where there is no distinction between inner and outer, subject and object. Clearly the native had this power under his voluntary control. Western dualism offers no way of accounting for it within our mode of consciousness except to say that the knowledge is "in the unconscious."

What is of special interest here is that the tribesman evidently took for granted this inner power of perception by which the psyche perceived an event occurring at some distance, as though this kind of awareness (clairvoyance) were happening all the time—instantaneously, effortlessly, and accurately—and needed only an inward glance to be seen by consciousness. Jean Gebser tells us that we moderns have invented radio and television to take the place of these powers now generally forfeited at our modern level of consciousness.[10] At the same time, as we press against the limits of what we will accept rationally, we are expanding our understanding of primal peoples, particularly their shamans and healers who practiced modes of consciousness other than our own. Do these men and women offer hints of the expansion of consciousness that is possible for us?

Toward a Field Theory of Projection

The native consciousness portrayed in Layard's example is best described as an immersion in a field of awareness, such that all the tribesmen were at all times aware of shifts and changes and cycles occurring within the field. Their own awareness detected the changes going on "outside" but not available to the eyes or ears. We can find a modern parallel in the child's immersion in the world of the family. A child who is not told what is troubling the family will nevertheless know with his whole being, though his knowledge may be of a subliminal kind. Probably it will take the form of symptoms or behaviors that are somehow expressive of what the turmoil in the family means to him, usually behavior distressing to the parents. Then the child himself becomes a focus of parental concerns, as if he were the cause instead of the mirror reflecting the turbulence in the field of the family.

When the mother, upset and alarmed at the child's behavior, brings it to the therapist, shall we say that she is "projecting" the family difficulties onto the child? Or that the child has "introjected" the family disturbance? From the standpoint of each family member, there appears to be an unconscious taking in and then casting forth. From the standpoint of the family as a whole, we may better speak of radiating influences that together form the psychic atmosphere that accompanies the family's external interaction, so pervasive and encompassing that it cannot be apprehended consciously until one has moved "outside" it. The sorting out of these "radiating influences" within the field of the family becomes a necessary and arduous part of each person's maturation.

This brings us to a very significant issue that must be raised in connection with projection. In a forward-looking essay called "The Psyche and the Transformation of the Reality Planes," Erich Neumann was among the first to examine projection in the context of different levels of consciousness.[11] The polarization of the world into subject and object, said Neumann, is a product of the human perceptual system attached to a conscious ego that can apprehend only a limited world field composed of separate persons and objects. This polarization is not intrinsic to the nature of the world itself. It is a dualistic state that cannot be a final condition. If I am a subject to myself while you are an object to me, at the same time I am an object to you while you are a subject to yourself. We are both, at all times, subject and object. We cannot say that one of these states is true while the other is not. From another standpoint, we can say that the separation of subject and object depends on our perspective—from my perspective you are the object, but from your perspective I am the object. Neither one perceives a final truth.

Knowledge and experience gained within a particular psychic structure are bound up with that structure, says Neumann, and do not seem valid when another psychic state supervenes. Charles Tart uses the helpful term "state-specific knowledge" to point to the fact that knowledge or experience gained in one state or level of consciousness is not normally available in another state or level. This is most evident in our dream life, whose knowledge is not easily available to consciousness. According to Neumann, "There is a marked tendency on the part of the ego-conscious system to repress the extrane knowledge" (that gained in what we might call an alternate state of consciousness).[12]

To illustrate what is meant by psychic structure, Neumann, like Jung, turns to the world of the "primitive." He sees primal people as beautifully and precisely attuned to the conditions of their world in ways that resemble the adaptation of animals. Their sense of unity with the natural world makes for stable and long-enduring ways of life, but any change in the environment with which they form a field can lead to chaotic confusion or even to the destruction of the tribe. Accordingly, over the eons, human beings have developed the kind of consciousness that separates them from the natural world, creating an apparently objective world "out there" which they can manipulate for their own purposes. This has led to greater freedom and the ability to survive in many environments, but it has also isolated and separated human beings from an outer world with which they no longer form a unified field.

When we say that these ancient peoples were identified with the landscapes, the moods, the life and rhythm of the natural world, we do not mean that they could not make necessary distinctions. We mean, rather, that they experienced their own being contained within the same "stream" that quickens all life. Their experience of the life pulse that animates tree and grass and animal life made all living things a unity. This was a state of being, not a philosophical idea, and it is not necessarily archaic. Known as animism, it is being put forward in various forms by an increasing group of modern scientists, particularly those who focus on ecology and the marvelous interdependence of all life forms.

In regard to this unity of landscape and mindscape, Neumann makes a significant comment:

> In *participation mystique*—usually, to my mind not too accurately called an "unconscious state"—oneness is experienced in a multiplicity of connections and relations, between man and man, man and animal, man and world, and so on, which does not hold in the reality field of ego consciousness. But *participation mystique* (the unconscious identity of subject and object) is something more than a "subjective" means of perception, especially since the subject is merged in a field situation in which the boundary between "subject" and "object" dissolves (that is to say, it is not in force). The relations valid for this reality are called illusory by a consciousness which can only partly understand them. But ego consciousness is not fully competent in a reality field other than its own, and the reality to which *participation mystique* relates is certainly also only relative, though not for this reason illusory or false.[13]

Here Neumann is distinguishing between modern subject-object consciousness and another state in which the division between subject and object is not in effect. The two states give access to different realities, he is saying, each having its own validity. There is not merely state-specific knowledge, but also state-specific *worlds* that correspond to the knowledge and level of selfhood we bring to the encounter. This is what makes us co-creators of our world.

The reality field changes as our state of being changes. To say that the reality apprehended in ordinary consciousness is the only valid one is to hold to a kind of parochialism. Our difficulties arise through having approached these other states from the perspective of pathology, by observing persons overwhelmed by the unconscious and unable to return voluntarily to the ordinary state. In that context, ordinary consciousness is seen as the only real and valid state.

Now, if a tribesman asserts that he gets his knowledge from a bird that told him a secret, it is not correct to say that he is "projecting" into the bird, in the sense that the knowledge is really "in him" though unconscious, but he discovers it only by projecting it outward into the bird. That formulation belongs to our ego consciousness, not to the native consciousness. Rather, both native and bird are embedded in a field situation in which this kind of communion is ever present. The knowledge, Neumann insists, is in the living field that contains both human and bird.[14] The bird does not form part of an "objective world" in which it remains separate from the native. And the native is not a cool observer, but afloat in his world and its sights and scents and currents. Neumann suggests that the concept of projection does not necessarily refer to knowledge originally "within" us, though unconscious. Rather it is "field knowledge . . . present or emergent in a living field" in which both subject and object are contained. We might call this a "meaning field," or a field of awareness. This means that knowledge is as much a real existent within the field as the persons or things active in that field, while the field itself functions as a carrier of knowledge, a field of awareness. As such, the field begins to have a sentient nature. Says Neumann, "It follows that we must learn no longer to regard it as self-evident that every knowledge is 'inner'—in our consciousness, in our psyche, in us, in some living thing. The more so when we remember that inner and outer are categories of our system of consciousness, valid only for its reality, but not, for instance, for the reality of *participation mystique* nor hence of projection."[15]

This interpretation will sound strange to us, Neumann admits, since it assumes knowledge to be something as concrete in essence as human and bird. Nevertheless, it is a provocative way of formulating the kind of events he describes. The effect of Neumann's approach is to *relativize the form of consciousness in which we ordinarily live.* Ordinary consciousness can no longer be seen as the standard against which all other forms should be measured.

We come to recognize it simply as that form in which I, as subject, stand at the center of a world of objects separate from me and, in a sense, alien to me. This divided world is my "reality." My claim to its exclusive validity is threatened by the idea of "field knowledge" not connected to the ego and made conscious only with difficulty.

If we are wrong in saying that the native tribesman projects knowledge into the bird, for what he learns is field knowledge emerging from his attunement to his natural environment, then isn't it reasonable to think that many projections represent just such an intuitive taking in of knowledge, and not at all a casting forth, as was proposed in the beginning of the chapter? This is a possibility that now cannot be ignored: that all such knowledge is field knowledge apprehended through the intuitive faculties, not through the ears, eyes, and central nervous system. And the reason it tends to be flawed in many interpersonal situations is that we have not cleansed ourselves of the personal desires and demands that keep us from seeing clearly. Perhaps the knowledge gleaned from the field is knowledge that this particular ego is not prepared to accept. Or perhaps the knowledge becomes twisted in the act of interpretation but was accurately perceived in the beginning. If the knowledge was not originally "in" the native, so that he could project it out onto the bird, perhaps my "knowledge" of my irresponsible neighbor is also not "in" me but is generated whenever we are involved with each other. In our effort to make sense of projections, we have attributed a spatial dimension to unconscious feelings and attitudes (they are "in here" or "out there"), which Jung acknowledges are not spatial in form any more than ideas or feelings are spatial.[16]

This question involves a whole shift of perspective that we are scarcely able to make in the absence of more evidence. Our thoughts are not "in" us? They don't necessarily belong to us? They are "field knowledge"? Such ideas are not to be taken up lightly, for they undermine some of our most basic assumptions. But as we begin to reconsider our understanding of space and time, in line with modern physics, such ideas will again come to the fore, along with a number of other questions having to do parapsychological phenomena.

Projection and Intuition

The idea of projection suggests a one-way traffic between person and world at unconscious levels—but why not a two-way traffic? It cannot be doubted that the movement goes both ways. Freud uses the term *introjection* to refer to the unconscious "taking in" that would be the counterpart of projection, but Jung makes almost no use of this term.[17] For a Jungian equivalent we would have to turn to the word *intuition,* meaning "perception by way of the unconscious." Jung includes intuition as one of the well-known four functions, along with sensation, thinking, and feeling, by which we orient ourselves in our environment.

Jung does not appear to see intuition as the reverse of projection, but in one of his letters he equates it with "paranormal cognition" and relates it to the whole field of parapsychology.[18] He is thinking, evidently, of that knowledge that comes to us without the use of any of the five senses, suggesting that there is no difference between intuition (i.e., "you don't know how you get it") and paranormal cognition. He offers the interesting idea that intuition is perception by way of the unconscious in a relative or "elastic" time and space. He adds that time and space appear to be psychic functions rather than attributes of external reality. In most of his writing, Jung tends to ignore the paranormal aspect of intuition. At the time of the letter quoted (1945), he appeared to despair of our ever understanding what is called "paranormal."

The idea of projection is incomplete without a mention of its counterpart, intuition. While we as subjects are casting forth our projections onto the object, we at the same time are taking in the projections being cast forth onto us, just as the "object" is similarly taking in our projections and casting forth her own. Knowledge born in this way is not always a misinterpretation. It is sometimes said that people "sniff each other out," a hint that we can take in by way of the nose, the organ of intuition. For those whose intuitive faculty is not well developed, such insights are often fascinating but not always reliable. People who have frequent subliminal perceptions of this kind may find them very disturbing because they do not know consciously whether or not something unexpected or even dangerous is about to occur. But if the knowledge is translated into conscious meaning, and if it is veridical, it is telepathy or clairvoyance. The native who got his knowledge from a bird was using clairvoyance.

It is probable that all of us are continually giving and receiving impressions of this kind as such a constant accompaniment of living that we are as unaware of them as of the pull of gravity. The presence of such impressions would attest to the subliminal presence of the unitary world, still there, unrecognized, beneath the stream of ordinary consciousness, like the stars on a cloudy night. Highly intuitive persons are especially gifted in this kind of awareness, and it has been suggested that it is a capacity originally possessed by the entire human race, but now lost upon maturation or kept dormant by all but a few.[19]

The outward movement, projection, is more akin to speech at the level of ordinary consciousness, while the inward movement is more akin to hearing. Speech is more active and hearing more receptive, but both have to do with vibrations in the air or psychic field that embrace persons in relationship. If we hypothesize that this kind of communion comes from a level beyond that which human speech and hearing give access, then Neumann's suggestion that the knowledge is "in the field" takes on greater significance. In support of this view, without going into the studies of modern parapsychologists, is the report of early-twentieth-century adventurer and Buddhist scholar Alexandra David-Neel, who claims that messages were frequently sent "on the wind" in Tibet. She writes that she herself received such messages from lamas under whom she had taken mental and psychic training. This communication, she suggests, was facilitated by the great silence and solitude of that land, where the air was untroubled by the interaction of large crowds, and where the minds of the people tended toward calmness and placidity.[20] To the Tibetans, according to Madame David-Neel, these powers were very much a part of ordinary life, not to be regarded with special awe or wonder.

Unlike the native tribesman or the Tibetan, the modern Westerner cannot look directly within him- or herself to find a picture of what is happening at a distance. He or she is obliged to make a journey back to a realm of meaning that was immediately accessible to many of those living in previous ages. Although we live in a divided world and use a dualistic language, we are never entirely separate from the friend and neighbor who is our companion (from the Latin *com,* meaning "with" or "together," plus *panes,* "bread"; one who shares our bread in a sacred act that celebrates our unity). Only when we sacrifice some of our separateness in favor of immersion in the wholeness do we become fully human and gain access to our latent creativity. This must be by an act of returning, a homecoming that can be made once our own boundaries have been established. Our sense of community will then be secured in a way that supplements our individuality and does not overwhelm it. Community is also promoted by the work of creative persons who tune into the spirit of the time and place and give form to the latent intuitions of the people.

In the illustrations I have given here, I have taken it for granted that projection lies on a continuum with telepathy or other parapsychological powers of the psyche. Perhaps we should explore this more thoroughly. As we have seen, the idea that projections are mainly illusory is open to question. What seems a projection may represent the ego's confused response to knowledge apprehended by the deep psyche but known only dimly and fleetingly to consciousness. Such knowledge may in fact coincide with the outer reality. We then have a parapsychological event—telepathy, clairvoyance, or perhaps precognition. Von Franz gives an example of a patient of Jung's who came to therapy with numerous phobias. These gradually dissipated as he came to a more realistic understanding of his inner fears, except for one stubborn phobia concerning outdoor stairways. Years later it turned out that the patient, while standing on an open stairway, was killed by a stray bullet fired in a street battle. In retrospect, then, one could say he had good reason to be fearful of open stairs, and his "projection" was a case of precognition. But this could be determined only with hindsight by one acquainted with the inner circumstances of his life. A case like this prompts von Franz to say that psychologists should use great caution and discretion in dealing with projections![21]

What this says is that a projection may turn out to be not a projection—in the sense of a mistaken attribution—at all. It may be the very truth. In that case, it never was a projection; it was an instance of telepathy or some allied unconscious psychic mechanism—evidence that the unconscious may be aware of the actual configuration of outer happenings that could not possibly be known by way of the five senses. Jung refers to this possibility in a late essay on unidentified flying objects (UFOs), or flying saucers as they were then called.[22] His preferred explanation for UFOs is that they represent psychic contents constellated in the unconscious of modern humanity and "forced to manifest indirectly in the form of spontaneous projections" because we have no way to assimilate their meaning consciously. Since they are actually seen in the sky, they would have to be called apparitions or hallucinations, but Jung does not say this. Instead he mentions "the possibility of natural or absolute 'knowledge,' when the unconscious psyche coincides with objective facts."

The unconscious, in other words, reveals an ability to comprehend outer situations in ways consciousness is unable to do, free of the limits of space and time. Jung speaks of a number of instances of absolute knowledge seen not only in humankind, but throughout the organic world. He does not overlook the possibility that the UFOs are real material objects that happen to coincide meaningfully with the psychic situation of modern humanity—that is, that they are synchronicities. Thus the concept of projection opens up the larger question of synchronistic or parapsychological phenomena, the subject of the next chapter. In the meantime, we might underscore von Franz's warning to therapists to be cautious in dealing with what appear to be projections, but may not be projections at all.

The Paradox of Projection

One other problematic issue arises from our consideration of projection: this has to do with the great world-creating factors that Jung called the "archetypal contents" of the psyche, particularly those intuitions of the divine, the paradisiacal, or the glorious by which humankind comes into relationship with the healing and redemptive aspects of reality. Unfortunately these powers can also be destructive if we are not rightly related to them. They are generally seen first in projection, formerly onto gods and goddesses, but in our secular world perhaps onto political leaders or movie stars. They are the common heritage of humanity, not individual possessions. We know them through their symbolic representations.

The word *symbol* is a key to thinking about the archetypal powers. For Dante, Beatrice becomes a symbol of infinite worth, says Huston Smith.[23] The poet sees in her no longer an ordinary, flesh-and-blood young girl but a reincarnation of the timeless figure of the Virgin. The leap from the temporal to the eternal, from the individual to the universal—the projection—is made unconsciously, without ego participation. We do not know why we choose our heroes, our fools, our scapegoats, and our goddesses—or, perhaps, why they choose us. All we know is that they "grip us," exerting a hold on us quite different from that maintained by the ordinary contents of consciousness. Often they seem more like a fate that descends on us than anything we choose. The archetypal powers are experienced under the aspect of eternity; they reveal the insights that poets try to glean from the world.

The projection of such archetypal contents can fall equally on an innocent young girl, on a cult leader, or on a Hitler or a Stalin. They may call up the higher powers within us or our own disowned evil. Usually the projection involves undeveloped aspects of the psyche that are ready for manifestation. Two transformations are needed, both unconscious: the discovery of those powerful contents in another person or group, and the leap from the human to the transpersonal level.

During World War II, the negative projections of Americans as a people fell on the Japanese following the bombing of Pearl Harbor. The enemy was no longer a group of humans but "the Jap," a gap-toothed figure who was the very personification of treachery, who smiled to your face while plotting to stab you in the back. Under the sway of this projection, Americans believed that the Japanese deserved—yes, *deserved*—to have the atom bomb dropped on their cities and fire bombs sear their land. The projection of such archetypal images, with their trailing clouds of fear and hatred, probably made it more likely that the United States would drop the atomic bomb on Hiroshima and Nagasaki. After the war, when America treated the enemy with generosity, the gap-toothed marauder retreated back into the seed stage, but remained ready to spring into action again should an unscrupulous leader come along. This kind of negative projection seemingly has an eternal form of existence.

In Shakespeare's *Merchant of Venice,* Shylock the Jew says, "Hath not a Jew eyes? Hath not a Jew hands, organs, dimensions, senses, affections, passions? . . . If you prick us do we not bleed?"[24] Shylock is here claiming his humanity, in that he has hands and ears and feelings like anyone else. He is not an eternal figure; rich, powerful, and yet somehow contemptible (and therefore endangered), he is a human being who bleeds when wounded and cries out when wronged. The Bard understood the archetypal projections that fell on the Jews and knew that such projections were flourishing in his time, as they are today in many parts of the world.

To counteract the danger of these negative archetypal projections, we need to call up the images capable of sustaining and renewing human life. These images of the great healers and saviors are humanly constructed analogies by which we portray or envision the mysterious activity within the divine realm that gives rise to human life and heals and renews it. It was because of the potentially healing power of these images that Jung spoke of the great world religions as ancient therapeutic systems.[25]

In the previous chapter, we began to see the kinship of symptom and symbol. The former is a "falling together" of mind and body, and the latter, a "throwing together" of different levels of being. In connection with a disease, a symptom is, paradoxically, at once crippling and potentially healing. We see the same paradoxical quality in projections: they may bring either wounding or healing. Humans have always recognized something pathological in relentless, smoldering hatred, especially when it is enacted in cruelty to our fellow humans or passed on to future generations, for at such times the ego does not take up arms against the wayward tendency but actually conspires to join the fight. But when the ego holds fast to its fallible human nature while experiencing the eternal forms as they emerge on the stage of the world, we can attain new levels of consciousness. Somewhere within each of us is the healing truth. Symptom and symbol—wounding and healing—dance together as the lights go up, and fall into darkness if we lose the precious insight. We are not gods, nor are we necessarily in the grip of the gods unless we consent to our subjection. To be human is great enough.

A Diaphanous Worldview

We return now to the topic of subject-object consciousness, where the meanings we extract from the welter of experiences are relative to our point of view.

Each individual has his or her own perspective, yet at the same time each is affected by the perspectives of all others.

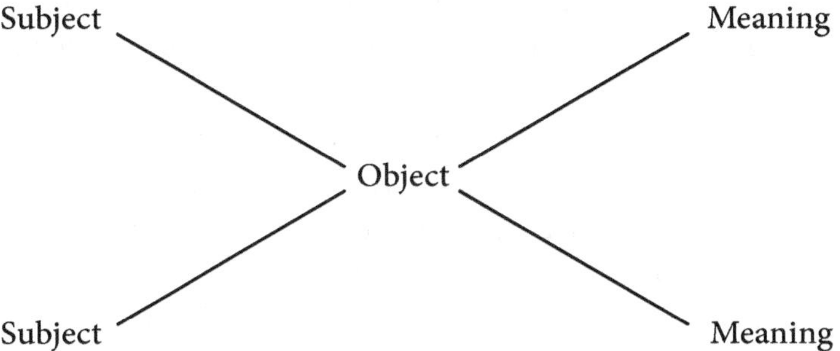

Suppose for a moment that we could see from all perspectives at once. Gebser suggests that this is the particular leap of consciousness that we are now engaged in making. He calls it a movement toward an "aperspectival world."[26] The perspectival world is basically visual and leads us to make visual representations or images. It is a world where space and time establish the relationships between different entities. Things are before or after each other, far or near; they are separated from each other, each located in time and space. This is the world we have lived in, and it was the worldview of science until very recently. Our difficulties in comprehending a phenomenon such as synchronicity arise in part because of our tendency to think of such events in perspectival terms. Perspectival thinking *spatializes*. By its very nature it is partial and limited by the possibilities afforded by other perspectives. The aperspectival world is *diaphanous*, in Gebser's language; one experiences situations in their symbolic wholeness as they gleam with many facets of meaning.

Aperspectival thinking is holistically focused. Relationships are understood less by their juxtaposition in time and space than by contemplation (*con*, "with," plus *templum*, "temple"; from the art of divination practiced in the temple). In contemplation, events become transparent and we "see through" them; they are seen in process, revealing their tendency in arising and becoming. In aperspectival thinking, we move from a spatial to a temporal view, which opens our imagination to the possibilities and promises that could arise within the particular situation. Since the future is already present in a state of latency, what is revealed as we look through events is not simply imaginary but the seeds of the future—divination. The distinctions by which we establish our time world—past, present, and future—tend to become transparent in the aperspectival vision. Would projections become rare or cease altogether in the aperspectival world? I suspect they would continue but might become conscious more easily, and the illusory nature of our reality would be lessened.

Our study of projections in this chapter has called attention to the subject-object nature of our consciousness, a division that is built into our form of perception. Projections can be the means of bridging the gap between subject and object, though whether our "bridge" is more illusory than real remains unanswered. Do projections actually belong to "our" consciousness, or do they emerge from a field of awareness that is created by people and things in interaction? As we pondered these issues, the question of whether projection involves a parapsychological element (clairvoyance) began to surface. In the next chapter we will take a step in the direction toward a more unified form of consciousness through a study of synchronicity.

CHAPTER 4

SYNCHRONICITY

When I see the immense order of the universe (and especially the brain of man), I cannot escape feeling that this ground enfolds a supreme intelligence.

—David Bohm

What is above is like what is below. What is below is like what is above. The miracle of unity is to be attained. Everything is formed from the contemplation of unity, and all things come about from unity, by means of adaptation.

—The Emerald Tablet of Hermes Trismegistus

Make no mistake about it: when we come to the subject of synchronicity, we are talking about marvels, miracles, and the occult. Now that even the most exotic of sexual practices, along with all manner of human perfidy, have been opened to public scrutiny, it would seem that only the occult, the hidden, is still a dark secret. Much that is unexplained and unexplored lies in the human mind itself.

But while the study of the occult has led some in the directions of phantoms, ghouls, vampires, and other nocturnal horrors, we seek contributions to a rational approach. We will be asking particularly what metaphors and analogies can be brought forward to throw light on this subject. This is one area where we have empirical evidence of the activity of another world order operating within our familiar reality. Those who deny the existence of parapsychological phenomena in the name of empiricism are hardly consistent, since many of these events are quite evident to the senses, though they cannot be understood by the many schemes we apply to ordinary physical reality. The effort to understand takes us outside the thought structures by which we make sense of our world. Whereas in previous decades many were willing to overlook the evidence offered by parapsychologists in the interest of remaining undisturbed in their mechanistic worldview, we may be more open to the evidence today, as that worldview recedes into the past.

Jung's exposition in his 1952 essay "Synchronicity: An Acausal Connecting Principle" has formed the starting point for many later investigations.[1] Of these, the most helpful is *Synchronicity: The Bridge Between Matter and Mind* by F. David Peat, a physicist and collaborator of David Bohm.[2] The difference between Jung's pioneering work and Peat's presentation measures the distance we have traveled in a very few years in opening ourselves to a changed worldview. Jung in his search turned to the ancient Taoists as well as the Hermetic philosophers of the West, whose ideas foreshadowed the needed changes, while Peat was able to turn to certain modern developments in art, science, and philosophy to lend support to his work.

I will begin by tracing Jung's path, since that is the way many of us have traveled, but I will draw on Peat's suggestions for further exploration. It is necessary to add that this material does not allow for a logical approach; we cannot think our way to an understanding of synchronicity. Rather, we are required to move tangentially, hoping to discover the outlines of our subject as we approach from different angles. Our purpose will be to learn whether synchronistic events allow us to probe more deeply into the nature of reality and aid us in the search for wholeness. That should lead to a more encompassing worldview, and to more creative and healthful living. But let us begin at the beginning.

Synchronistic phenomena or meaningful coincidences are easily recognized in practice. For example, during the first hour with a new female patient, I was startled by a sudden rustling outside my window, no more than four feet from my head. Peering out in the darkness, I saw a pair of beady eyes staring into mine—an urban-dwelling raccoon had climbed up the large bush outside my window and turned around to look at me. He climbed to the top of the bush, lingered a moment, and then crawled down and away. We had not seen a raccoon around our property for more than a decade. The appearance of the animal at that moment had a numinous effect: raccoons belong to the bear family and are thus linked to the Great Mother; they are nocturnal creatures, hibernating in winter in cold climates, wild but capable of being tamed. This spoke to the nature of my patient, who all her life had lived in close attachment to a dominant mother.

Another example occurred as members assembled for the first hour of a psychological group that I was conducting in a nearby community. We were startled when the light beside the fireplace suddenly went out with a splintering of fragments of glass. Our host, as he replaced the lightbulb, assured us that this had never happened before. But as if to rekindle our astonished speculations, as the group broke up at evening's end, the same lamp exploded again. The two events coincided in a remarkable way with the psychic situation of our host, who was going through an extremely critical life experience at the time, with no apparent way to extricate himself.

Some experiences seem to suggest the activity of a mind and will above and beyond that of the person involved, as in this account related by a woman who had been struggling with matters of religion:

I had been raised in the Catholic faith, but as a young woman I made the decision to read the Bible cover to cover, a chapter a day. Some of my Catholic friends said I should not do it; they saw it as dangerous. But when I went to church I began to hear a male voice saying, "You are going to leave this place. You shall leave this place." I argued with the voice, but I kept hearing it, and soon I began to have anxiety attacks whenever I went to church. Then the voice began to tell me to remove the crucifix that had hung at the head of my bed since the time of my marriage. I came to have the same anxiety every time I went into the bedroom. "Remove that. Remove all the icons in the house," the voice now said. At last I spoke to it. I said, "I can't do it; you do it." A few days later the crucifix fell off the wall.

The woman did not doubt that this was a synchronistic event. It was a situation of deep emotion and inner conflict, and also one of "impossibility," where she could not take the step that was demanded of her. Indeed, she did not know whether to trust the voice and only later came to accept it as expressing the fatedness of her life.

Synchronicities frequently involve animal life.[3] Here is a striking example from ancient times, a synchronistic event in the life of Pythagoras as told by the Neoplatonist Iamblichus:

> When . . . he happened to be conversing with his familiars about birds, symbols, and prodigies, and was observing that all these are the messengers of the Gods, sent by them to those men who are truly dear to the Gods, he is said to have brought down an eagle that was flying over Olympia, and after gently stroking, to have dismissed it. Through these things, therefore, and other things similar to these, he demonstrated that he possessed the same dominion as Orpheus over savage animals.[4]

A fine example of synchronicity is told by Roger Jones, a physicist and author of *Physics as Metaphor*.[5] As he was working on his book, he had just finished a paragraph on cardinal numbers when he glanced up and saw a beautiful red bird—yes, a cardinal—on his lawn, quite out of season. At first, preoccupied with his work, he did not see the connection, but then he saw it and called it a visual pun. Such synchronicities, he notes, seem like rare and precious gifts.

Synchronistic events usually seem to call for a symbolic reading. It is possible that in translating them into thematic terms we do a certain violence to them, as if they should be allowed to speak in their own dramatic immediacy, a kind of wordless speaking. A young physician made a house call at a home located on a T-shaped intersection in a lonely and desolate part of town. When she came out of the house, she found her car had been sideswiped. At that time, she was recently divorced and had returned to live with her mother. One whole side of her life, like one side of her car, had been crushed in. The outer desolation matched her inner despair. Even the T intersection, where one of the four directions was cut off, seemed to fit the total picture; the fourfold wholeness of her life had broken down. In the sideswiping, the car had become the analogical stand-in for that which in the physician herself was battered—her sexual life, her self-expression as a woman. Although it was only an accident, it was also a metaphoric description of the unfolding pattern of her life, and it spoke of the devastation that she had not quite admitted to consciousness. I suggest that this kind of event is analogous to symptom formation: a falling together that is characterized by meaning.

Chance and Meaning

Synchronistic events combine chance and meaning in a way that baffles the rational faculties. The term "meaningful coincidence" encompasses this paradoxical quality. Here is Jung's definition:

> The simultaneous occurrence of a certain psychic state with one or more external events which appear as meaningful parallels to the momentary subjective state—and in certain cases, vice versa.[6]

A strict reading of Jung's view would say that synchronicities cannot even be defined, much less explained, by the objective methods of traditional science, for the subjective element is an intrinsic part of the occurrence. In general, Jung's understanding of synchronicity includes the same phenomena now studied in parapsychology. Today they are often grouped together as "psi" phenomena. Jung differs from the approach of the parapsychologists in that from the beginning he includes the subjective meaning as a part of the event, while the parapsychologist strives as far as possible for an "objective" approach. The difference is crucial. Consider the following example:

> A young man was driving rapidly along the freeway headed toward a city where he expected to meet some strangers. He was in a mildly uneasy frame of mind, having been warned against these people, but at the same time he was excited by the prospect of an adventure. On the way, the front of his car was hit by a heavy beam that accidentally fell from a passing truck. Though his car was not damaged, he turned off at the next off-ramp and headed home, concluding that the universe was telling him not to go to this meeting. He later learned that he had indeed made the right decision.

For this sequence of events to unfold as it did, it was necessary for the young man to see the falling of the beam in a particular way, as Moses saw the burning bush. It has been well said that if Moses had not been able to see the burning bush in a sacred light, he would have seen only a brush fire in the desert, to the great detriment of our spiritual tradition. As it was, he saw the fire as a bearer of special meaning, and heard the voice of God coming from it. Our modern young man took a similar stance, allowing the incident to speak to him with a very personal meaning, although, from another perspective, it could be seen as a mere accident.

In such cases, the attribution of meaning is an act of the observer who sees the event; it is not necessarily inherent in the event itself. The one who sees draws the conclusion that the universe is coming down on one side of his dilemma, that it is speaking to him personally. This would be better called a sign than a synchronicity. The ancients paid close attention to signs.

Such meaningful events—if they are meaningful—are not explained by causality. Indeed a cause is not even thinkable.[7] The term *synchronicity*, Jung is careful to say, "explains nothing, it simply formulates the occurrence of meaningful coincidences which, in themselves, are chance happenings, but are so improbable that we must assume them to be based on some kind of principle, or on some property of the empirical world."[8] This property, whatever it is, cannot act causally in the sense of pushing and pulling things around. He holds that we are likely to posit a transcendental cause for lack of any demonstrable one, but that a transcendental cause is a contradiction in terms. "A cause can only be a demonstrable quantity." Causation as a principle is ruled out, in Jung's view.[9]

Synchronicity hints at a connecting or organizing principle that operates between mind and matter or between mind and mind, and that arises from an affinity of meaning, not from any mechanistic force. The presence of meaning, in turn, hints at the participation of mind. The full implications of such a principle operating throughout the world, or possibly throughout the universe, call for a real shift of consciousness.

As meaningful coincidences are not explained by causality, they are thus not affected by distance. J. B. Rhine's experiments at the Duke University Parapsychology Laboratory showed that certain subjects could guess the order of a sequence of cards to a number exceeding the law of probability at a distance of many miles. As with space, so with time: Rhine's subjects were able to guess the order of the cards before the cards were turned up—again to a number exceeding probability. Such instances of precognition are particularly baffling, because they cannot begin to be explained by causality. How can an event that has not yet occurred cause us to know it in the present? A cause acting now can only bring about an effect in the future, for causality requires space and time as independent realities.[10] Synchronicities must accordingly be related to the deeper layers of the psyche where space and time as we know them consciously are not in effect. We say, therefore, that they are related to the unconscious, using modern terminology that does not dispel the mystery. Jung suggests that synchronistic events are rare phenomena; however, he adds that if mind and body are linked synchronistically, then they would not be rare at all. We have assumed in our earlier discussion that this is the case, for we have taken many symptoms to resemble synchronicities—meaningful but not explained by any physical cause. Jung allows for this as a possibility without adopting it as a consistent view. He says that if mind and body are finally shown to be linked by way of synchronicity then his views "would have to be corrected."[11]

Synchronicity and Emotion

The one factor invariably present when positive results were obtained in Rhine's experiments was a subjective one: enthusiasm, high expectation, emotional involvement. Synchronistic events also often involve a time of transition, when situations roll over into new configurations. These are likely to be archetypal moments with life-changing implications for the persons involved—birth, death, illness, the loss of a child or lover, situations of "impossibility,"[12] and similar occurrences—all of which have the effect of setting aside the ego with its customary interpretive patterns, and of opening the person to the deeper levels of the psyche. Indeed, Jung suggests as a therapeutic technique that we observe toward what situation of "impossibility" the psyche of the patient is tending, for this may well herald the breakthrough to another level of functioning and may be accompanied by synchronicities. This suggestion recalls the "double bind," a well-known modern therapeutic technique.

Speaking of the link between these emotionally charged situations and the occurrence of synchronicities, Jung notes "that this is by no means a new idea, but was already known to Avicenna and Albertus Magnus." He goes on to quote the latter writing on the subject of magic:

> I discovered an instructive account [of magic] in Avicenna's *Liber sextus naturalium,* which says that a certain power to alter things indwells in the human soul and subordinates other things to her, particularly when she is swept into a great excess of love or hate or the like. When therefore the soul of a man falls into a great excess of any passion, it can be proved by experiment that it [the excess] binds things [magically] and alters them in the way it wants. . . .[13]

Using a figure of speech, we might say that the heat of emotion seems to be the bonding agent that melts together the outer event and the inner state of the soul to bring about a meaningful coincidence. Or, putting it another way, we could say that in states of high emotion, mind and matter begin to move in a new and faster rhythm. The high emotion is characteristic of an activated archetypal field, but it cannot be said that the high emotion causes the synchronicity; rather it is a synchronistic accompaniment. A release of emotion frequently occurs after the synchronistic event with the awakening of conscious meaning. A crucifix falls; a car is hit in a way that speaks to the inner state of the driver. The events appear almost as answers to questions the person was unable to ask.

Of emotion Jung says,

> Emotions are needed for the final precipitation of the precious substance [the gold, the new insight], and not passing emotions only, but passion. People are afraid of passion; then passion overtakes them. They think passion is a mistake, but they need it, and really seek it. The more they know, the less they will deny passion; rather they will accept it, because they know it is the purifying fire needed for the production of the pure gold.[14]

The new insight, the birth of consciousness, is the pure gold, Jung is saying. And emotion tends to have a rhythmic quality, involving both body and mind. Indeed, we immediately recognize the trembling that takes over the impatient lover, the angry warrior, the soldier entering combat, the performer about to go onstage. We speak of "waves" of anger and "shudders" of fear. Experiences of high emotion endure long in the memory, so that there is a definite connection between vibration, emotion, and memory. We will later raise the question of whether memory may be carried not only within the human being, but by the continuing vibrations surrounding an intensely emotional event. Of course once conscious knowledge is born, the synchronicities stop—they belong to the threshold of consciousness.

Synchronicity and Meaning

In all these happenings, psyche and matter, inner and outer, come together in a meaningful arrangement. Although the fact of meaning is paramount in them, Jung tries resolutely to deal with chance as a way of seeing them. He thinks that in dealing with the subject of chance, the "need for a statistical evaluation of the events in question forces itself upon us."[15] By this means, it should be possible to separate out those events having a causal explanation from those that appear as random happenings. He was also perhaps impressed by Rhine's statistical evidence for the existence of extrasensory perception, or ESP. Such a statistical analysis may offer convincing evidence to the modern mind, if that is needed, but it cannot in itself supply an explanation of synchronistic events. His lengthy discussion of a statistical experiment he conducted on the horoscopes of married couples adds little to our understanding except to underscore what is said above, that a certain emotional intensity seems to be a factor operating in synchronicities.

Here Jung begins to lead us into some very deep waters. He says, "We are so accustomed to regard meaning as a psychic process or content that it never enters our heads to suppose that it could also exist outside the psyche."[16] If we do make such a supposition, then meaning begins to take on an independent existence of its own, or to inhere in events whether or not apprehended by a human mind. It is as if these events come to embody a psychic or meaning-laden aspect. They participate in a larger order, and derive meaning from the context in which they occur. Insofar as phenomena display an underlying order, they strike us as meaningful. Meaning and order are closely related, and meaning is something we discover in the universe, and sometimes co-create.[17] Although Jung never quite gives up the idea of chance as a way of viewing these events, his further explorations, as we shall see, increasingly call it into question.

If for the moment we put aside the idea of chance, then the question of meaning comes forcefully before us: what does it mean to be "meaningful"? Is meaning a mere human interpretation laid on the surface of an essentially meaningless universe? Is meaning simply one of our human projections? Or does it have a deeper significance? Regarding this question Jung says, "Although meaning is an anthropomorphic interpretation it nevertheless forms the indispensable criterion of synchronicity. What that factor which appears to us as 'meaning' may be in itself, we have no possibility of knowing."[18] Jung thus assigns "meaning-in-itself" to Kant's noumenal realm. Yet he ventures to question our Western bias in this respect by drawing on Chinese philosophy as found in the I Ching, which sees meaning not as a human construct imposed on reality, but rather as self-subsistent within the universe in the form of the Tao, a word that Richard Wilhelm interprets "brilliantly" (in Jung's opinion) as "meaning."[19] In the Chinese view, the fact of meaning is interior to the phenomenon itself, not laid on from the outside in some arbitrary or subjective fashion. Thus, in describing a phenomenon as meaningful, we are actually apprehending it in its essence.

"Synchronicity postulates a meaning which is a priori in relation to human consciousness and apparently exists outside man," Jung affirms.[20] And in a footnote he adds that since synchronicity may occur "without the participation of the human psyche, I should like to point out that in this case we should have to speak not of meaning but of equivalence or conformity."[21] Another appropriate word would be *parallelism*.

Parallelism figures in the fine geographical analogy that Jung mentions from the writings of Schopenhauer, who preceded him in the study of synchronicities.[22] The nineteenth-century philosopher, attempting a causal approach to synchronicity, pictured the North Pole of the world as a transcendent first cause from which emanated an indefinite number of causal chains in the form of meridians. The parallels along the earth's surface would link up the simultaneous "cross-connections" of events related by meaning and correspondence, but not by direct causation. Events along each level would be meaningfully interconnected and would give rise to the events lying below on the causal chains, thus preparing the shape of the future. Jung takes issue with this analogy on the ground that it would make synchronistic events so regular as to be obvious to all. He also says that the first cause is not necessarily a unity but may be a multiplicity, though later on, departing from some of the positions of modern science, he himself suggests the possibility of a "unitary idea of being."[23] Such an idea, Jung suggests, leads toward abolishing the division between the observed and the observer, and requires a new language for its expression. We have already encountered this issue in our chapter on projection.

When he approaches his subject from the standpoint of meaning, Jung appears to hover on the verge of revising his own views as well as those of the scientific community at large. Originally the meaning attached to synchronistic events appears as something apprehended by the human mind in states of high emotion. A crucifix falls off the wall when a woman is in a state of extreme anxiety about her faith. The event has an irreducible subjective aspect. But as the meaning begins to attach to the event itself in the sense that the phenomenon embodies an inherent meaning, then that meaning appears as the working of mind, but not necessarily any human mind. What is being suggested is that there are happenings in our visible world that fall outside the categories of space, time, and causality, but that, having meaning (or equivalence or parallelism), seem to call for rational explanation and to be attributable to a quality of "mindfulness" in the universe itself. Though approached through our subjectivity, the meaning has its own being, its own objectivity. It works through us, not by us.

Synchronicity and Causality

Although we cannot prove the existence of an objective meaning that is not just an idea in someone's mind, we are driven to assume such if we do not want to regress to a magical causality, Jung tells us.[24] Any such idea as magical causality ascribes to the psyche a power it does not have. Let me illustrate the problem with a case of precognition:

> A minister's wife, having sent her little daughter to play near the railway embankment, was suddenly seized with terror and violent trembling. An inner voice told her to bring the child back or something dreadful would happen. The lady immediately summoned the servant to get the child, and the two returned safely some fifteen minutes later. But that afternoon, an engine and tender jumped the rails in precisely the spot where the child would have been, and three men were killed.[25]

Magical causality would lead us to assume either that the lady's panic caused the train wreck, or conversely, that the wreck caused her terror. Neither of these makes ordinary common sense. Causality cannot be invoked in either direction.

We could use the concept of causality only if we were willing to take a holistic view that includes the mental and emotional aspects of the situation as well as the physical. In that case, we could say not that the train wreck caused the lady's panic, but rather that the *horror* of it, anticipated in advance of the outer event, was the cause. Additionally, we would have to say that causality in the subjective world can act from the future to the present rather than invariably from present to future. This accords with our actual experience, where anticipated pain or joy affects our present moods, feelings, and actions. There is no mystery to this, of course, when we know of the approaching event that "causes" our present feelings, but when, as in the above case, there is no known way by which the coming event could be consciously known in the present, our rational minds are totally baffled. When such feelings arise, it is usually very difficult to judge whether some dreadful event is on the horizon or whether we are merely "imagining things." An experience of foreboding that actually anticipates a coming catastrophe in time to avert its effects makes us think of magic, or perhaps of the intervention of God.

To discriminate between a harmless wish or sudden fear and a genuine precognition is no easy matter, but the occasional appearance of these latter events, scattered unpredictably among the more common "imaginings" like diamonds in a coal bin, gives us food for thought. In the meantime, if we hold that synchronicities are not causally determined, and are certainly not caused by our momentary conscious fears or wishes, we shall eliminate one source of superstition. We are happy to be rid of that fallacy, but the alternative—that the psyche can leap over the barriers of time and space to prophesy the future—is not an idea we can easily entertain. Even if we assign this ability to the "unconscious," that does not necessarily dispel our doubt.

Jung is inevitably drawn into questions of time and space, which set up the conditions for causality, since a cause acting now can reveal its effect only to an observer along its event horizon in the the future, not the past. He is alluding to a meaningful interconnection of events that may be known subjectively but is not visible from a merely external perspective, and he raises the question whether this meaningful interconnection is not in fact present whether or not apprehended by a human mind. This leads us to the possibility that the human mind in some way participates in a larger mind that knows in ways we ordinarily cannot know, and that pervades and envelops the whole situation in both its inward and outward aspects, operating independently of space-time. He mentions that philosophy assumed precisely such a secret correspondence or meaningful connection between events until well into the eighteenth century in the form of the correspondence theory. The consequence of this approach is that the overarching meaning would have to be ascribed to an existent such as a Universal Mind having creative power, or to the Platonic World Soul. While Jung does mention Plato, he refrains from adopting either of these as possibilities, though his mention of "absolute knowledge" seems to move in that direction.

We intend to go into the issue of time and space more thoroughly later, but in the meantime an example of telepathic communication will illustrate the difficulties:

> A scientist of my acquaintance reports that when he and his wife were in India at the close of the Bangladesh war, he was asked to visit that country to make an assessment of the damage done to scientific equipment by the war. He agreed to do this, though

> travel to Bangladesh was not easy, after planning first that his wife should go to Calcutta, where he would meet her for a few days' holiday before returning to Delhi. He completed his assignment, and then tried to book a flight to Calcutta, only to find that no planes were taking off from Bangladesh to Calcutta. The only plane he could get would take him back to Delhi. Worse yet, communications had not yet been restored, and there was no way to reach his wife to tell her of the change of plans, either by wire, phone, or post. In the circumstances he resorted to the only means of communication possible—he sent her a "thought-wave," and himself took an early plane to Delhi. His wife, having got his "message," flew in an hour later from Calcutta.[26]

In all experiences of this kind it does appear that a message is moving through space and time, but no time is taken in transit. This assuredly would defy our common experience. Jung, in one of his late letters, seems to throw up his hands: "The question is, in short: shouldn't we give up the time-space categories altogether when we are dealing with psychic existence? It might be that psyche should be understood as unextended intensity and not as a body moving with time."[27] But if we give up time and space, where are we?

In the course of his discussion, Jung tries to deal with the various dilemmas posed by his material by introducing a more abstract principle, that of acausal orderedness.[28] Synchronicity would then be a special case of this more general principle. Acausal orderedness would represent a fourth principle to be added to the familiar triad of space, time, and causality by which we orient ourselves in the phenomenal world. That fourth has to be added "by force," for it differs from the other three in forming a link to a realm beyond the phenomenal. He finds this principle at work probably in biological morphogenesis, in the properties of the natural numbers, and in radioactive decay.[29] These he sees as related phenomena in the sense that they involve the unfolding of meaningful patterns that cannot be explained as the effect of a physical cause. Whereas these latter are eternal events, synchronistic events are acts of creation in time.[30] Something erupts into our world of space and time from another realm not limited by these categories. Thus, while acausal orderedness is a constant factor in the world, synchronistic events are sporadic and exceptional, in Jung's view. They are more difficult to understand than the repetitive patterning found in ordinary causal orderedness, bearing the stamp of timelessness as they emerge in the world of time.

How are we to think of acausal orderedness? Is it to be understood as a mechanical or an organic order? If organic, is it in truth another name for God? If chaos can happen by itself, as we tend to think, but orderedness requires a preexisting intelligence to establish the order, then is acausal orderedness the means by which God manifests his presence in the phenomenal world?

Synchronicity and Perspective

The difficulties here are illustrated, though not fully clarified, as we think about precognition. Take the example of the lady who received an inner warning in time to save her daughter from the train wreck, along with the many other documented cases of mothers saving their children by just this kind of sudden intuition. If, as Jung insists, synchronicities are acts of creation in time, hence almost by definition unpredictable, how is it that foreknowledge can occur? How can we know in advance what has not yet happened? Is any message transmitted through space and time that permits the mother to become aware of the possible future event? The "transmission" would have to move backward through time (from the future back to the present), or so it would seem from our time-bound perspective.[31] Referring to such situations, Jung remarks, "There is good reason to doubt whether it is a question of transmission at all."[32]

Consider a hypothetical example: A woman, stepping out on her front porch just as the tip of the sun appears over the low hills to the east, observes a car rounding the crest of the hills and coming along the road toward her. She will experience the sunrise and the appearance of the car as a coincidence, but not a meaningful one. However, suppose she had awakened in the night with a dream saying that as the sun arose her son's car would appear at the top of the hills. Now she will await the approach of the car with excitement to see if her dream has "come true." When it is indeed her son's car, she feels a moment of surprise and disbelief—there is magic in the world! How did she happen to dream that dream? All the happenings—the sunrise, the coming of the car, and the dream—are causally unconnected, but vibrant with meaning. If we add that the mother has been anxiously awaiting the return of a son from whom she has not heard in many months, the event becomes all the more meaningful.

Now suppose that a plane is flying high above the house at this time, on a course parallel to the hills to the east. The pilot, whose height permits him to see over the hills, has long seen the sun coming up as well as the car as it climbs the eastern slope. To him there is no simultaneity in the appearance of the car and the sun, no special meaning, and of course no causal connection. The synchronicity is a meaningful event only in the mind of the mother; to the pilot it is not even happening.

It is as if the synchronicity depends upon one's perspective—with the wrong perspective it does not even occur! What is very meaningful to the mother is for the pilot a non-event. Are we back to saying that meaning is an "anthropomorphic interpretation" laid on events by the human mind, but lacking any deeper significance?

But wait: What appears magical in the occurrence is only the telescoping of time in the "unconscious" insofar as the dream precedes the events. The mother's psyche experiences meaning spread broadly across time, much as a telescope's field of focus spreads broadly across space. This is very like the train-wreck example, except that in that case the anticipation came in the form of the mother's emotional reaction of trembling and dread and a voice that spoke with seeming foreknowledge. Contemplating this, we are obliged to ask whether there is a level of the psyche in which time as we understand it consciously is not in effect. We often observe that in the dream state the individual may be carried forward and backward in time, enjoying a freedom from the limitations of time that is unknown in the waking state. The two states resemble the experience of a surfer who, when riding atop a wave, can see all around himself, but when tossed into a trough sees only the next wave bearing down. It is as though our ordinary consciousness lives in a trough of the waves of time.

Telepathic dreams are actually quite common. Ordinarily the coming event would be pictured in a symbolic rather than a literal way, but dreams are perfectly capable of speaking the literal truth. The simplest description of such a dream is to say that the dreaming psyche anticipates an emotional state that will be experienced in the waking state in an accompanying future event. The psyche anticipates its own future state, not the actual outer event. It can move backward and forward in the time dimension in the same way the person in ordinary reality moves backward and forward in space.

From within the dreaming psyche, mother and son seem connected by a patterning activity that involves the mother subjectively, but is not subjectively caused. Having already rejected magical causality, we cannot say that the mother's dream or her accompanying anxiety about the son's return caused the later events, but we could suggest that the unfolding of a meaningful pattern was somehow already present in a timeless realm, and became known to her in the dream state, where she, too, participated in the pattern. That "realm," wherein the patterns are "contained," could be Jung's collective unconscious or the "psychic ether" of the occultists. Or we could use Jung's description of synchronicities as "the continuous creation of a pattern that exists from all eternity, repeats itself sporadically, and is not derivable from any known antecedents."[33] In this case, the pattern represents the archetype of the Return of the Son, a story told in virtually all the sacred literature of the world, involving an internally felt connection that is not causal, but somehow intuitively comprehensible. From this perspective, we would find the event best described not by a factual account, but by a dramatic and poetic rendering that would include the mother's love, her yearning, and her hope for the son's safe return. The intermingling of the feelings of both mother and son is also involved.

From the mother's point of view, the whole experience is emotion-laden, pulsing with meaning, and independent of her causing—in a word, magical—while the pilot, whose position in space and time permits him to see the same events from a more elevated perspective, remains oblivious. The patterning activity and the meaning do not involve him. Just as the mother in her dream would be generally described as "unconscious," the pilot could be described by the same language, since a significant event in his vicinity escapes him.

What is happening here is that the two participants, the pilot and the mother, find themselves within two different frames of reference. The pilot sees the event from a predominantly spatial perspective, while the mother, in her dream, slips through the meshes of our ordinary space and time and catches a glimpse of the event before it actually unfolds. Her perspective is atemporal. If we follow Einstein's dictum that all frames of reference are equally valid, we cannot say that one view is correct while the other is wrong.

Language is not well adapted to bring forth the nature of an event occurring at the margins of our ordinary space and time. To say that the meaningful pattern "preexisted" perhaps attributes to it a spatiotemporal form which is not appropriate. It is like asking where a thought goes when no one is thinking it. One might say that the synchronicity is "context- or field-dependent" because only within certain contexts does it emerge and become visible. Given the context or meaning field, the unfolding of the pattern has a certain inevitability once set in motion.

Jean Gebser, in *The Ever-Present Origin*—a monumental work that occupied him for many years—sees consciousness as manifested in three different structures: the magical, the mythical, and the mental.[34] He does not use the term "levels" because he does not wish to suggest that one is superior to the other. However, he argues that each structure in turn has moved humanity further away from awareness of the ever-present origin. He thinks that we are now in the process of developing a new structure which he calls the aperspectival or integral consciousness, and he sees this already exhibited in the work of forward-looking artists and poets, who are typically the first to explore new possibilities of consciousness.

Gebser's magical structure is characterized by the primacy of sound and rhythm, a timeless, spaceless form of consciousness where all things are united in magical harmony. Events are related by what Gebser calls the "vital nexus," an organic connection more feelingful than mental, resembling more the relationship of lovers than of mere acquaintances. It was a time before causality was invented, so to speak, when synchronistic events could be described as "pre-causal" rather than "acausal" on the ground that space and time, which set up the conditions for causality, did not exist for the human psyche.

In our example of the returning son, we might suggest that the mother, in her dream, represents the magical structure, while the pilot, flying high above, represents the modern mental structure, and the distance between them measures the move we are obliged to make to gain some comprehension of synchronicity. This helps us to understand why happenings of this kind resist the embrace of science, because they are not experimentally repeatable, and they are subjective. Raynor Johnson, a physicist and mystic, makes a telling comment:

> It is the level on which awareness is focused which determines what world will be described as objective: experience on levels

> interior to this will then be described as subjective. This distinction is one of great convenience, but it does not correspond to anything significant in the levels themselves: it describes only the relationship of an individual to these levels or worlds.[35]

By describing a dream's foreknowledge of a subsequent event as "subjective," we are saying nothing about the level of events in themselves, but only about our ego relationship to them. This means that the events have their own legitimate mode of being that can be distinguished from the path by which we approach them. In truth, nature has many aspects, and there are many frames of reference through which nature can be viewed. Nature reveals to us only the aspect we are equipped by the level of our consciousness to see. In this sense we can say that we make our world by the mode of our participation in it.

If the pilot represents the modern consciousness, and his difficulty in perceiving the synchronicity is like our own, we might ask what he would have to do to begin to take it seriously. A first suggestion would be that the pilot should begin to take account of his dreams, which would reveal that the timeless, spaceless level of the psyche really exists and is readily accessible. In this way, he would begin to realize that the deep psyche, which does not depend upon outward seeing or hearing, may yet open up an awareness of outer events. We may even suggest that this kind of perception goes on all the time but may not enter consciousness, and so we do not know about it.

However, if the pilot wishes to remain undisturbed in his present views (and he would have much of his culture behind him in doing so), he could say that the mother's dream is merely wish fulfillment; she wishes her son to be returning, and in her dream actually sees it happening. The fact that the son does appear as predicted would then be seen as pure chance or coincidence, and this could be the origin of Jung's repeated effort to look at these phenomena as chance occurrences. From the modern level of consciousness, that is what they are. Thus do our presuppositions about the nature of reality shape what we can see.

But, if we take Raynor Johnson's remark seriously, then we are obliged to become more "subjective" and to enter the mother's nighttime feelings—the intensity of her love and yearning for her son, her knowledge of the joy awaiting her on his return, her immersion in a state of mind quite outside her daily preoccupations or ego concerns. Only by this route can we approach the nighttime state where nature's own ways are secretly and marvelously in process outside our willing.

When we take account of the eminently personal nature of the meanings involved in synchronicities, we are led to think that they cannot possibly be subject to natural law, for the laws of nature, as we understand them, are always impersonal. However, these events embody a meaning that is at once personal and at the same time universal or archetypal; they stand as individualized representatives of universal patterns, uniting the universal with the particular, the general with the unique. That their emergence can be foreseen from within the dream state suggests that even before manifestation they have a certain form of existence.

The fact that the synchronicity is observed only by the mother and not by the pilot does not mean that it is not real. It is perfectly real. We have already pointed out that it is frame-dependent. An eclipse of the sun is also perfectly real, but it can be seen only where the observer has the right perspective. When an eclipse is predicted, astronomers fly off to remote parts of the world intent on measuring and filming it to see if it conforms to their predictions. We can imagine that in certain times and cultures where the movements of the heavenly bodies were not understood in this way, these events were called coincidences, or a god was introduced into a narrative to bring about the eclipse. If this does not happen in our society it is because we understand how the orbital paths of sun, moon, and earth come into alignment to create eclipses. Conversely, we do not understand the patterns that are found in synchronicities, and so we call them coincidences—meaningful, to be sure. A deeper view would inquire what patterns are in motion to bring about a synchronicity, and how the psyche is involved.

In an eclipse of the sun, the three bodies—sun, moon, and earth—must be properly aligned in time and space to allow the eclipse to appear. In addition, the observer must also be properly aligned, or he will see nothing. Just so, observing a synchronicity requires a particular alignment. The psyche of the observer must be aligned with the significance or meaning of the happening, or he will not be aware of it. That was the problem of the pilot in our example: he was properly aligned in time and space, but not psychically aligned to the meaning of the synchronicity so as to be aware of it. The mother, on the other hand, was psychically aligned, and observed it.

Mind Is Inherent in the Universe

Over and over, synchronicities tease the mind with the sense of something at work outside the natural order (at least as it is now understood). They spill over the edges of the thought structures we have built to describe and contain reality. We have mentioned the unaccountable telescoping of space and time that occurs in clairvoyance and telepathy, as well as in the dream state. Jung speaks of the "unconscious foreknowledge" that seems to be shown not only in precognition, but also in cases where a series of events having a common meaning take place within a short period of time. He points out that goal-oriented processes in biology, such as those seen in the development of the embryo, suggest the possibility of foreknowledge, and this again would be knowledge not found in the human psyche: "as soon as we begin seriously to reflect on the teleological processes in biology or to investigate the compensatory function of the unconscious, not to speak of trying to explain the phenomenon of synchronicity," we are driven to think of foreknowledge.[36] "Final causes, twist them how we will, postulate a foreknowledge of some kind." This is knowledge not connected to an ego; he calls it "absolute knowledge."[37] It is a foreknowledge of goal or purpose much like Aristotle's entelechy, "that which carries its goal within it" like a seed.

Jung is not attempting to say that the foreknowledge in the unconscious causes the accompanying synchronistic events to occur; that would be a reversion to causality. Rather, he is suggesting that both the foreknowledge and the accompanying outer event emerge from the same timeless substrata (the same archetypal field) that is characterized by an indwelling meaning or pattern. We might call it a "meaning field," having both a subtle physical and psychic aspect. The more these events "multiply, and the more exact the correspondence is, the more their probability sinks and their unthinkability increases until they can no longer be regarded as pure chance, but, for lack of a causal explanation, have to be thought of as meaningful arrangements."[38] He rejects the possibility that they can be explained away as projections of the observer.[39] This suggests that in the appearance of the raccoon at my window, the meaning was not merely my projection, but was "self-subsistent," having its own reality inherent in the situation—or field, if you will. Thus the more Jung explores the phenomena of synchronicity, the more he is forced to abandon the idea of pure chance and to move toward the idea of plan or "meaningful arrangement."

He therefore speaks of synchronicity as "associated with the activity of unconscious operators."[40] He quotes the writer Wilhelm von Scholz as saying that these events "are arranged as if they were the dream of a 'greater and more comprehensive consciousness, which is unknowable.'"[41] Jung refers more than once to the "absolute knowledge of the unconscious."[42] All this would seem to suggest the presence of some higher mind, an "arranger," or "operator" at work, unless we assume that mind is immanent within the creation itself, in which case created nature must be seen as having qualities not now attributed to it. Indeed, it seems to me that this formulation—that all the universe is infused with the quality of mind—forces itself upon us as the most natural way of expressing the inherent meaningfulness of such phenomena. In other words, the "arranger" is not exterior to the thing or event, but is immanent within it as an inherent principle of order and meaning.

Jung quotes the Chinese philosophers (as brought to us in the work of Richard Wilhelm), who make precisely this assumption in their concept of the Tao, sometimes called "Nothing." "'Nothing' is evidently 'meaning' or 'purpose,' and it is only called Nothing because it does not appear in the world of the senses, but is only its organizer."[43] Jung goes on to quote the Chinese view "that there is in all things a latent 'rationality.' This is the basic idea underlying meaningful coincidence; it is possible because both sides have the same meaning. Where meaning prevails, order results. . . ."[44] And, we would emphasize, where meaning prevails, mind is at work. Here we see Jung moving quite away from the idea of chance and toward that of order, plan, or arrangement.

Plainly, though, it is not the order of the so-called rational, everyday world, certainly not when an automobile is wrecked in a way that expresses the inner turmoil of the driver. Such an event is more like the "order" of a symptom that suddenly erupts in the body to express what the conscious mind of the patient has been unable to acknowledge. It is as though the necessity to express the neglected meaning rises up with a powerful thrust, driving all else before it. Another world order, and a powerful one, suddenly thrusts itself into the conventional world to speak the unspoken, to reveal what was hidden—to bring a revelation.

The Meaning Field

Let us invoke the concept of a unified field to frame the idea of an immanent principle of order and meaning, as considered in the preceding section. We have said before that synchronicity is "context- or field-dependent" because only within certain circumstances does it emerge and become visible. We are supposing that when a synchronicity arises, both the psychic condition and the accompanying outer event emerge from an indwelling meaning or pattern, which we call a "meaning field."

A most convincing description of such a field comes from the teachings of Alfred North Whitehead, philosopher and mathematician.[45] Though his ideas are shrouded in a dense terminological fog, they may nonetheless be explained simply without doing violence to them. In Whitehead's view, telepathy and clairvoyance become an activity of the cells of the body, and the atoms, molecules, and electrons. Whitehead calls all these microscopic elements "enduring individuals." They are aware of their environment in the sense of "internally taking account of it." This means that they do not act merely as recording devices, like the concentric circles that form in the trunk of a tree, but have their own form of awareness. This kind of perception Whitehead calls "prehension" (compare *comprehension*). It belongs to the microscopic level of reality. While we perceive sporadically through the sensory organs, our cells are perceiving all the time; they are the primary means of perception. Our eyes and ears serve as a secondary form of perception. Thus, the primary elements of our constitution are themselves suspended in and participate in a meaning field that enfolds them.

Recall the example of synchronicity told by physicist Roger Jones. As he wrote a paragraph on cardinality, he saw a beautiful cardinal land on his lawn. Recognizing this synchronicity, his mind freely associated other entities that would belong in a meaning field of cardinality: a high official of the Roman Catholic church is called a cardinal, who, incidentally, wears a bright red hat; a deep rich red color is called cardinal red; a red bird is an astrological term for the pioneering spirit. There are the cardinal numbers, the cardinal points of the compass, and the cardinal virtues and vices. The *Oxford English Dictionary* says that "Cardinal is often associated with the number four, where it is connected with wholeness in Jung's symbol system." Jones' example illustrates an archetypal field whose meaning centers on cardinality. The entities within the field are held together by their relation to cardinality. Synchronicities, we understand, may give rise to such a field, but we need the concept of the activated field to make sense of the data. We assume that it was Jones' sudden lively interest that powered the subsequent activity.

In John Layard's story of the anthropologist traveling through the African bush with his native companion, the native suddenly fell on his face, saying that the neighboring chief was dead. This knowledge came to him by way of clairvoyance. Layard added, "the knowledge was in the field." He recognized a field of meaning. The tribesmen were beating drums, but the knowledge was not found in the rhythm of the drums. The native was open to the field, and he could grasp the meaning of the field consciously as he looked within and saw the face of the dead chief.

Synchronicity and the I Ching

Jung's discussion of the Tao as a meaning field becomes most fruitful when he points out that the ancient oracular and intuitive methods take for granted the presence of a psychic aspect at work as an ordering principle in the universe. Of all these methods, the I Ching is far and away the most impressive. It is an expression of the Chinese tendency to grasp situations as a whole rather than focusing on details. The details then are seen against the larger order established by the interaction of Yin and Yang, the two great cosmic forces operating throughout the manifested world.

To get an answer to a significant life question, an inquirer of the I Ching uses one of two methods, either dividing forty-nine yarrow stalks in a way that produces a random ordering, or tossing three coins. The yarrow-stalk manipulation or coin tossing is repeated six times, and the result, called a hexagram, provides a graphical key to one of sixty-four texts that the inquirer is to read in the I Ching. In his discussion of the I Ching, Jung says that "the coins fall just as happens to suit them."[46]

The procedure may make no sense to a naive observer, one who does not recognize that there is an equivalence of meaning linking the psychic state of the questioner and the physical happening—the fall of the coins. To such an observer, it seems that an unintelligible answer is given to an unknown question. Such a person might wonder, does asking a question cause the coins to fall a certain way? If we say that we have previously eliminated causality as an explanation, then the next question might be, if causality is eliminated then is it not mere coincidence how the coins fall? The naive observer can think of no alternative between causality and accident or pure chance.

But the great sages of ancient China, "basing themselves on the hypothesis of the unity of nature" and assuming "the same living reality was expressing itself in the psychic state as in the physical," intuitively worked out the meanings of all the possible patterns formed by the six throws of the coins or by the division of the yarrow stalks. They took for granted a meaningful correspondence between inner state and outer event (parallelism). The sixty-four hexagrams in the I Ching constitute sixty-four situations, together with dynamic interconnections that change one into another. In this way "an inner state can be represented as an outer one and vice versa," and "these interpretations formulate the inner unconscious knowledge that corresponds to the state of consciousness at the moment."[47]

The statement that the coins "fall just as happens to suit them" is true only for an observer taking no account of the inner state of the questioner. Even a skeptical questioner will discern that the pattern that arises from the coins is linked to his state of being. It is simply a fact that the outer pattern—the fall of the coins—is coincident with the questioner's inner pattern, and inner and outer thereby form a meaningful relationship. When the inquirer then turns to the text in the venerable book indicated by the hexagram, and thoughtfully reads its contents, its message appears to be specifically relevant to the question. It is as though the meanings assigned by the ancient Chinese sages to the sixty-four hexagrams form a complete map of the collective unconscious, and one's own situation can be fitted into its geography by the throw of the coins.[48]

Synchronicity and Correspondence

The idea of *correspondence* fits very well here, for the patterns of inner and outer form parts of a single whole—a unified field, or meaning field. Though Jung, in his essay "On Synchronicity,"[49] expressly speaks of the correspondence theory as "obsolete," he does not hold to this view consistently, and in other contexts brings it forward as a reasonable hypothesis. It was because the Chinese took for granted the idea of correspondence that they depended on synchronicity to link the questioner and the meanings set forth in the I Ching. The sages were setting aside the schemes and preconceptions of the conscious ego, allowing nature to speak for herself by the way the coins fell or the yarrow stalks divided. The meanings they developed are not "interpretations" or explanations so much as symbolic representations, like the battered car of the female physician, whose damaged vehicle symbolized the damaged state of her life. The meaning must be allowed to *shine through* the symbolic representation, as the latter becomes transparent to our view, and nature is seen as encompassing the organic wholeness of the situation, both inner and outer; accordingly, there cannot but be a correspondence—actually a unity—of the two aspects.

The theory of correspondence goes back to what Aldous Huxley has called the Perennial Philosophy, the metaphysical doctrine that underlies the whole of human wisdom, from the dawn of civilization to the present day. Whereas the idea of synchronicity considered alone seems to hang in the air without a supporting theoretical structure, the idea of correspondence fits synchronistic phenomena into the entire body of ancient truth.

That Jung was aware of the ancient knowledge embodied in the principle of correspondence is shown in his writings on synchronicity.[50] He refers to Leibniz and Schopenhauer, both of whom had preceded him in studying synchronicity, and both of whom were influenced by ancient metaphysical thought. In *Aion* he refers to the "principle of correspondence, or as I have called it, synchronicity," showing that he was well aware that he was giving a new name to phenomena long recognized under this principle.[51] In a letter written in 1952 to John Raymond Smithies, an English psychiatrist interested in parapsychology, he says, "I propose a new (really a very old) principle of explanation, viz, synchronicity, which is a new term for the time-hallowed sympathy or correspondentia."[52] Jung goes on to say, "If you think of it as being something not unlike Leibniz's preestablished harmony, you are not far off the truth. But whereas it is a constant factor with Leibniz, it is a thoroughly inconstant one with me and mostly dependent upon an archetypal psychic condition." (As earlier pointed out, Jung was not wholly committed to this view and did take account of the possibility that the mind-body relationship was a synchronistic one.)

In her book *Number and Time,* M. L. von Franz follows Jung's views and makes this careful formulation:

> In this sense, synchronistic phenomena are spontaneous two-manifestations of the primal unity, and this particular aspect

> lends them their numinosity. In other words, synchronicity requires two essentially heterogeneous world-systems, whose sporadic interlocking causes certain aspects of wholeness to manifest themselves. For this very reason the term *unus mundus* emphasizes more the oneness of existence, while the visible aspects of reality lead us to posit the duality of psyche and matter, of observer and object. The coincidence of the two realms in synchronistic phenomena is our only empirical indication of unified existence to date.[53]

As we explore the issues underlying synchronicity, we begin to see the possibility of a broadening of the modern consciousness that would place us in line with the primordial wisdom of humankind going back to the shamanic experience of the hunting and gathering cultures and of course including our modern knowledge. If Jung is correct, such wisdom is not as remote as it might seem, for it is continuously alive within the collective unconscious. By going into our own depths, we might come in contact with aspects of the ancient tradition. Wilhelm tells us that the writers of the I Ching had mediumistic powers. To go forward we will need to explore types of consciousness previously known only to mystics and spiritual seekers of the East and the West, but starting with a new language and a different understanding. We also need to reexamine Jung's formulations. How, for example, to explain the intermittent operation of the powerful patterning factors that seem to enter human awareness only with the arousal of extraordinary human energies? Isn't it more likely that such an arousal merely allows us to become aware of something operating all the time beneath our notice, somewhat as we become aware of the beating of the heart only during intense exertion, though it is obviously beating all the time?[54]

The above quotation of von Franz emphasizes the intermeshing of two world orders that occurs in synchronicity. Their "sporadic interlocking," which brings about a sense of the ultimate unity of existence, may well be a form of correspondence in force at all times by reason of a sympathetic connection arising at all levels of the universe. To pursue this further will be the aim of our continuing discussion.

CHAPTER 5

Psychic Phenomena

Implications

The Middle Ages never forgot that all things would be absurd, if their meaning were exhausted in their function and their place in the phenomenal world, if by their essence they did not reach into a world beyond this. . . . The more this perception converges upon the absolute One, whence all things emanate, the sooner it will tend to pass from the insight of a lucid moment to a permanent and formulated conviction.

—Huizinga

The ultimate meaning of the world—fate, the world as it is, how it has come to be so through creative decision—can be apprehended by going down to the ultimate sources in the world of outer experience and of inner experience. Both paths lead to the same goal.

—The I Ching

The modern study of parapsychology was initiated by the Society for Psychical Research (SPR), founded in 1882 and based in Great Britain. SPR's work comes closer to the issues involved in synchronicity than does that of today's investigators because it begins with individual cases and tries to explore them in their life context, where they have great meaning for the person concerned. In this way, it connects to the idea of synchronicity. Dispensing with the aggregative, statistical method, and less concerned with experimental techniques, it reveals some of the very issues the modern laboratory approach tends to obscure. It has a freshness and aliveness that the latter approach tends to eliminate. For my part, I am convinced that it offers one important way to understand not merely parapsychology but a deeper reality, and it accordingly opens a vision of a spiritual life grounded in the idea of harmony between the life of the individual and that of the universe as a whole.

The connection between Jung's meaningful coincidences and the more exotic phenomena studied by these early parapsychologists may not be immediately apparent. They so seem related in that none of them can be accounted for by reference to many of our ordinary categories of understanding. All take place in the sensory world but cannot be explained by way of sense data. More positively, all appear to occur at the margins of the space-time world and to lie on a single continuum, which at its lower end is reminiscent of certain ordinary experiences such as hunches or premonitions, but at the upper end verges on the miraculous. It is not unthinkable, of course, that such phenomena are far more varied than we know, and it is only our ignorance that connects them. Our rapid survey will begin with apparitions.

One of the early projects of the Society for Psychical Research was to collect a census of apparitions. They succeeded in uncovering 1,684 cases, which they studied with admirable care and objectivity, using the methods of historical research, checking the reliability of witnesses, and securing corroborative evidence. They were intent on establishing that something out of the ordinary was happening and on clarifying, if possible, what this was. A great question motivating their research had to do with the possibility of survival of bodily death. Could parapsychology throw any light on this subject? Despite being one hundred years old now (or perhaps precisely because they are old), these cases have a freshness and a fascination about them that is lacking in much of the modern parapsychological literature.[1]

Another collection and evaluation of spontaneous cases of extrasensory perception was made by Louisa E. Rhine of the Duke University Parapsychology Laboratory. Her book *Hidden Channels of the Mind* was based on letters sent to the laboratory by persons who had had parapsychological experiences.[2] Rhine did not attempt to interview the percipients, but made the assumption that they were writing in good faith and that any errors of recollection would be insignificant among the large number of cases she studied.

Still a third census was reported in a 1958 book by Aniela Jaffé.[3] These cases came to light when the Swiss bimonthly magazine *Schweizerischer Beobachter* published a series of articles in 1954 and 1955 on prophetic dreams, premonitions, apparitions, and similar occurrences. At the conclusion of the series, the editors invited a reply from readers whether they had ever had similar experiences. An astonishing 1,200 letters were received and turned over to Jung, who entrusted his associate, Aniela Jaffé, with their interpretation. Again the cases have the ring of simple truth, whatever their value as scientific evidence may be. Many of them had occurred years before and could not be checked.

It is of interest not only that so many cases were reported in these three censuses, but also that there is considerable agreement in the findings of the different studies. Modern research continues to point to the frequency with which these paranormal phenomena are experienced in the general population.

Dream Maker and Apparition Maker

The earlier census of the Society for Psychical Research is discussed in *Apparitions* by G. N. M. Tyrrell, a British physicist, mathematician, and parapsychologist. Published in 1953, Tyrrell's book is based on material gathered before the findings of modern depth psychology were widely known.[4] In order to make his thinking more accessible, I will cite one of the many cases of apparitions he studied. I have chosen an example that provides enough information to attempt a psychological approach:

Mrs. P. and her husband had gone to bed, but she, wrapped in her dressing-gown, was lying on the outside of the bed, waiting to attend to her baby, which lay in a cot beside her. The lamp was still alight and the door of the room was locked. She says, "I was just pulling myself into a half sitting posture against the pillows, thinking of nothing but the arrangements for the following day, when, to my great astonishment I saw a gentleman standing at the foot of the bed, dressed as a naval officer, and with a cap on his head having a projecting peak. The light being in the position which I have indicated, the face was in shadow to me, and the more so that the visitor was leaning upon his arms which rested on the foot rail of the bedstead. I was too astonished to be afraid, but simply wondered who it could be; and instantly touching my husband's shoulder (whose face was turned from me), I said 'Willie, who is this?' My husband turned, and, for a second or two, lay looking in intense astonishment at the intruder, then, lifting himself a little, he shouted, 'What on earth are you doing here, sir?' Meanwhile the form, slowly drawing himself into an upright position, now said, in a commanding yet reproachful voice, 'Willie, Willie!' I looked at my husband and saw that his face was white and agitated. As I turned towards him he sprang out of bed as though to attack the man, but stood by the bedside as if afraid, or in great perplexity, while the figure calmly and slowly moved towards the wall at right angles with the lamp in the direction of the dotted line. [A diagram is included with the account.] As it passed the lamp, a deep shadow fell upon the room as of a material person shutting out the light from us by his intervening body, and he disappeared, as it were, into the wall. My husband now, in a very agitated manner, caught up the lamp and, turning to me, said, 'I mean to look all over the house and see where he is gone.' I was by this time exceedingly agitated too, but, remembering that the door was locked, and that the mysterious visitor had not gone towards it at all, remarked, 'He has not gone out by the door!' But without pausing, my husband unlocked the door, hastened out of the room, and was soon searching the whole house."

> Mrs. P was wondering if the apparition could indicate that her brother, who was in the Navy, was in some trouble, when her husband came back and exclaimed, "Oh no, it was my father!" She continues, "My husband's father had been dead fourteen years; he had been a naval officer in his young life."
>
> During the following weeks Mr. P became very ill and then disclosed to his wife that he had got into financial difficulties and, at the time of the apparition, was inclined to take the advice of a man who would probably have ruined him.[5]

An apparition, Tyrrell posits, after consideration of this and many other cases, is a three-dimensional drama that embodies a message or an idea pattern. In the present case, the drama is made visible to both the husband and wife. It is a representation that appears to be enacted for the benefit of the consciousness of the percipient. There is no physical occupant of the space where the apparition appears. Though apparitions are not physical entities, they are also not "spirits," according to Tyrrell; but the present case shows that it is possible to see an apparition of a deceased person, even one never known in life.

The apparition is a telepathic phenomenon wherein an agent, while undergoing some crisis (possibly but not necessarily death) becomes linked in a nonspatial way to a percipient, who embodies it in sensory form. Since it is a "drama" that is "staged," Tyrrell speaks metaphorically of a "producer" and "stage carpenter" who unite to create the phenomenon, the one providing the theme and the impetus, and the other contriving the form that is seen, heard, or sometimes touched. Extraordinary energies are involved, such that the percipients often testify years later that they will never forget the experience. What happens when an apparition is seen is rather like what happens when a hypnotist as agent says to the subject, "You will now see a brick," and the subject obediently sees a brick—but with an apparition, the impetus is given telepathically rather than verbally. In addition, the apparition seems to have a measure of "substance," for it is usually experienced by other persons in the same room who become involved in the drama as spectators, who see from their own perspectives, and who make the appropriate interpretations. In this case, the darkening of the light as the apparition passes by the percipient adds to the impression that it has substance.

It is possible to see an apparition of oneself, thus to be both agent and percipient, just as one can dream about oneself. Such incidents seem to be wholly subjective, not requiring the presence of another person, although what is seen is "outside" in the form of an apparition. In such cases, the personality appears to be divided into two parts, the one observing, the other acting to produce the drama. These two parts, the agent and the percipient, must be at a certain distance from each other if a startling dramatic production has to be staged. But what is this distance? Evidently it is a psychic distance, not a physical one, that separates the two parts. Psychic distance must mean (among other things) such a difference in the construing of reality that the conscious part cannot directly take in what the deeper levels would communicate. It might involve strongly held belief systems that disallow any contrary thought or image to arise, or resemble the differences that separate two people who speak different languages. Or it might involve powerful emotions of dread or anger that prevent one part from hearing the cautionary voice of another part. We would then speak of a person "at war with himself" or of a "split personality." Whereas physical distance is shortened by a physical movement, psychic distance would be shortened by a psychic movement, that is, a change of psychic state or attitude or an increase of insight. The startling experience of seeing an apparition may well bring about such a change, unifying what was formerly divided in the personality.

If, on the other hand, the agent is a separate personality, then there is obviously a physical distance between the two, but the distance between them is bridged instantly in the telepathic situation. The physical distance appears to be annulled in a process of psychic unification. Just as the apparition "breaks through" the psychic distance between estranged parts of the single personality, so it breaks through the physical distance that separates the two parties no matter how great that distance may be. The idea pattern that is the driving impetus for the occurrence is instantly present to both parties; a relationship of a nonspatial kind is formed between them—or, as Tyrrell would say, between the midlevels of their respective personalities. He takes telepathy to be the normal means of communication between these levels and asks whether these midlevels are "in" us or "outside" in the form of a neutral background (the collective unconscious, perhaps?). At the same time, Tyrrell suggests that the question is probably unanswerable in terms of the spatial presuppositions we bring to it. The mind waffles in uncertainty as it tries to take in an idea pattern that is communicated nonspatially and yet takes the form of a three-dimensional presence occupying space. (The feeling of a "presence" is often the most striking aspect of the apparition, and that is what makes it appear that we have been visited by a ghost.)

The apparition of a deceased person inevitably leads to the question of the survival of bodily death. In ancient times, such apparitions were undoubtedly interpreted as evidence that something of the living survives in the form of a shade or ghost. It seems that Tyrrell would prefer to avoid such an interpretation, but as an unbiased observer he is obliged to admit toward the end of his book that certain cases are difficult to explain in any other way.[6] He studied a great many "post mortem cases," such as that of the deceased father appearing as an apparition. Since his theory calls for an agent, he would probably think of the deceased father as the agent, though he does not seem particularly attached to this view. This brings up the whole question of communication between the living and the dead, on which we have little more information than the ancients. As an alternative he might consider the husband to be the agent, since the wife apparently never knew the father and was not emotionally involved with him.

The latter view would mean that the whole event is a subjective experience of the husband, but this introduces another problem: how can the purely subjective experience of the husband be witnessed by the wife as well, and in such a material form as to cause a shadow when the ghost passes the light? If this is a purely subjective experience—a hallucination—how is it visible to both parties? Tyrrell works hard to explain cases where two or more persons witness the apparition. Here he holds that the driving message, or idea pattern, behind the drama requires that any observer present must see the apparition just as they would see it if it were a physical person occupying space. The metaphoric "producer" and "stage carpenter" are required to collaborate with the principal percipient, who is drawn into the whole drama and becomes part of the picture in somewhat the way people are drawn into a highly emotional situation or a mob action.

The modern reader will perhaps be thinking here of a hologram, a possibility unknown to Tyrrell. In a hologram, a three-dimensional image is produced in space by two beams of laser light or coherent light split by a semitransparent mirror, one beam of which has encountered an object in the course of its travels, while the other has not. The information contained in the two beams is recorded on a photographic plate or other medium, and when this plate is illuminated by coherent light, the object appears in three-dimensional form. A holographic image and an apparition are both so lifelike that they deceive a casual observer. Is something like this involved in the construction of an apparition?

Let us return to the question of the message. The idea of a messaging system implies a number of things: two different parties in communication, or at the very least two different parts of the same personality; a distance between them; and a signal passing between. Underlying all this are our assumptions and experiences of space and time. By this definition, does an apparition constitute a messaging system? From the standpoint of the dualistic consciousness it does, but in unitary consciousness we can say, as Tyrrell does, that there is no action across distance. We place ourselves within a form of awareness like a deep dream state or a state of profound rapport with another person. In this case, the awful shock that would befall the husband were he to lose the family fortune is paralleled by the shock of seeing the father literally standing before him to warn him. Both husband and wife are absorbed in the drama—recall that "to absorb" means "to suck in," and this in turn implies a very bodily way of taking in nourishment or knowledge. The sudden entrance of the ghostly visitor appears as a creative and compensatory act by which the knowledge of the deep awareness drives through to the consciousness of husband and wife with shocking impact.[7]

This would come closer to the point of view of depth psychology. In that view, one would agree that the apparition serves to bring badly needed insight to the husband, and drives it home in an unforgettable way, but one might tend to think of it as a dream of the husband, who projects the image out into the room. All psychological complexes—in this case the husband's "father complex"—have a tendency to exteriorize, as Jung says, generally in the form of outer behavior, but sometimes appearing as visions. If this is the case, then the admonishing figure of the father, who, after all, had died fourteen years before, would be interpreted as an older and wiser aspect of the dreamer's unconscious who comes to warn him against an impending ruinous decision. The fact that the wife sees the figure first suggests that conceivably she is the agent of the apparition (if we return to the dualistic view), for we may assume that she was drawn into her husband's dilemma at unconscious levels and was seeking a way out. Or we might suggest that husband and wife are brought into momentary psychic unification in the experience. In that case, we might say that his anima—either the inner or the outer woman—takes the lead in warning him when his own ego is stubbornly set in another direction. (The stubborn set of the husband's consciousness would give rise to the "psychic distance" of which we have spoken.)

His subsequent illness as he comes to an unwilling recognition of the tangled state of his affairs forms a part of the price of an awakened consciousness, as is often seen in psychotherapy. From this angle, the event looks like a drama whose emotional impact is sufficient to turn the husband back from his wrong course, and the question of whether the father's ghost actually invades the bedroom seems less important. Therapeutically we are first of all interested in a right adjustment to the needs of this life and less concerned with the metaphysical aspects of the affair, though these aspects are not to be ignored in a larger view. The metaphysical standpoint requires the intervention of an inner guide or orienting factor, personified by the father and capable of intervening when ego consciousness is inadequate to the demands of life. We could call it the Jungian self.

If we assert that the dream maker and apparition maker represent essentially the same capacity or outflow from the deep psyche, then in contemplating either dream or apparition we place ourselves in alignment with a power able to apprehend the ego's purposes and the larger context within which the ego operates. In this way, we link the apparition with the experiences we have called synchronicities, in the sense that both lead us back to a patterning activity that lies behind both dream and apparition, a form of awareness or "arranger" with the power to apprehend meaning and express it in either the inner or the outer world. We are not merely trying to appropriate the message of dream or apparition for ego purposes. A possibility suggested by this approach is that dream-making and apparition-making form a single capacity of the deep psyche, and that to this faculty the categories of "inside" and "outside" are not very significant; it can produce a drama to either the inner eye, where it appears as a dream, or the outer eye, where it becomes a vision or an apparition. Clairvoyance, the experience of an inner vision that is a veridical representation of an outer occurrence, may also be an activity of the dream maker who comes alive at night while the ego sleeps. Telepathic dreams—in which, for example, the dreamer senses the thoughts of remote others or perhaps even participates in the dream of another—would be another aspect of this same psychic function. From this perspective, the stage on which the dream maker works embraces both the inner and outer aspects of life in a single sweep. The deep psyche acts at once with wisdom exceeding that of either the dream maker or apparition maker, and sometimes acts with powerful will and intentionality. Powers that appear miraculous to ordinary consciousness are available to it to carry out its purposes. When we treat the experience in this manner, it seems to me that we are trying to rise imaginatively to the level of the dream maker; we may see the lives of the husband and wife as a dream, and the nighttime visitation as a dream within a dream, briefly opening up the deeper levels of the world to their view. We attempt an intuitive approach to the situation to match the ways of the dream maker. Their life situation becomes transparentized, and another level of meaning shines through.

We might compare this apparition with the reports of extraordinary dramas witnessed by multitudes at religious festivals in Tibet, or, on the other hand, with the famous Indian rope trick, where a person climbs into the air on a rope that appears not to be tethered to anything above. Many of the modern UFO sightings probably fall into this same category. Or again we might think of the visions reported by mystics throughout history. For the most part, such experiences are reported as the fruit of prolonged spiritual practice; they are said to appear somewhat intermittently at certain intermediate levels of practice, and then to become stabilized at higher levels. However, if such faculties are possessed by all of us in rudimentary form, there is no reason why they could not be discovered spontaneously by ordinary persons, especially in times of intense need. The apparition would then be seen as a creative response of the deep psyche, drawing on powers but little understood by the modern consciousness.

In making this interpretation, I do not wish to deny the possibility that the husband's deceased father actually played a role in the affair. Though we may have a preference for a particular interpretation, we have no basis on which to dictate that interpretation. For example, we do not know whether the travail of the son might somehow have penetrated to the realm of the ancestors. If that were somehow established to be true, then the deep psyche of husband and wife would have to be seen as receptive rather than active, as open to a visitation from an objective realm outside their conscious awareness, as though a being from the beyond in the likeness of the father appeared in answer to their profound dilemma.

Apparitions Linked to the Death Experience

There are cases in which the conditions definitely invite the strange interpretation of a visitation from the dead. Here is one from the collection of Aniela Jaffé:

> I was still a young girl and engaged to a young man. We wanted to get married in four months' time. And yet the engagement was broken off. I tried my best to forget the whole affair, and indeed I succeeded, deeply convinced that this marriage would never have brought happiness. It was six years later, on a fine summer day—I had completely forgotten the young man—when something strange happened. In the afternoon I was busy tidying up the kitchen when suddenly I felt a strange restlessness. What occurred in the next hour is still inexplicable to me, for I did not act according to my conscious will, but under some invisible compulsion. My restlessness forced me to finish my work in almost feverish haste. Then I took the key to the attic, went upstairs, unlocked the door and closed it again behind me. It was a room in which only old suitcases were kept. I opened one of them and took out a box containing the letters of my former fiancé. Six years before, full of bitterness, I had put them away. I now sat down on the suitcase and began to read, feeling more and more disturbed. Suddenly I was overcome by a deep pity for this man who had again and again assured me of his love, and I began to cry. I was sitting there in tears, quite beside myself, when all at once I had the feeling that I was no longer alone in the room. I looked up in fear and before me stood my fiancé. He was looking at me quietly but almost urgently, and said without any movement of his face: "You must forgive me everything I did to you, I was a poor creature." I stared at him as though hypnotized and said aloud: "I forgive you everything, you were a poor creature." When I had finished speaking the figure dissolved into nothingness. First of all I thought I must have been dreaming, but outside it was the loveliest summer day, and I knew that I had not been asleep. I went to bed that evening quite crushed by the experience, and fully convinced that my nerves were thoroughly disturbed, otherwise such things would not have happened in broad daylight.

> But next day I saw the notice of my fiancé's death in the newspaper. As I was told later, he had died the same afternoon when he had compelled me to forgive him everything.[8]

Here it is as if the ghost of the fiancé has an independent existence and an urgent need for forgiveness. Jaffé comments:

> The act of forgiving a deed or a transgression brings peace not only to the soul of the deceased, but also to that of the woman who forgives. . . . Again the ghost of the fiancé may be explained as the personification of a psychic content of the woman's soul, as an image of memory, and equally as an apparition independent of her. In fact, only the interplay of both aspects leads to a meaningful interpretation.[9]

This is to say that the apparition cannot be seen as a wholly inward experience of the woman, involving the different levels of her psyche, even if we assume that these levels are capable of reaching out to indefinite physical distances. It seems rather to be a manifestation of the spirit of the dying man. Many such near-death apparitions have been recorded, and they formed a high percentage of all the cases uncovered by the Society for Psychical Research. Nowadays a substantial body of literature has accumulated on the subject of near-death experiences; these reports make our subject less strange, but they are clearly different from the present case in that the subject returns to earthly life to tell his story.[10] Here, the fiancé is definitely passing on to the death state, but it is as if his soul insists on completing the task unfinished in life.

The woman speaks of being in a restless state and acting "under some invisible compulsion," which then becomes visible in the shape of the fiancé. Since only one day elapses before she receives word of his death, it is possible that she experienced some precognitive knowledge of the immediacy of death and acted from a sudden compelling though unconscious need to speak to him. Again we have a "message" driving through from the deep psyche and revealing a purpose and a knowledge beyond the ego's domain.

The details also suggest that the souls of the two people involved were somehow intertwined in life at some very deep level, so that their coming together in the first place would not appear merely accidental, and the final act of forgiveness seems a necessary conclusion to the life drama that involved them both. I do not consider this experience as differing from a dream because the person is fully awake throughout; actually the woman appears to have been in an alternate state of consciousness during the whole experience. Rather it is because the impetus and the theme come from the dying man, as though her will were completely subordinated to the urgency of his need. By going to the attic and reading his letters, she places herself in contact with his psyche and in a position to gain awareness of his thoughts and his feeling state. In Tyrrell's language, he is the agent and she the percipient, but here we are calling attention to the importance of the meaning field and the tension that connects man and woman. It is as if he has only a short time to conclude his earthly business before going his way.

Incidentally, note that the man speaks "without a movement of his face." We may suggest that the woman, in turn, hears without her ears—that the sound is not made with the vocal chords, but telepathically, as if inserted into her mind. It is as if the two minds are so connected that the thoughts of one become the thoughts of both.

I would refer the reader back to our chapter 3, where Erich Neumann struggled with the idea of projection and asked how it was that a native tribesman could receive secret knowledge from a bird; was it not more likely that the native already possessed this knowledge at an unconscious level, and then "discovered" it by projecting it outward into the bird? Neumann believed that this was not the case and theorized instead that projection occurs within a field of meaning in which the distinction between subject and object disappears. A state of unity prevails in all parts of the field. Neumann was suggesting that the knowledge was "in the field," that the reality field changes as our state of being changes, and that knowledge does not have to be "in" us or in some other living thing. Although he was speaking of projection, his thoughts apply equally to the state of unification in which this apparition appears. We can compare the native's attunement to his environment with the woman's attunement to her fiancé's psyche; in both cases, their heightened receptiveness to the field of meaning enabled them to acquire knowledge that would otherwise have been unavailable.

Another case linked to death was reported by Lord Brougham, who afterward became an active member of the SPR. At the time of the event, he was reportedly twenty-one years old (though his narrative suggests an age more like thirty-one) and was traveling in Sweden with friends:

> We set out for Gothenburg, determined to make for Norway. About one o'clock in the morning, arriving at a decent inn, we decided to stop for the night. Tired with the cold of yesterday, I was glad to take advantage of a hot bath before I turned in, and here a most remarkable thing happened to me—so remarkable that I must tell the story from the beginning.
>
> After I left the High School, I went with G., my most intimate friend, to attend the classes in the University. There was no divinity class, but we frequently in our walks discussed and speculated upon many grave subjects—among others, on the immortality of the Soul, and on a future state. This question, and the possibility, I will not say of ghosts walking, but of the dead appearing to the living, were subjects of much speculation; and we actually committed the folly of drawing up an agreement, written in our blood, to the effect that whichever of us died first should appear to the other, and thus solve any doubts we had entertained of the life after death. After we had finished our classes at the college, G. went to India, having got an appointment there in the Civil Service. He seldom wrote to me, and after a lapse of a few years I had almost forgotten him; moreover, his family having little connection with Edinburgh, I seldom saw or heard anything of them, or of him through them, so that all this schoolboy intimacy died out, and I had nearly forgotten his existence. I had taken, as I have said, a warm bath, and while lying in it and enjoying the comfort of the heat, after the late freezing I had undergone, I turned my head round, looking toward the chair on which I had deposited my clothes, as I was about to get out of the bath. On the chair sat G., looking calmly at me. How I got out of the bath I know not, but on recovering my senses I found myself sprawling on the floor. The apparition, or whatever it was, that had taken the likeness of G., had disappeared.
>
> The vision produced such a shock that I had no inclination to talk about it even to Stuart; but the impression it made upon me was too vivid to be easily forgotten; and so strongly was I

> affected by it that I have here written down the whole story, with the date, 19th December, and all the particulars as they are now before me.

Lord Brougham later wrote:

> Soon after my return to Edinburgh, there arrived a letter from India, announcing G's death, and stating that he had died on the 19th of December.[11]

Here we have a case where the motivation for the event seems to have come wholly from the dying person, who at the time of death recalls his pledge to his young friend. However, the interior view would attribute such a happening entirely to the "unconscious" of the percipient; it would say that Lord Brougham had an unaccountable vision of extraordinary power as he sat in the bath, such as to throw him sprawling to the floor, less a waking dream than a waking nightmare. Ordinarily, the interior view is appealing because it connects such happenings to our everyday experience. For example, we are constantly constructing little dramas for ourselves out of the stuff of ordinary life: we see a threatening father in our boss and act accordingly, or we expect all women to be as domineering as our mother or older sister—that is, we attribute meaning to events in a stereotypical way and begin to act in the outer world on the basis of these mistaken unconscious attributions. We make our friend, supervisor, parent, or neighbor out to be the incarnation of our own unconscious drives and impulses. The less conscious we are, the more we do this. Thus our inner world expresses itself on the stage of outer life as a projection or as "acting out." Many therapeutic hours are spent sorting out such attitudes.

We have earlier discussed projection as a "casting forth" or exteriorization of unconscious emotional complexes; an apparition can be seen as a more sudden and vivid example of a similar mechanism, where the deep psyche actually constructs a visible other with whom the life drama is enacted with shocking immediacy. Hence one could speculate that the young Lord Brougham produced a drama in which his dying friend remains true to his oath and answers the question they had put to themselves many years before. But this does not seem very plausible, because there was no driving need for him to conjure up the ghost of his friend at that time—although we might imagine that he was placed in sudden telepathic communication with the dying man, and from his own deeper self staged a drama that completed the relationship. Alternatively we could say that his deeper self anticipated the letter that arrived only later in waking life, which was to bring up the whole complex of emotions that belonged to that friendship. The fact that Lord Brougham was in a relaxed and receptive state in his bath might have facilitated a telepathic or precognitive experience.

Actually, the whole impetus seems to come from the dying man himself. Like the fiancé of the woman discussed previously, he apparently needs to complete his earthly business before going on to the next phase of his journey. In both of these cases, there seems to be a pattern involving the two parties that requires closure, as though each of the dying men remains faithful to a preestablished purpose, and somehow acquires the power to carry out that purpose. In such a view, the death experience (in which the ego retreats into the Self, the larger life from which it emerged) appears more complex and more meaningful than we have imagined, while the patterning activity we have discussed so often appears more compelling. I think here of the "life review" that is said to occur with lightning speed in a dying person, frequently reported in near-death experiences. Here one might suppose that the dying person, in the context of the "life review," discovers the power to initiate one final gesture of closure before passing on.

Apparitions and the Unconscious

In the series of apparitions we have discussed so far, we have moved from one that is perhaps satisfactorily discussed on the level of a dream to other cases that seem to arise from the death experience. Is it possible that in that experience the soul gains access to powers that in ordinary life we attribute to the "unconscious"? Or that death itself lies on a continuum with life, linked by the knowledge and the power of the deep psyche? Is the ghost or apparition in such cases a temporary manifestation of the soul as it passes from the state of materialization to that of nonmaterialization? Are dream and apparition actually the same, divided only by the discriminating activity of the conscious mind—particularly in view of the possibility (amounting to a certainty) that the deep psyche passes over these boundaries with apparent ease? We seem to gain an awakening sense of the continuity of psyche and world, life and death, as we ask these questions.

Possibly our concern with questions of "inner" versus "outer," or "subjectivity" versus "objectivity," is another reflection of our modern preconceptions. We tend to think in terms of causation, as if an outer event must be "caused" by an inner one (or vice versa), and we are convinced that direct willing must somehow be involved, as when I choose to move my chair to the table. It is baffling to us to think that a state we see as inward can shape outer events not by willing, but "unconsciously"—synchronistically. Our conscious mind separates inner and outer. But here we see a state of inner tension, need, or desire, unacknowledged at the conscious level, such that outer things and events are drawn into configurations that carry out a preestablished purpose. In such events, the boundary between "inner" and "outer" is annulled; it is all one unified pattern, and the pattern itself becomes the paramount reality.

Earlier we have noted that the category of space appears to change depending on whether we think in terms of physical space or psychic space. As to time, we have indicated that past and future tend to merge in the depth experience when the partition that divides past and future becomes penetrable. By way of the "unconscious," we come to know of events that are distant in the time dimension. This faculty is called either precognition or retrocognition, depending upon whether it reveals the future or the past. In all these experiences, the divisive activity by which consciousness establishes itself is reversed in a countermovement of unification, culminating in what Jung has called the experience of the Unus Mundus.

Out-of-Body Experiences

We must let go of some of the categories of the conscious mind in order to free ourselves to apprehend a deeper reality, for it is becoming clear that many of the orienting factors employed by consciousness to make sense of its reality are, on another level, limiting to our perception; they must be transcended before a different reality can shine through. The entire spiritual experience of humanity goes to show that the surrender of these categories, given the aid of a competent teacher, need not be disorienting, but can lead to a whole new experience of the world. Indeed, some further steps are required of us if we are to take account of out-of-body experiences, or OBEs. The following OBE case, recounted by Raynor Johnson, is chosen because of the individual's excellent powers of observation and description:

It was an airless torrid night of June, when I was working hard for my examinations. . . . I had been obliged to yield, completely exhausted, to an imperative need for repose, and had thrown myself on the bed . . . without extinguishing the paraffin lamp. An unconscious movement of my arm probably overturned the lamp between the table and the bed, and instead of going out it gave off a dense smoke which filled the room with a black cloud of heavy, acrid gas. . . . I had the clear and precise sensation of finding myself, with only my thinking personality, in the middle of the room, completely separated from my body, which continued to lie on the bed. I saw—if I may call by that name the sensation I experienced—the objects around me as though a visual radiation penetrated the molecules of the objects on which my attention rested, as if matter dissolved at the contact of thought. I saw my body perfectly recognizable in all details, the profile, the figure, but with the clusters of veins and nerves vibrating like a swarm of luminous living atoms. . . . I saw the objects, or rather their almost phosphorescent outlines, melt together with the walls, under the concentration of my attention, allowing me to see in the same manner the objects in the neighboring rooms. My thinking self was without weight, or rather without the impression of the forces of gravity or the notion of volume or mass. I was no longer in the body, since my body lay inert on the bed. I was like the tangible expression of a thought, an abstraction, capable of transferring itself to any part of the earth, sea or sky more swiftly than lightning, in the same instant that I formulated the wish, and therefore without any notion of time and space.

If I were to say I felt free, light, ethereal, I should not express at all adequately the sensation I experienced in that moment of boundless liberation. But it was not a pleasant sensation: I was seized with an inexpressible anguish from which I felt instinctively that I could only free myself by freeing my material body from that oppressive situation. I wanted therefore to pick up the lamp and open the window, but it was a material act that I could not accomplish, as I could not move the limbs of my body, which I felt should move with the breath of my spiritual will.

> Then I thought of my mother, who was sleeping in the next room. I saw her clearly through the dividing partition, quietly asleep in her bed; but her body, unlike mine, seemed to emanate luminosity, a radiant phosphorescence. It seemed to me that no effort of any kind was needed to cause her to approach my body. I saw her get hurriedly out of bed, run to the window and open it, as if carrying out my last thought before calling her; then leave her room, walk along the corridor, enter my room and approach my body gropingly and with staring eyes. It seemed as though her contact possessed the faculty of causing my spiritual self to re-enter the body; and I found myself awake with parched throat, throbbing temples, and difficult breathing, while my heart seemed to be bursting in my chest.

The narrator here rules out any possibility of suggestion as responsible for the experience, and continues:

> Neither could it have been a dream . . . because never have I had so vivid a sensation of existing in reality as in the moment when I felt myself separated from the body. My mother, questioned by me soon after the event, confirmed the fact that she had first opened the window, as if she felt herself suffocating, before coming to my aid. Now the fact of my having seen this act of hers through the wall while lying inanimate on the bed entirely excludes the hypothesis of hallucination and nightmare during sleep.[12]

This narrator is clearly struggling for words to describe the strange sensations that came to him in the out-of-body experience. He has become "the tangible expression of a thought," weightless, able to move anywhere in a twinkling. While his mother's body seems to emanate luminosity, his body on the bed does not—as if he has become the luminosity, and traveled with it outside the physical body. The occultist would say that the consciousness has retreated into a more subtle vehicle or body, the astral body, which interpenetrates the physical body. But this luminosity, this radiant consciousness, has the power to see into objects, "as if matter dissolves at the contact of thought," becoming insubstantial, yet dancing with vital energy. What the luminosity cannot do is to move a material thing, but it does appear able to communicate with the sleeping mother without sounds or words. His consciousness is clearly intent on getting back into the physical body—perhaps that explains his feelings of anguish and desperation. He wants to resume his work in the "real world" and pass his examinations, not to explore alternate realities, indicating that the intentions of consciousness have some effect on the deeper process.

This experience is by no means typical of OBEs, many of which seem quite pleasurable and unthreatening. Jung gives an account of his own experience in 1944 following a heart attack:

> In a state of unconsciousness I experienced deliriums and visions which must have begun when I hung on the edge of death. . . . My nurse afterward told me, "It was as if you were surrounded by a bright glow." That was a phenomena she had sometimes observed in the dying, she added. I had reached the outermost limit, and do not know whether I was in a dream or an ecstasy. At any rate, extremely strange things began to happen to me.
>
> It seemed to me that I was high up in space. Far below I saw the globe of the earth, bathed in a gloriously blue light. I saw the deep blue sea and the continents. . . . My field of vision did not include the whole earth, but its global shape was plainly distinguishable and its outlines shone with a silvery gleam through that wonderful blue light. In many places the globe seemed colored, or spotted dark green like oxidized silver. . . . I knew that I was on the point of departing from the earth.
>
> Later I discovered how high in space one would have to be to have so extensive a view—approximately a thousand miles! The sight of the earth from this height was the most glorious thing I had ever seen.[13]

Two things can be said here. One is that when we stand at the rim of the space-time world and look out to what lies beyond, we encounter a threshold that cannot be passed by ordinary consciousness or language. If we speak of this as the spiritual world, then the whole treasure house of spiritual experience known to humankind through the ages becomes available to light our way. However threatening it is for the modern consciousness to enter those worlds voluntarily, we know that they have been explored by spiritual teachers throughout history, all of whom attest to an inflow of wisdom from that source. That there are risks involved we cannot deny.

Second, the kind of parapsychological events I have chosen to mention so far do not testify directly to the survival of bodily death because they can be explained in other ways. Nonetheless, Jung has taken them as indirect evidence of survival because they show that the psyche at some level participates in the timeless and spaceless realm, the realm of eternity. One could say that at that deep level, the psyche already has eternal life and does not need to win it. It is the very nature of humanity to arise from that larger life, to be sustained and nurtured from within it, and to return to it at the transition we know as death. Our whole living world takes on a quality of translucence as we contemplate these transitions.

Apparitions, OBEs, and Projections

We have now brought forward three cases of apparitions: In one case, the boyhood friend of Lord Brougham was dying in India at the very time his apparitional form was observed in Norway. In another case, a young woman was compelled to go to the attic to read the letters of her former fiancé, whose apparition also became visible in bodily form at the precise time of his death. In still another case, a young husband and wife, at a time of crisis in their own lives, saw the apparition of the husband's father, a naval officer whose death had occurred many years before. All these cases are linked by the experience of death, though the connection is more remote in the last case. If we assume that at the time of death the soul takes leave of the body, pausing only briefly along the way to release some of its aspects, this might account for the urgency displayed when appearing as an apparition. Perhaps the soul is still in a visible phase of its journey, but will soon go on to a state where it can no longer be a visible manifestation. However, the apparition of the naval officer, who appears after an interval of fourteen years, contradicts this theory. Alternatively we might speculate that the urgency expressed in the other cases is simply the desire to depart this life with a sense of closure, and there are no spatiotemporal constraints on reappearance. In the meantime, we see an affinity between the apparition and the phenomenon of projection. In both cases something moves outward, and there is something that bridges the gap between inner world and outer. In the same way, we may propose an affinity between apparitions and OBEs, both involving a movement outward toward separation of body and soul.

Seen by a friend or observer, an apparition has a bodily form, but its inner life is unknown. It may not even have an "inner life." Presumably the conscious part of the person, along with memory and purpose, remains with the body lying immobilized on the bed. The apparition, in other words, appears to be a shell, not the reality of a person. In an OBE, by contrast, the traveling part of the person speaks from within; it sees, hears, feels, has thoughts, memories, purposes, and consciousness, and is capable of making choices. Sometimes its perceptions are reported to be especially vivid. Our knowledge of OBEs comes from persons who return to tell their story. The thinking and feeling part of the person—the soul—with its memories and consciousness, has traveled out and away, while the physical body remains catatonic on the bed. OBEs are known from the inside, as reported by persons aware of having all their faculties, but apparitional experiences are known to us only from the outside, as reported by persons who see and, in many cases, recognize the apparition. Since we cannot concede that knowledge and feeling are present only when observed, it must be that they are present throughout the OBE. This implies that the soul can exist independent of a physical body.

Memory in Nature

Turning now to precognition, we may consider a case chosen by Raynor Johnson, the physicist and parapsychologist who drew most of his examples from the proceedings of the SPR. The following was the experience of a woman known personally to him and for whose credibility he vouches:

> Late in October I was having a few days' holiday on Mount Macedon [near Melbourne, Australia] by myself. One morning I walked through the forest to the Cross, but once there I did not stay long to admire the view because I noticed some smoke curling up the Mount . . . and come blowing towards me. Not wishing to be involved in a bush fire, I decided to take the path leading directly to my home. I discovered that it crossed a firebreak, and once past that I entered the forest again and sat down under a tree to eat my lunch and to read Wordsworth. But for

> some reason I felt uneasy and was unable to concentrate. Was it fear of the fire, I wondered, or could there be some woodcutter of evil intent nearby, or was it merely the soughing of the wind in the tree-tops, which by now was making rather an eerie, lonely sound? I stood up and listened. There seemed nothing of which to be afraid. It was barely one o'clock and still sunny. Telling myself not to be foolish, I found a hollow, where I crouched down so as to be hidden from the view of anyone approaching the firebreak, and waited.
>
> Then suddenly it happened. Over me flowed a wave of acute terror, loneliness and pain, amounting almost to an agony. After a moment of paralyzing suspense, I turned and ran through the forest. Nor did I stop until I reached home, panting. The feeling slowly subsided, but I decided not to venture out again that day. Instead I sat down and wrote a brief account of it in a letter to my friend, Miss Y, but unfortunately this has been lost. However, she remembers the description and my efforts to explain it.
>
> I faced all the physical possibilities that could have induced fear, but decided that the overwhelming character of the sensation was not justified by any known physical cause. I rather tended to think that, having had similar experiences twice in my life before, it was associated with some event that had occurred in that place in the past, as were the other two experiences.
>
> A week later a Douglas DC3 air-liner crashed in the firebreak close to the very spot where I had been sitting and both pilots were killed, one immediately, one dying after an hour's agony of mind and body.[14]

In trying to explain such an experience, Johnson speculates that a place can hold a record of events occurring within it. That a place can hold a memory of the past he is willing to assume; he considers it possible that what we think of as "our" memory is in fact only our share of the common memory, which might be considered the memory of nature. We think of it as "ours" because we experience it as coming from within ourselves.[15] It is said that old battlefields or places where massacres occurred hold memories of the high and tragic emotions of those who fought and died there. All this would belong to the memory of nature. But here we have a "memory" of an event that has not yet occurred. In this baffling situation, Johnson considers it more plausible to regard the incident as one of "precognitive telepathy," meaning that the lady achieved a rapport with the emotions experienced a week later by the pilots who died in the plane. She was not traveling backward or forward in time, but was drawn into attunement with the powerful emotions still to be experienced in that place. These emotional energies do seem to have a certain relationship to the spatial realm in that they are tied to that particular place and no other.[16] Perhaps the lady was involuntarily doing what prophets have always been able to do.

To put it another way, we might say that she was attuned to a world pattern that was destined to reach its agonized conclusion on the mountainside in the near future and was somehow already in process, like a musical chord that has not yet been struck, but whose reverberations are portended by the whole tenor of the music. This idea is strengthened by the fact that the woman did not get an actual picture of the event, but rather an emotional apprehension of its pain, as though she took it in with the whole body. The case may be compared with the one given earlier in which the mother was able to save her daughter from the train wreck when she was seized by terror and trembling and heard an "inner voice" telling her to bring the child home. In a sense that, too, was "prophecy." In both cases, the partitions that keep the individual psyche confined to a narrow slit in the time dimension are broken through.

From the perspective of time, the cases given so far appear to have a certain linkage. Perhaps Lord Brougham witnessed "precognitive" telepathic knowledge of the death of his friend, which was then occurring but lay in the future of his conscious time. Likewise, the lady whose fiancé was dying may have experienced telepathic knowledge of his death at the time of its occurrence but before she gained the knowledge consciously. Even the husband and wife, Mr. and Mrs. P., may have gained a kind of foreknowledge in time to save them from financial ruin, though their case is less clear. However, it can be said that such cases open up important questions about the nature of time and our apprehension of it.

There are experiences in ordinary consciousness where we have a premonition or a "hunch" of impending disaster without being able to say what it might be; perhaps the incident on Mount Macedon is an extension of such occurrences. There are also experiences where we find ourselves taken over by the emotions of another person; we have mentioned in a previous chapter that this sometimes happens in the therapeutic situation. What is important for the persons concerned is to be able to discriminate between the emotions that belong to their own subjectivity and those that have an objective character, coming from some other source.

This applies to the woman in Johnson's case: if she had never learned of the plane crash, but had continued to view the strong emotions as belonging to her own psyche alone, then she might have interpreted the incident on the mountainside as an anxiety (panic) attack instead of a precognitive experience. And if she (or her psychiatrist!) had been unaware of the possibility of precognition or retrocognition, she would have been all the more likely to interpret the experience as wholly subjective. In that case, she might well have considered herself "abnormal," and this could have had a destructive effect on her psychic balance. Persons who have a good acquaintance with the flow of their inner life will find it easier to make these distinctions, but this is the fruit of much introspection, and not easily acquired.

Long ago in classical Greece such experiences were attributed to the goat-footed god, Pan, whose name gave rise to the word *panic*. The ancients knew how to discriminate between experiences belonging to their own subjectivity (the personal unconscious, in our language) and those coming from some source beyond (the collective unconscious), and they did not see the latter as pointing to a psychic abnormality in the individual. They knew that Pan roamed the hills of Greece and was liable to make sudden appearances before frightened shepherds and woodcutters. As a god, he had a certain lecherous quality, pointing to a hidden connection between panic and sexual excitement. I do not mean to imply that panics are "caused" by sexual excitation, but rather that such feelings may be a predisposing factor opening the person to the appearance of the god.[17] If we do not hold to the metaphysical standpoint that calls for a god presence, we are left with a personal emotion—panic; hence the gods, as Jung said, have become our diseases. Here we come again to where *ratio* (reason, rationality) links up with *sanus* (health, sanity). We need the gods for the sake of our psychic health.

Parapsychologists believe that experiences like this are apprehended by way of psychometry: that knowledge of an event of intense emotion—generally agonizing pain or sorrow—is found in the whole surroundings, such as old houses or places where a murder or tragedy once occurred. Powerful emotions apparently leave their record on the earthly stuff around them, to be picked up by persons who can attune themselves to their patterns. That the intense energies can be picked up before the decisive events have actually happened stretches our notions of time, energy, and emotion.

A Case of Retrocognition

By retrocognition is meant the perceiving of a situation or event that occurred in the past, unknown to the perceiver. This is usually considered very difficult to establish, because as long as there is a living person who was aware of the particular event, then the perceiver may be picking up his knowledge either through some causal channel or by telepathy with that person. He would not then be entering into the past, but only tuning into memories now present in the mind of another person. This difficulty arises if retrocognition is defined as the direct acquaintance with events now past without the mediation of another mind. However, if it is posited as another aspect of telepathy, and if that faculty, whatever it may be, operates not only in the present, but backward and forward in time, being free of the limitations of ordinary consciousness, then retrocognition would be the complement of precognition, both of them revealing essentially the same power of the psyche in the sense that both demonstrate freedom from the constraints of time as we ordinarily experience it. In any case, there are examples in which the information gained predates the memory of any living person. Consider an experience from the life of George Fox, founder of the Quaker faith, as told in his journal:

> As I was walking with several friends, I lifted up my head, and saw three steeple-house spires, and they struck at my life. I asked them what place that was? They said, Lichfield. Immediately the word of the Lord came to me, that I must go thither. Being come to the house we were going to, I wished the friends to walk into the house, saying nothing to them of whither I was to go. As soon as they were gone I stept away, and went by my eye over hedge and ditch till I came within a mile of Lichfield; where, in a great field, shepherds were keeping their sheep.
>
> Then was I commanded by the Lord to pull off my shoes. I stood still, for it was winter; but the word of the Lord was like

> a fire in me. So I put off my shoes, and left them with the shepherds; and the poor shepherds trembled, and were astonished. Then I walked on about a mile, and as soon as I was got within the city, the word of the Lord came to me again, saying: Cry, "Wo to the bloody city of Lichfield!" So I went up and down the streets, crying with a loud voice, "Wo to the bloody city of Lichfield!" It being market day, I went into the marketplace, and to and fro in the several parts of it, and made stands, crying as before, "Wo to the bloody city of Lichfield!" And no one laid hands on me.
>
> After this a deep consideration came upon me, for what reason I should be sent to cry against that city, and call it the bloody city! . . . But afterwards I came to understand, that in the Emperor Diocletian's time a thousand Christians were martyr'd in Lichfield. So I was to go, without my shoes, through the channel of their blood, and into the pool of their blood in the marketplace, that I might raise up the memorial of the blood of those martyrs, which had been shed above a thousand years before, and lay cold in their streets. So the sense of this blood was upon me, and I obeyed the word of the Lord.[18]

Fox, a spiritually gifted man, had a ready explanation for his experience: it was the Lord who tugged at his sleeve. Like the lady on Mount Macedon, George Fox cannot see at the time of the experience exactly what happened in Lichfield; instead he suffers the living agony of it. What is revealed to him is the blood and the excruciating pain, as if the very paving stones still run red, though many, many years have passed. Or perhaps the whole world still groans with the memory of that anguish, but it is only apprehensible by consciousness there, at the source. Rufus Jones, editing Fox's journals, explains that Fox, a very active man, had just gotten out of prison after a year's confinement, and the new freedom, combined with his old restlessness, may have created an "irresistible force" so that he was "in no condition to inhibit suggestions." Some subconscious memory or some tale heard in his boyhood may have given him the suggestion, according to Jones. In 1612, forty years before Fox's experience, a man had been burned at the stake in Lichfield, an event known to persons still living in the town. It is possible, then, that what Fox experienced was telepathic communication with the minds of living persons. William James, who quotes this account in his classic *The Varieties of Religious Experience,* sees Fox as a religious genius, of the kind to whom religion is an "acute fever." Such persons, he thinks, often show symptoms of "nervous instability" and are subject to "abnormal psychical visitations." They are creatures of "exalted emotional sensibility," often with a "discordant inner life." He mixes high praise of Fox with language of a different kind, mirroring our own ambivalence toward such faculties.

What is suggested here is that certain persons with a particular sensitivity may at times find themselves drawn into sympathetic attunement with their environment in such a way that they are given access to information labeled past or future by ordinary consciousness. Whether their knowledge comes by way of the minds of other persons or by way of a "memory" within the locality remains unclear; very possibly both can happen. It may be significant that Fox was commanded to remove his shoes, thus putting his bare feet in touch with the paving stones. Perhaps the form of the experience—whether by way of an inner or an outer perception, as in a dream versus an apparition, or bodily sensations versus a visualization of distant events—would depend on the special faculties of the perceiver.[19]

A Case of Psychometry

Certain sensitives can apparently discover information about a person who has previously handled an object by making contact with the object. Given a scarf, wallet, watch, or trinket—any object will do—belonging to an unknown individual, they can provide details about that person's life and character. Raynor Johnson calls this a key phenomenon because it helps reveal the invisible isthmus that runs between mind and matter.

Once again an example will be helpful, this one taken by Johnson from the work of Eugène Osty, a French physician, who writes:

> In absolute ignorance of the person whose book this might be I put it into the hands of Mme. Morel, hypnotized, asking her to speak of the life of the person to whom it belonged.
>
> She said "A young man appears to me tall and rather slight. There is nothing very characteristic in his appearance but his eyes, which are not like those of other people. There is nothing wrong

with them, but their form is peculiar. . . . I see this young man for a long while in a place where there is no danger. . . . He was there with many other men. . . . Then one day, one morning, he departs with others . . . a long march. . . . He then goes in a train. I see him a little later with others in a kind of hole. He is standing up with shining eyes. . . I hear much noise. . . I see fury in his brain; he goes up. . . . What a noise I hear! He feels a blow and falls . . . gets up . . . receives another blow, and falls afresh with others on a road. . . . On one side I see grass and cultivated land, on the other side gray mud. He is wounded in the throat and head by a piece of iron." [Then follows a description of his being carried away, dying, and the place where his body was laid.]

Two days later this account was sent to M. B., who had supplied the object to be analyzed to Dr. Osty and his team. M. B. supplied the following information:

The little book I gave you was a manual of Esperanto taken from the civilian clothing left at my house by the son of one of my friends. The young man to whom it belonged, G. M., was afterwards a second lieutenant in the 27th Regiment, killed or missing on December 12th in a trench attack at the Bois-Brule. G. M. was aged twenty-five or twenty-six, tall, slight, face rather long, and his eyelids had a slight fold like the Chinese, serious and quiet expression. . . . As far as is known he was wounded leading the attack, but continued at the head of his men, then fell at the edge of the German trench which was still in the hands of the enemy. The first wound seems to have been in the shoulder, the second in the head. The body is supposed to have been taken up by the Germans and buried by them, but there is no certainty. He was returned as "missing." The vision is therefore correct, with some particulars that cannot be ascertained. I can state that the little book was touched by G. M. some months before the scene to which it gave rise.[20]

This case suggests that the sensitive was able to make contact with what may be called the transcendental self of the dead soldier, which was aware not only of his life, but of the circumstances following his death. There seems to be no other source of the knowledge concerning the young soldier's death and burial, unless we assume this to be lucky inference on the part of the sensitive. Surprising as it is that the little book could have evoked such information, it is even more surprising that the information could be known to a surviving aspect of the human being, as though the discarnate self retains knowledge that is otherwise lost. Or it may be that the psychic tuned into the timeless knowledge that the young officer had below the level of consciousness as he led his men toward the enemy lines. The Greeks would say that the soul is bathed in the waters of Lethe, forgetfulness, while today we would say that the knowledge is "in the unconscious." I do not see that we have improved our understanding.

Psychometry and Unconscious Connectedness

Important facts for our study can be uncovered by the careful analysis of examples of psychometry. First, the sensitive does not necessarily have to handle the psychometrized object; it is sometimes enough to establish a mental rapport or psychic bonding of some kind with it. Given this, Johnson maintained that even the previous owner need not have physically touched the object; simply caring for it or somehow investing psychic energy in it would establish the necessary contact.

The object is not necessarily the source of the information, according to Johnson. It may be an intermediary, like a telephone line that affords contact but does not in itself provide information. In our example, the sensitive gained contact with the facts about the former owner that occurred after the object had passed from the owner's hands. This would be especially hard to understand if we assume that the knowledge is conveyed by the object. But it has been demonstrated that once contact is established, the object may be removed or destroyed without effect on the communication process. In other words, the object bears some imprint of its former owner, and opens up that knowledge when contact with it is established; however, the essential contact is not with the object, but with the mind of the previous owner.

This is disputed by other investigators, who say that the object is indelibly stamped by the personality and history of the former owner. Some students of psychometry have suggested that the sensitive responds with his or her own associations to certain clues provided by the object in the same way that a person responds to words in the word association test which

Jung studied extensively. Presumably, though, the psychometrist moves beyond personal associations to veridical images that are awakened by the object, these images offering revelations of the life story of the former owner. It is known that the best telepathic connections are made by people who know each other—husbands and wives, parents and children, brothers and sisters—perhaps because these people share a larger fund of common experiences, memories, and associations which can be put together to set forth the meaning of a telepathic "message." However, we are dealing with a connection between mind and object, so that whatever principles apply to mind-to-mind connections do not necessarily apply here. Note that we have evidence of knowledge of the afterlife experience of the subject. Such knowledge presumably must come from a very deep level of the psyche, far below consciousness.

Each person who had contact with the object can be separately and distinctly cognized; there is no confusion of one with another, any more than we confuse different voices on the telephone. The time intervening between contact with the former owner and that with the sensitive is unimportant; it may be many years or very recent. The object itself may have been in contact with other objects in the meantime, but their properties generally do not mingle.

In ordinary human contacts, the degree of affinity or rapport has a lot to do with how much information becomes available. So, too, with psychometrists, who are more successful with some subjects than others. The sensitive may make contact with various levels of the personality of the subject and be unable to distinguish them; he may report the hopes or fears of the subject as outer facts, being unable to differentiate the two. As the above example shows, he may make contact with the transcendent level of the subject's personality, and so come into information about his death. Once again there is the relativization and blending of inner and outer, life and death, that we have seen before. The fact that the sensitive is often unable to distinguish between the thoughts and actions of the previous owner suggests that the distinction between the inner and outer life is somehow not very significant.

In the past, such occurrences were attributed to a "psychic ether" surrounding and interpenetrating the material object that enables the psychic rapport to be established. Johnson takes this theory very seriously. It is as though the "etheric double" of the previous owner has impregnated the "ether" surrounding or within the object, and the sensitive makes contact by means of her own "etheric" level. Johnson thinks that the existence of the etheric level may help us understand hauntings; perhaps the atmosphere of particular places becomes impregnated with the feelings of events occurring there, which would explain George Fox's experience in Lichfield. This invisible "ether" seems to participate in both mind and matter—matter in the sense that it has a certain quality of locality, and so belongs to the spatial realm, and mind in that it is a bearer of psychic information for those who can read it.

Johnson suggests that this may help explain why certain talismans and the relics of saints have always been treasured by religious people for their ability to convey some of the imprint of the saintly life. Jung refers to the *churinga* of the Aboriginal Australians, a sacred object "which was handed down from generation to generation, [and was] not only endowed with the magic power put into it when first it was made, but has gained some kind of virtue from every individual to whom it has belonged."[21] This "magic power" or subtle energy may be related to what we now call psychometry.

We are also led, it seems to me, to think in terms of a kind of wave motion that some scientists have referred to as "consciousness waves." The very individual nature of the sensitive's contact with the former owner or owners of the object, such that each one seems to have placed a unique stamp or vibration on the object, also suggests a very distinctive kind of wave motion for each personality, and even for different layers of the same personality. Layers deeper than the superficial ego are being tapped, as in the dream state.

Psychometry and Projection

The aspects of psychometry we have discussed, particularly the fact that the previous owner of an object need not have physically touched it, raise questions of great moment when we try to reconnect to the idea of projection. Jung has something very interesting to say about this in the context of discussing sacrifice and gift giving.[22] He says that objects are "projection carriers"; they are not simply objects but also symbols. What is "mine" is a representative of myself; it speaks for me, symbolizes who I am. If I give it away, it carries something of me with it. It is stamped with the quality of "mineness," my identity. This sometimes reaches comical proportions, when I am personally offended if an object of mine is treated disrespectfully. My children also "speak for me" and carry my projections, as we all know. These layers of meaning that attach to objects lend them more than a physical nature, for they become unconscious symbols. Jung refers to this in his familiar terminology, calling it "unconscious identity" or "participation mystique"; however, as suggested in our earlier discussion of projection, we need to see objects in their symbolic aspect (especially if those "objects" are persons), allowing them to open us to the symbolic world, as Dante was led through the sight of Beatrice to an apprehension of divine glory. In their magical, symbolic aspect, all things sing the world song.

But now if a psychic can make contact with my nature through an object of mine, what does this tell us about projections? The object seems to have "absorbed" ("sucked in") my nature, acquiring the quality of "mineness," which it can hold for an indefinite time. And isn't this true of persons also? Those I have known and loved must have been impregnated with my nature, while I, in turn, have been impregnated with theirs. Doesn't this point to the idea that by way of projections we are each permeated by the objects and the persons around us, so that all things and people are connected? This gives new meaning to the idea of the unitary world.

What does this suggest about the nature and goals of psychotherapy—or even of human life? Should we attempt to be so conscious and so well defended, each in his fortress, that we neither give nor receive projections? Is this even possible? Or do we need to be ever more aware of that other level where all things and people are one, which may be mediated to us by way of our "projections"? (And, as I have argued, those projections should not be denigrated as "merely unconscious," since they are the doorway to the divine, and to the whole present and past of the race.) It could be said that modern urban life does not afford enough opportunity for these kinds of projections; our human contacts are too casual, lack intensity. This may be one reason for the modern breakdown of community and the loss of the sacred dimension of life, as well as for the loneliness and isolation of the modern individual. Let us be clear: what we are talking about is the loss of human love, though our love is not "in" the projection, but rather in the energies awakened in us by the process of projection. We should not be in the business of denying what was plain to long ages of the past—we are all one.

Taking this issue in a psychological rather than an ethical direction, we may say that in truth we do not know very much about projection. Just as quantum physicists cannot say whether their elementary units are waves or particles, we cannot identify the fundamental nature of projections. We know that there are many levels on which projections occur, so that there may be a level where these projections are perfectly objective, uncolored by our personal foibles. What the psychometrist reads seems to have an objective quality; it is not the same as a personal projection, colored as the latter may be by our desires, longings, hopes, and fears. One line of inquiry would be to study what has now been observed about transference in modern psychotherapy, in which many projections occur.

Many other examples of psychometry, most of them naturally far less impressive than the one concerning the young soldier, are to be found in the literature. In its rudimentary stages, psychometry can be practiced by almost anyone, without the need for prior training or discipline, and in such cases it appears to be no more than a chance occurrence. However, as the above example shows, it can be far more than that.

Psychometry and Psychokinesis

Suzanne Padfield is an English psychic who has given much study to her particular gifts, psychometry and psychokinesis. She offers information on these phenomena deriving from her own subjective experience. She has done scientifically controlled experiments in psychokinesis by moving a straw beam within a large glass bottle, deflecting it to an angle of up to ninety degrees, and holding it for a required time. She reports a series of up to fifteen runs at a time with 70 percent success, until fatigue set in. She was later able to move the beam successfully from an adjoining room by the use of a video camera for visual contact. She can also do psychometry, or "object reading," and the two abilities—object moving and object reading—seem to be linked in her case. Both have been documented in her report "Mind-Matter Interaction in the Psychokinetic Experience."[23]

If I may interpret the author somewhat freely, she is theorizing that objects are coded microscopically with the events that have happened to them—rather as a magnetic tape is coded with the audio signals or sounds that will be heard when the tape is played—and the coding consists of structural changes within the atomic organization of the object. This theory is reminiscent of the ideas of Alfred North Whitehead, discussed in chapter 4. Both the object and her own brain are visualized as societies or organizations of atoms in motion. When the psychometrist "tunes into" the object, she is not reading the past, but experiencing a new event that is very like (but not identical with) the original event with which the object has been coded. One could perhaps say, shifting metaphors, that with her mind she moves into the "dance of the atoms" within the object.

As she dances with or "becomes one" with the object, Padfield reports a feeling of scanning the past events of the object in such a way that she becomes aware of sequences or memory traces, some actual, some possibilities. She feels herself to be a participant in these events or possibilities. In psychokinesis, she becomes aware of the future possibilities open to the system (which now includes her own consciousness), and can choose one possibility, giving it the status of an actuality. With the straw beam, that is, she can choose the new position it will occupy next from the various possibilities open to it. Apparently she cannot devise a wholly new pattern or direction, or impose an alien will upon the atoms, but she can somehow influence the choices already inherent in their nature.

Psychometry, as understood by Padfield, is closely allied with psychokinesis. Here she does not attempt to cause an object to move, but she is again aware of operating at the atomic level, seeing her mind as a society of atoms that is able to scan the past encounters of the object, both the actual ones and the possible ones. She tries to differentiate the actual from the possible. It is as though she herself were experiencing the moment-to-moment process of choice and change. The "codings" within her own brain, she thinks, become identical with those of the object (the atomic organization) she is handling. This sounds somewhat like the ordinary experience of being involved with a person who trembles on the edge of a decision, where it is clear that the decision could go in any of several directions, except that she is apparently bonding at some microscopic level.

Each object is changed atomically by its encounters with other objects, and each encounter (including the one with the psychometrist) is a new event. How this new event comes to resemble so precisely the events that have previously occurred to the object, so that she can report its history, Padfield can only explain by saying that all the prior encounters of the object are connected in a "similarity space" where distances are defined by similarity, not by the ordinary time and space coordinates. Again, at the macroscopic level, the person trembling on the brink of an important decision will throw all his relevant past experience into the decision-making process—his memories of past choices, together with their outcomes (which were once possibilities). The process is very like some of the ideas proposed at the beginning of this study in regard to the analogy. A person will seek orientation when advancing into a new situation by analogy with past experiences of a like kind. He will be aided by past successes, limited by past failures, and, if without prior experience of any kind, will feel himself stepping off into the unknown. At that point, his dreams, coming from a deeper level, may well throw up helpful analogies, either from his own past or from the past of humanity (the collective unconscious). This means that the deeper levels of the psyche are drawn into the decision-making process. Similarly, we might say that an object can be "oriented" by drawing upon its past encounters, both actual and possible, encoded at the microscopic level.

In psychometry, instead of moving the microscopic particles within the object, Padfield "reads" a life history she believes is coded within it. Apparently the particles composing the object not only move into new configurations with each encounter, they actually encode the meaning, history, and nature of the persons encountered—not just at the moment of encounter, but in the entire history of the person. It is as though a whole life story can be encapsulated in a unit having vanishingly small, perhaps subatomic proportions. This is not as strange to us as it would have been before the discovery of the wealth of information found in the DNA molecule. The particles appear to encode this knowledge, like a magnetic tape, but whether they actually comprehend it we do not know. If they are merely recording the information, they are acting like a machine; if they also comprehend it, they are acting with intelligence. These atoms are active, not merely passive, in their encounters with persons, and they are not limited to the "now" moment in what they will record.

The "similarity space" of which Padfield speaks sounds rather like the "psychic space" which we postulated when discussing apparitions. We discovered that when a person sees an apparition, she is evidently going through a very energy-consuming process to tell herself something, as though her psyche were divided into levels separated by a considerable distance from each other. This psychic distance, we suggested, might be created by such a difference in the construing of reality that the conscious ego cannot comprehend what the deep psyche tries to convey. Thus, strongly held convictions can impede the communication process, while flexibility and openness facilitate it. This has application in the realm of practical affairs when we are urged to "love our enemy," for this makes communication possible. Similarly in psychotherapy, we may be urged to try to love the hateful aspects of our personality as an aid to intrapsychic communication and healing. Whether it is psychic space or similarity space, we are evidently getting at something real, though difficult to describe. We are making use of spatial metaphors to describe a psychic process that is more like scaling a wall. Perhaps the term "affinity space" might be more helpful than "similarity space."

Regarding the insights suggested by our study of psychometry, memory is not the laying down of a precise copy of an image, but the creation of some structural change which encodes an event, while memory retrieval is an active process of "breaking into the code," or, shall we say, moving into the dance. It is not the case, says Padfield, that objects pick up traces of what has happened to them, which in turn stimulate analogous memory traces in the mind of the psychometrist.

Padfield's insights appear to rest on a set of analogies from the field of electronics, using the language of atoms, encoding, and programming. Her "societies of atoms" suddenly come to acquire wholly new qualities as they participate in the "similarity space" and encode the history, the destiny, the life patterning of the person who touched them or attended to them. Such powers stretch the concept of the atom beyond previous limits, but as we open our minds to larger possibilities, we must find room to consider intelligences beyond our own, including, potentially, an intelligence within the atoms.

By this time, we have touched on questions that go far beyond our ability to answer with the knowledge and the experiences available to us. Raynor Johnson concludes that the psychometrist need not handle the object, for the requested information can be obtained by establishing mental contact with it. Similarly, the former owner need not have had manual contact with the object; it is enough to have invested some care or attention in it. Johnson's interpretation would lead us to believe that we are dealing with a contact of mind to mind, whereas Padfield's language suggests a contact of mind to matter. When one of our narrators reported that "matter seemed to dissolve at the contact of thought," I suspect he was on the right track. There is no question that our materialistic biases are called into question as we try to come to greater understanding.

Questions Raised by Parapsychology

Just as we are obliged to assume that the psyche has many layers, so we must assume that material objects are many-layered things. Indeed, this is not news to us, for we have long been acquainted with molecules, atoms, and subatomic particles. As now described by scientists, the ultimate particles have only a tenuous connection to the material realm, being more like waves, flashings, "tendencies to be," than solid things. The billiard ball analogy by which subatomic particles were seen as solid spheres, passive and inert, has come to the end of its usefulness, for we must now see these units as active, and as having their own level of intelligence. Of course it is by no means certain that particular kinds of mental or emotional functioning can be traced to particular material levels such as the molecular, atomic, or quantum level. In the same way, we cannot link our own conscious mental functions securely to the physical brain. What seems clear is that there are possibilities of "communication," not well understood, between our own consciousness and the "consciousness" of objects, whether living or insentient. Material things reveal themselves to be permeable by mind, using its own inherent powers.

Implicit in this thinking is the idea that the human psyche consists of many living layers, such that the knowledge available to ego consciousness is only a small part of a much larger totality. Apparently there are wide gaps between the different layers, so that it is possible to "know" on one level what is wholly unknown at another level, and great energies are required to bridge the gap. While ordinary consciousness relies on speaking and hearing for communication, these other layers are more directly connected to the universal substrata, or, shall we say, open at all times to hidden channels. Speaking and hearing, after all, are vibratory phenomena; therefore we may think of a progression or a spectrum of vibratory energies that afford communication at different levels. We would be saying that at the deeper levels the psyche participates in a realm outside time and space—that these, indeed, are categories by which consciousness establishes its coordinates within the phantasmagoria of the universe, but that they do not set the boundaries or establish the relationships of events in other realms.

Another line of questioning raised by parapsychology then is, What is the nature of time and space? Are time and space attributes of our consciousness, or do they have objective reality? We will discuss this in the next chapter, but we cannot fail to be aware that both time and space become problematical in the context of this material. In his late letters, Jung struggled with this question. He wrote in 1957:

> I would not go so far as to say that the categories of space and time are definitely non-objective. I would rather ask on what level or in which world are space and time not valid? In our three-dimensional world they are certainly and inexorably objective, but we have the definite experience that occasionally—presumably under certain conditions—they behave as if they were relatively subjective, that is relatively non-objective. We are not sure how far the relativity can go, so we do not know whether there is a level or a world on or in which space and time are absolutely abolished, but we remain within the limits of human experience when we accept the fact that it is the psyche which is able to relativize the apparent objectivity of time and space.[24]

Other aspects of psychic phenomena raise still further questions, considered below.

What Is the Urgency of Recently Deceased Apparitions?

In two cases, apparitions of a dying person appear to the living at approximately the time of death. Between the moment of death and the appearance of the seemingly material form at a considerable distance, there may or may not be any lapse of time. It is doubtful that anything has passed through ordinary space, yet the form takes on a visible and spatial nature when it is seen. To the observer, it becomes known as though perceived by the physical eye. It is unclear whether an agent is sending a message to the percipient, though information is certainly shared. In Tyrrell's language, we would say that a preexisting pattern or drama is enacted involving the two parties, and that the agent and percipient, at the moment of death, unite to carry through the pattern as though acting mind to mind. A sense of urgency pervades both cases, as we have suggested, as though this possibility is either fleetingly available or emotionally urgent to the deceased.

If the opportunity is only fleetingly available, we would be saying, for instance, that the woman who forgave her fiancé at the time of his death and the fiancé himself were both acting under the compulsion of a psychic field whose nature we can only dimly picture forth. A driving intentionality seems to be present in this, as in many other such cases. The manner of the perception, whether through eyes, ears, scent, or the awareness of a lurking presence, seems to be somewhat incidental, depending on the particular nature of the percipient.

Is Direct Mind-to-Mind Contact Possible?

In another case, a man in an out-of-body state is able to summon his mother to his aid, not by ordinary communication, but by a kind of instantaneous mind-to-mind contact. His distress reaches her without any audible sound. The idea of a psychic energy not available to ordinary consciousness arises, or perhaps the idea of a vibratory energy that is not commonly known. Along with this comes the idea of a psychic space in which all minds participate, except that death seems to mark the entry to another "space" requiring the crossing of a threshold.

Is the Fissure Between the Living and Dead Permeable?

In yet another case, we have not ruled out the possibility that the distress of a son and his wife penetrated to the realm of the deceased, so that a father appeared to warn his son against an unwise decision. Perhaps the fissure between the living and the dead is a flexible one, impassable in many places but capable of being crossed in others.

Our questions point to the secret of the second tree in the Garden of Eden, the mystery Adam and Eve could not resolve: that of life and death.

An Explorer of the Hidden World

To pursue these questions, we shall have to develop mental powers new to most of us, though perhaps not unknown to the spiritual masters of the past. In this task we are aided by a totally unrelated scientific exploration coming from the field of biology, which was never intended to throw light on parapsychology. This exploration was undertaken by someone who belongs to that most rarified of groups, female Nobel Prize laureates. Barbara McClintock was awarded the Nobel Prize in Medicine for her discovery of moveable genes in maize.[25] Although some of her chief discoveries came in 1951, her work was scarcely understood even by her colleagues, much less honored, until 1983. She had cultivated a kind of insight little known in scientific circles, which enabled her to "see" into the microscopic stirrings at the chromosomal level, becoming herself a microscopic eye that wandered among the chromosomes as among a gathering of friends. Looking through the microscope, "I was right down there with them and everything got big," she explained. "I was even able to see the internal parts of the chromosomes." And she added, "As you look at these things they become a part of you. And you forget yourself. The main thing about it is you forget yourself."

This power came to McClintock as a kind of revelation fairly early in her career when she was invited to Stanford University to work on the cell structure of *Neurospora,* a bread mold. Finding herself blocked in her work, she left the laboratory and went out to sit on a bench under the giant eucalyptus trees that line the driveway at the center of the Stanford campus. After sitting there in silence for half an hour, she suddenly jumped up, knowing she was going to make sense of the data. What actually happened during that half hour McClintock did not say, but it was clearly a time of intense concentration, integration, and creative insight, when many threads of meaning came together. The findings that followed were later confirmed by colleagues. Many years of careful preparatory work doubtless went into that fruitful half hour under the eucalyptus trees.

McClintock continued this method of "seeing" throughout her career, working mostly alone, without the support of understanding colleagues. She could at will move from the macroscopic to the microscopic level of the plant species she studied, so that by looking at the growing plants she would know what corresponding structural alterations in the chromosomes she would later find under the microscope. And she was always right, she said. Her colleagues, having had no similar experiences, and having quite different presuppositions in approaching the evidence, were for many years unable to credit her findings. McClintock emphasized that she approached the data without presuppositions; while the majority of her colleagues continued to hold that genetic change is random, she came to believe that these changes are under the control of the organism. This is to say that genetic change, and therefore evolution, is not a random happening but comes about through the adaptive effort of the organism as a whole. McClintock was very cautious about putting forth her conclusions, but their startling nature inevitably led to misunderstandings with many of her colleagues.

It seems to me that McClintock's ability rested on a kind of transcendence of our ordinary assumptions about time and space. When these spatial assumptions are let go, then size drops away, and one can become a tiny knowledgeable eye inspecting the cellular level of reality. McClintock said that "her computer was never wrong," relying on an analogy with modern technology to explain what she did, but she had studied the practices of Tibetan lamas, who teach the skill she had mastered for herself. We see this skill as allied to psychometry and are led to ask whether her journeyings among the chromosomes affected their dancing; did she influence them as they affected her? That, of course, would be psychokinesis, but it might also apply to some kinds of "spiritual" healing in which the healer is assumed to intervene at the cellular level to bring about change. Influences going the other way would also seem possible. I am reminded of the remark of the modern philosopher Charles Hartshorne, that when we have a sense of bodily well-being it is because our cells are feeling happy; our satisfaction grows out of theirs, which is somehow communicated to us.[26]

Notice McClintock's half-jesting remark that the chromosomes became her "friends." I believe she began to relate to them not only by quantifying them but by somehow uniting with their life, feeling their feelings, sensing their ways. They had choices to make, things to do before they slept. She brought a whole personality to the inquiry, allowing herself to care for their hidden world. With that step, the whole universe suddenly took on a new dimension of aliveness, vibrant with new meaning. And this is not merely a "projection"; it is the aliveness of the world swarming and bubbling and speaking to us on all the levels of being, using a language we must try to learn.[27]

Divine Presences

We are now led to one more "unanswerable" question: are there not powers or intelligent energies in the universe that stand over and above our ego position and yet understand and are involved with our personal concerns? If not, then we will continue to worship the great god Chance. But if so, then we need to discover new ways of communicating with these powers. Our own psychic depths could be assumed to derive from them, forming a concentrate of them as a fish forms a concentrate of the potencies of the sea.

Related to this question are the powerful patterning factors we call archetypes. In the world of the unmanifest, they are like spiritual seeds which must enter the world of time in order to be played out as life dramas. The birth of a person into ordinary time and space then would be like the planting of a seed into the earth that will unfold in time into a shrub or tree. We might assume that every individual entering into birth comes equipped with certain seeds that he is destined to live out; these constitute his fate or calling. Those who have tried to change their fate have learned that the archetypal patterns have extraordinary stability, and are very difficult—though not impossible—to change.

What is so bewildering to the modern mind is the personal nature of the meanings expressed in these life dramas. In synchronicities, the patterns seem to be alight with intelligence and to connect in an extraordinary way with human emotions and intentions. A woman in the process of losing her Catholic faith finds the crucifix falling from her bedroom wall. Faced with a situation of impossibility, she finds her life's meaning somehow expressed through the dramatic activity of material things. The unspoken cry of the human being—the cry she is unable to make—is made for her from the depth of the universe. The "arranger" of the occurrence, though transcendent to the human ego, yet displays a knowledge of—or a connection to—the ego's aspirations and frustrations. There are certain resonances between this and the occurrence of psychometry; just as the human mind displays an ability to "read" the knowledge encoded in the atoms, so the higher intelligences appear to "read" the emotionally laden thoughts and feelings of the human being. And just as the human being can rearrange the possibilities open to a society of atoms, so the higher intelligence can reorganize material objects in a dramatic presentation meaningful to the personal ego. There is an intelligence that leaps over the gap between mind and material objects. Or perhaps we should say that that intelligence operates at a level where there is no gap.

After giving a great deal of thought to these matters, I find that instead of speaking of archetypes, I often prefer the ancient language that Jung also used in many contexts: there are "spirits" or "presences" in the world that must be admitted to have superior intelligence and some attributes of personality, as well as the power to "arrange" events. To give them names that signify these qualities seems a reasonable step—they are gods, powers, divine presences. Jung's mentor, the winged being Philemon, who conveyed spiritual knowledge, would belong to this realm of experience. We may also be instructed by D. T. Suzuki, whose interpretations of Eastern traditions have enlarged our Western understanding of spirituality. In Tibetan Buddhism, "The highest reality is not a mere abstraction, it is very much alive with sense and awareness and intelligence, and above all, with love purged of human infirmities and defilements," according to Lama Anagarika Govinda, who goes on to comment:

> This is why Suzuki emphasizes that even the Dhyani-Buddhas [enlightened beings realized in the course of concentrated contemplation] have all the characteristics of personality, in the sense of a living, self-sustaining, conscious force, and that they are not merely "personifications" of an abstract concept.[28]

The wise of both East and West are agreed on this fundamental truth. The highest truth is living truth. John Blofeld has an excellent way of describing the deities who personify this wisdom: they "hover on the frontier between symbolic entities and actual beings that are scarcely distinguishable from gods and goddesses," he says. "The reason for their existence," he adds, "is that there are certain levels of consciousness which cannot be reached by the ordinary processes of logical thought." These deities, then, are "instruments for communication between those levels and the 'normal' or everyday state of consciousness." At the same time they are seemingly endowed with life and embody the secret energies that operate in living things and in the universe as a whole.[29]

The nearest approximation to these entities that I have found comes from the near-death experiences that have now been widely reported and studied. A fair number of the survivors of these experiences come back to speak of encounters with Beings of Light (or Love), who somehow confer knowledge upon them and allow them to experience such bliss and love as they have never known in earthly life. Such experiences are life-changing and life-renewing, and the experiencers report that they no longer fear death. If these entities can be properly compared with the Dhyani Buddhas of Eastern contemplation, it would suggest that Eastern adepts have learned to consciously move into experiences that we of the West know only in the extremity of death or near death.

In synchronicities we discover a mysterious kind of activity in the world that happens at the very margins of our consciousness, like a strange sound in the night that stops as we come to wakefulness. What was that? we want to say. Does it suggest the presence of something unknown that we almost recognize from out of the past? Some half-remembered reality? An important area of study opens from our consideration of these events. It has to do in part with our ability to experience the ways of a higher reality. When we can do this voluntarily, we shall be able to turn to that reality with assurance for the guidance of our lives, thus bringing ourselves into harmony with its purposes. In the following chapter, we will try to face squarely the nature of the reality that opens before us as we explore further into the meaning of synchronicity. At the same time, we will be exploring some of the shifts of consciousness that have to be made to apprehend that reality.

CHAPTER 6

Time, Space, Synchronicity

Part I

In every transformation of reality, in every change of form, or every time the status of a thing is altered, the abyss of nothingness is crossed, and for a fleeting mystical moment becomes visible. Nothing can change without coming into contact with this region of pure absolute Being which the mystics call Nothing.

—Gershom Scholem

The interplay of forces that determine a historical moment sounds as a single chime.

—Helmut Wilhelm

It is understandable that reason should have the greatest difficulty in granting validity to the peculiar nature of telepathic phenomena. But anyone who does justice to the facts cannot but admit that their apparent space-timelessness is their most essential quality.

—Jung

In this study, we have found ourselves pacing along the edges of the ordinary world, rather like prisoners behind a fence, trying to spot any holes in it that will permit us to see what lies beyond. The holes appear to us as anomalies—unexplained gaps in our ordering systems. How can a person have a visionary experience that brings immediate veridical information about events at a great distance or a future time? What do such visions mean? How is it that I impress my "signature" on a material object in such a way that a psychometrist can read my life history as she takes it in hand? What is the nature of the secret tie between inner world and outer reality that seems to be revealed in these happenings? To what changes of consciousness are we led as we focus on such questions? What is the nature of our reality, anyway?

We observe all events, including synchronicities, through various frames of reference, which can lead to different conclusions. In the hypothetical case of the mother and the pilot who observed the same happening, the former saw a meaningful coincidence, while the latter, flying high above, saw nothing extraordinary. We thus came to the idea that all our theories represent different "takes" or perspectives on a reality that stands beyond any single perspective. This, in turn, led to a reexamination of some of the basic tenets of our own view of reality, particularly space and time. Here, at the very basis of our theories, we met with stubborn facts we could not explain. Our questions then began to converge toward the wholeness of the reality that lies behind all the different theories and perspectives. In this chapter, we will examine the nature of that reality and the ways in which it can be known.

Synchronicity and Time

In a number of cases we have examined, synchronistic events did not conform to our previous understanding of time. One case was that of the woman who saw an apparition of her former fiancé at what later proved to be the time of his death. When this happened, she had no conscious knowledge of the impending death; a day later, the news reached her by way of the newspaper. But even before the apparitional form appeared, she was in a state of agitation, hurrying through her chores before going to the attic to read his letters. The urgency seemed to come from the man, but it was experienced as a mounting anxiety within herself, probably brought about by deep intimations of what she was to learn from the newspaper the next day. Her actions are those of a person torn between opposing motives, and she was hurrying to make sense of the signs coming from within. Her task was to bring to consciousness that which was already stirring in the depths of the psyche. What was the task of the man? Perhaps he knew he had only a few moments, as his soul passed to the disembodied state, when the apparition could appear in a visible form. That would explain his urgency, but not hers. The case shows a discrepancy between conscious time, in which nothing had changed, and unconscious time, in which new insight was forming.

Another case that bears on the theme of synchronicity and time is the story of the woman vacationing at Mount Macedon who hurried to her lodging in a panic, which she later attributed to the crash of an airplane nearby and the death of the two pilots—a crash that did not happen until a week later. If we accept the woman's explanation, we are left with unanswerable questions. Raynor Johnson called this precognitive telepathy. The woman did not predict the future or recognize what was to happen. She experienced a terror that was like the fear and agony later experienced by the two pilots. Quantum physics has raised the question of whether there can be faster-than-light signals in which effects could happen before their causes, meaning causality could work backwards in time. This certainly stretches the usual concept of cause and effect. Could the later event on Mount Macedon have "caused" the woman's panic? At present we have no explanation for such happenings—if they really do happen. Jung would call them synchronicities—acausal events—though this does not explain them; it merely relieves us of the necessity of finding a cause. In the case of the plane crash, could the region already have been pervaded by the intensity of emotions still to be experienced in that place?

In some cases, the connection between synchronicity and time (as we understand it) goes far beyond a mere discrepancy and amounts to a headlong collision. This happens in prophecy and precognition. Our life experience tells us that the future is unknown, yet stories of prophecy and precognition continue to be told—and believed—today. In his book *Soulmaker*, the modern philosopher Michael Grosso tells the story of having three dreams of Ronald Reagan in the two months before the president was shot on March

30, 1981.[1] On February 13, he dreamed that President Reagan was shot in the left shoulder. On February 25, he again dreamed that the president was shot, with much confusion and people running about. On March 12, he dreamed of the president again; this time he saw him stripped to the waist and in excellent health. He told a friend of these dreams before the shooting occurred. The dreams naturally made a powerful impression on him, and he wrote them down, convinced that the president would be somehow restored to health. Who can fail to believe a story like this, which has echoes in biblical times? Yet we have no idea how a philosopher's dreams could foretell the future of the president—or, for that matter, how any prophecy can occur.

We recall the ancient Oracle of Apollo at Delphi, which was frequently consulted by kings, generals, and leaders about to embark on significant undertakings. The Sybil, or Pythia, a simple virgin dwelling in a cave beneath the temple of Apollo, delivered the prophecies. But her utterances required interpretation by a committee of elders, as they typically were not intelligible to the layperson in their raw form. Answers often seemed ambiguous and could be interpreted multiple ways, perhaps to help them appear plausible no matter the outcome. But that ambiguity did not deter people from consulting the oracle.

The State Oracle of Tibet at Nechung Monastery was established during the reign of the fifth Dalai Lama in the seventeenth century. It was served by a ferocious deity named Pe Har, who was originally opposed to the introduction of Buddhism into Tibet, but was subdued and brought to order by Padmasambhava, the Indian master who had been invited to bring the new teaching to Tibetans. As this memorable example shows, in contests between gods and humans the gods do not always win, and Pe Har was converted to Buddhism. It was said that the medium chosen to speak the prophecies was not a fragile woman given to tremors and premonitions, but a vigorous male active in public affairs. He had to be strong to confront the god, for it was Pe Har himself, not a human being, who prophesied the future. The most famous of the Tibetan oracles, the Nechung Oracle continues to this day, though the medium now resides in India with the Tibetan government in exile.

In classical Greece and Tibet—as in many other societies—prophecy stood near the heart of the culture, enjoying the support of the religion and the people.[2]

A Modern Prophecy

A story from the twentieth century shows how far the art of prophecy has fallen in modern times. It happened in a gypsy camp in England, as told by Phoebe Bendit, no mean psychic herself, in one of the many books she wrote with her husband, the psychiatrist Laurence Bendit.

> The swarthy, black-eyed woman asked me in the usual way to cross her palm with silver, then she lightly touched my finger-tips for a moment, shut her eyes and poured out a torrent of speech. Her character reading was astonishing; and she mentioned without hesitation a number of incidents in my past life. She was particularly clever in her analysis of my psychic abilities, seeing both their weakness and their strength.
>
> Eventually she began to foretell the future. It sounded incredible, not to say impossible. She sketched correctly the kind of professional life I was then living and said that it would change radically. "You will marry a man who is either a doctor or who is in a profession associated with sharp, bright instruments." She went on, adding various details about him. "You will work together and write books together. You will travel together and neither of you will work alone in the future." She then foretold a number of events that would lead up to this. Then, guessing my doubts, she said, "You don't believe me, so I am going to tell you three unimportant things, which will come true within the next seven days. When they do, you'll remember what the gypsy said, and you will see that in the next few years the big things will happen too."
>
> She then told me that I should very shortly receive a gift of stones; that I would also be given a ring; and that, on some very stony ground, I should find two sprays of white heather where no other white heather grew.
>
> I said nothing of all this to my hostess, but that evening while I was dressing for dinner she came into my room, bringing a box of unset cairngorm stones, beautifully cut. Three days later, a registered parcel arrived from London. It contained an old ring. Then on the fifth day, out for a picnic . . . when I had nearly reached the

> top of [a] rough and stony track I saw, growing in solitary beauty, two sprays of white heather. . . .[3]

Bendit adds that after her own session with the gypsy, the woman turned to her companion but had nothing to offer but the "usual fortune-teller's gibberish." Even her character reading was quite wide of the mark. The gypsy, who showed definite signs of being a gifted psychic, and whose prophecies for Bendit later proved to be accurate, failed utterly when she tried to work with her friend. These kinds of failures, multiplied many times, give rise to the claim that all precognition is fraudulent, but it seems to me that the difference between the successful reading a few minutes before and the failed effort so soon after ought to tell us something about the nature of the abilities that are involved here. Was this a personal matter, like the instant likes or dislikes that sometimes arise between two people who have never met before? Could personal feelings block access to deeper knowledge?

We have no recognized theory to account for the prophetic ability of the gypsy. Even some students of parapsychology believe that there is no such thing as precognition and prophecy.[4] After all, how can events that haven't yet happened be known to us in the present? Foreknowledge requires a deterministic world, but does not such determinism take our freedom away?

Some of the best evidence for precognition and prophecy comes from dreams. Future events are often pictured forth in dreams, either symbolically or realistically. It would be a worthy subject of research to take note of the many references to the future in the dreams of some people, but the references would be difficult to identify, since the events foretold would occur only later.

People appear to differ a great deal in their relation to time, both in dreams and in life, and in how far their dreams penetrate into the future. A dream that came to me as I began my Jungian training spoke of a period extending eight years in advance, and was one I recognized immediately as making use of symbolic language to refer to the future. For many years, I dreamed every night of events that were to happen two or three days in the future. I did not consider this to be in any way unusual, since it happened every night. Was I becoming a prophet every night when I went to sleep? I did not know what to make of it. The dream's knowledge was always quite personal; if there was any wider reference, I failed to get it. Sometimes the dream suggested bad news in the making, but I was never able to change what happened. The dreamer had it right. I came to believe that the boundary between past, present, and future is a flexible one, perhaps differing for each observer.

These examples point to a stratum of the collective unconscious in which time as we know it is not in effect, and the future is already portrayed. This stratum is somehow available to the dreaming psyche but apparently not to consciousness, at least not in our culture. The gypsy, however, penetrated to that layer, and so could reach times years ahead of the present moment. Instead of scoffing at her, we should be studying her (if she would allow it), for she is a bearer of an ancient knowledge that might be lost if we don't pay attention.

Do these experiences tell us something about the nature of time? If our physical bodies live in time, changing and growing and dying in time, is there another part of ourselves that does not live in time at all? Is it possible to make contact with that eternal aspect (if it exists) and come to learn its wisdom? Our religions have always spoken of the survival of death and of immortality. Do these claims deserve further study in the light of parapsychology?

Our questions have once again far outpaced our answers, so let us return to the subject of time and synchronicity, and to some aspects of the world that make the latter seem thinkable.

Chance, Time, and Synchronicity

When called upon to explain synchronicity, Jung often turned to the idea of wholeness and to the Chinese habit of thinking in terms of wholes. The I Ching—whose guidance is found by the throwing of coins or the dividing of yarrow stalks, both depending on chance—was one of his preferred examples of synchronicity.

The word *chance* comes from the Latin *cadere,* "to fall." Chance is that which befalls, a fortuitous happening or a contingency. It is connected to the fall of the cards or the dice, to fate (Lady Luck), to whatever comes without conscious design or defies our expectations. Jung referred to synchronicities variously as meaningful coincidences, chance events, contingent occurrences, and acts of creation in time. He also remarked that they seem to reveal an ordering principle within nature that he called "acausal orderedness" rather than "psi." In saying this, Jung was trying to make room for synchronicities within an ordered universe without invoking the usual ordering factors of space, time, and causality. Let us follow up these descriptive names, for they offer different insights on the nature of synchronicity.

Chance and randomness are not the same. Randomness is the stochastic probability of outcomes occurring across a range of trials, for example, the probability of drawing a particular card from a deck of cards. Chance is that which befalls in the moment; its result is the card actually drawn. The Latin *cadere,* "to fall," and *cadentia,* "a falling," are related to *cadence* and hence to such terms as measure, beat, or rhythm. Through synchronicity, chance reveals an order or rhythm, less the order of an imposed design than of an inherent beat or wavelike motion, much as a rhythm in music provides a framework upon which a melody can be erected. "To fall" in this sense means "to fall in step," as one says of a column of soldiers or a marching band—or, for that matter, "to fall out of step." There must be some prior order from which to fall or we could not identify it as a "fall." But such a fall, rather than representing disorder, might simply express a different kind of order, much the way that atmospheric turbulence is still an expression of the physical laws of gases. Consider chaos theory, which studies (among other things) the order hidden within turbulent motion.[5]

In the primordial tradition, the falling is not random but rather an expression of the ordered flow or rhythmic emanation from the primal unity. It is the descent from that unity (the Nothingness, the Void) into the realm of multiplicity according to definite cyclic or rhythmic patterns. What "befalls" is connected to the passing of time, both its rapid, momentary ticking and its great planetary cycles. On a mythic level there is the "Fall of mankind" that came biblically with the eating of the forbidden fruit and the separation of Adam and Eve from God. We can understand the Fall into sin as a dropping away from the original unity; it formed a meaningful part of the larger world process.

Perhaps a metaphor developed by David Peat will be helpful to understand the relation between chaos and synchronicity, and how these can lead to higher order.[6] He asks, if all the pieces of a jigsaw puzzle, having been thoroughly shuffled, managed to re-form themselves into a total picture, would this be an example of synchronicity? No, not in and of itself. Synchronicity is not the merely accidental arrangement of formerly disconnected parts into a particular order; it is the expression of a higher unity. The puzzle has been cut up in an arbitrary fashion, and the meaning is not organically enfolded within each of the parts. Synchronicities, by contrast, involve the coming together of a wholeness pattern that in an explicit sense appears broken, but in an implicit sense was always present at some fundamental level. Each part bears the stamp of the whole, like a hologram. The wholeness is greater than the sum of the parts, as though represented by a unique vibratory frequency that locks each part into its state of being, just as the harmonics of a musical tone are the expression of its specific vibratory frequency. This is to say that the whole is not a simple collection of separate parts; it is the expression of a higher unity. Synchronicities, then, are the empirical evidence of an unseen order expressing itself within the visible world; the meaning of this order arises from this evidence. We might speculate that this order has an eternal form of existence, and so it is present before it becomes visible on our plane. We might also note that things may participate in more then one whole.

Contingency

The word *contingency* comes from the Latin *con,* "with," plus *tangere,* "to touch" (for example, in mathematics, a line is *tangent* if it touches a curve or circle at but one point). Here, by way of a falling, we find ourselves in the realm of multiplicity, far from the center of the wheel of existence, the original and basic unity. Contingency involves that which is liable but not certain to occur; if something is *contingent,* it is dependent, subject to unforeseen conditions or chance. As a noun, *contingent* means a share, proportion, or quota, as in "a contingent of troops." This implies a latent wholeness of which each part forms a share or due proportion; thus the presence of the higher unity or order is not entirely lost. From this comes the idea of fairness or justice—each part should contribute its fair share to the whole and receive a fair share from the whole. Paradoxically, this is often achieved by chance.

Contingency thus embraces both the idea of chance and that of proportion, or due measure. From the idea of proportionality, we are led back to the analogy. As suggested by the Hermetic Doctrine of Correspondence, discussed in chapter 1, the realm of contingency, or the phenomenal world, stands in an analogical relationship to the transcendent world, linked by correspondence. It is another name for the sensible world. Since it involves touching on all sides, it also involves an aggregation, a multiplicity, perhaps of cells, molecules, or persons, along with the influence of each member on the others. It is a falling away from the original unity into a lower realm where particular conditions affect the emergence of the higher meaning or order.

Chance and the Whole

The casting of lots was an ancient way of arriving at a proper division of a wholeness among the separate parts. For example, to assign members to perform an agreed-upon task, a leader might break straws into short uneven pieces, and, hiding their uneven lengths in his closed fist, have each member take one with the proviso that the recipients of the shortest straws were chosen. Among the Hebrew tribes in Canaan, lots were cast to assign territory (Numbers 26:55–56). In a war among the tribes of Israel, the men to go into battle were selected by lot (Judges 20:9). Among the ancient Hebrews, as in all primal societies, the sense of group identity was strong, while the sense of personal identity was fairly weak. Courageous action by an individual could uplift the whole group; a shameful act shamed all.

In many societies today, this sense of group identity, of community, is attenuated, the organic unity of the whole all but lost, while the sense of individuality is very strong. The meaning of life is no longer to be found in loyalty to the group; it is every man for himself. While until recently we still used the method of casting lots to choose the men who would fight our wars, the procedure is now becoming anachronistic, for the warrior no longer sees his courage and sacrifice growing out of his roots among his people. This suggests that sacrifice is on the way out along with heroism—both depend on the cohesion and loyalty of the group. Our loss of the sense of community as the meaningful backdrop or context for our acts and choices frees us from the compulsion of the whole, but leaves us alone in a frantic search for meaning. Perhaps the terrible ethnic conflicts going on today represent last-ditch efforts by some people to maintain the sense of group identity, and with it the very meaning of life.

Time, Fate, and the Whole

From the above considerations, we see a connection between one's lot—that which befalls one—and fate, the emergence of a unique patterning in time. As the history of a group unfolds, so the story of each individual unfolds, everyone playing his or her appointed role. Without the prior existence of the larger wholeness, the casting of lots would be merely arbitrary, but given the preexisting wholeness and the organic connectedness of the parts, each one's role becomes a share, a due proportion of the whole. In primal societies, the tribal whole gained its significance by its allegiance to a still higher order, the tribal gods; thus each person could find the meaning of life and a link to the higher orders through membership in the tribe.

If we think of chance as mere randomness, then the idea that order can be restored by a chance operation such as a throw of coins or casting of lots seems totally wide of the mark. After all, we define randomness as the opposite of order. But the I Ching proceeds through the application of chance as the means of linking its teachings to one's lot. Puzzled by a life situation that cannot be resolved by conscious thinking, the inquiring individual throws coins or manipulates yarrow stalks to find an entry point into its teachings. Orientation within its guidance is thus achieved by way of chance. The connection between chance (the divinatory act) and order (the reading in the I Ching so selected) is thus linked to fate, to one's lot in life—hence the use of gambling terms to describe one's pathway through the changing circumstances of life. But while one's life choices may appear to the conscious ego as a gamble, given the ego's limited knowledge, those choices may be seen as wise by the deep psyche from its more fundamental perspective. Chance becomes a mysterious window that allows a larger vision to become visible through the lens of the I Ching.

How is it that chance—the fall of the coins—can lead us to a new level of order? Suppose on a trip you must exercise some creativity to choose a destination. You know that if you to try to think through the problem or make a calculation, you tend to remain on the same (conscious) level. Recognizing this, instead suppose you simply close your eyes and jab at a map with your forefinger, and accept that as your answer. Alternately, you might assume a meditative stance, sink into yourself, and allow the answer to come through your own depths in the form of a picture, an image, or a sign. Or you might turn to the I Ching, to access what Jung called the absolute knowledge of the unconscious.[7] In this way, instead of working up a rationale, you open yourself to possibilities you had not imagined. Such methods are useful when the possibilities of rational thought have been exhausted or are no longer fruitful. An answer comes by depending on a hidden connectedness between the psyche and the cosmos mediated by chance. These processes resemble what we mean when we say, "Let go and let God." By opening ourselves, we get out of the way so that some deeper knowledge can come through—along with either good or bad fortune.

Consider another example based on Mendeleev's periodic table of the elements. The table is arranged in a matrix as an ordered symbolic arrangement of all known elements. (Gaps in Mendeleev's original table showed where additional elements had to be discovered. It has been said that the development of the periodic table of elements was the breakthrough of alchemy into modern chemistry.) Suppose you put your finger down at random on a copy of the periodic table. Because of its underlying structure, in touching the symbol for one element you are in a sense choosing the whole. Similarly, the sixty-four hexagrams of the I Ching are arranged in a matrix, an ordered arrangement that includes a symbolic representation of all life possibilities, hence a whole. If you put your finger on any one hexagram, you likewise choose that one as a representative of the whole. The one is necessary to complete the whole, and in a sense presupposes and implies the whole. Notice that the parts of Mendeleev's table are not held together by causality but rather by a patterning, as the members of a family are held together, as a map is held together, and as the sequence of hexagrams of the I Ching are held together.

We see that chance can lead to a new level of order if the chance events form a bridge from our current circumstances into a reference framework, such as a map, the I Ching, the table of the elements, or any other orienting field, such as the position of the planets. But without the bridging function, chance events carry no meaning. In the example of the map, it would avail us nothing were we to allow our finger to point beyond the constraints of the map's edges. The chance event must lie within the boundaries of the selected reference framework in order to be meaningful to the perceiving individual's life-world.

The One and the Many

The concept of synchronicity opens this viewpoint still wider by positing an underlying meaningful unity of mind and matter, of the physical and mental, of the individual in his or her life-world. Synchronicity implies that our lives are lived in the context of an encompassing Whole and that this in turn informs the very meaning of our lives. If we cannot establish a meaningful life-world by returning to the unity of family or tribe, we are impelled by our very nature to discover other ways—which is at the root of our modern struggles for meaning.

The two terms of the synchronicity, the inner thought, dream, or vision and the outer happening (such as the fall of the coins) form a meaningful coincidence. We feel a certain delight in the moment when we recognize a meaningful coincidence because it meets our need for a sense of meaning we feel impelled by our natures to uncover.

Embedded within human history and language is an ancient teaching that all things unfold into this world bearing the stamp of the One from which they emerged. They are not separate and independent things that go their own way. The One from which they unfold is a reality, not a mere abstraction, and is not constrained by the limits of time and space as we experience them; therefore the movement into this world is a movement into the time and space we know, out of a higher unity. A further study of these ordering factors will clarify this.

In depending on chance, we are not moving outside the region of laws and meaning. While a preliminary view suggests that chance cannot be meaningful, this is not the case if chance can refer to a higher order, as we have seen above. Our problem then becomes one of reconciling two different and apparently disconnected orders, as a composer brings the different vibrations and textures of the many musical instruments into the higher order of a symphony. An act of creativity is involved. Let us take this in the beginning as a working possibility. To be able to see chance as anything but random, we must see it in the larger context of the whole. It becomes simply what "befalls," the way time unfolds, and yet it has a certain meaningful orderedness or rhythm deriving from its connection to the higher order.

Synchronicities, then, are the empirical evidence of this unseen order expressing itself within the temporal world, or the restoration of the primal order within the subordinate one, as though the latent unity of the whole, its meaningful coherence, is reestablished by an act of nature herself. Our own deep inner connectedness within the wholeness of nature is briefly set forth in a symbolic enactment. The higher order that flashes into visibility can be seen only from a holistic perspective. It is a view that links up especially well with Eastern spirituality.

AN EASTERN VIEW

The old Taoist masters approached these matters with a viewpoint that grew naturally from ancient shamanic and tribal experience. They did not have to prove to themselves that chance events could be meaningful; they simply recognized the meaningful connection between the patterns of mind and matter: in throwing the coins to get a reading from the I Ching, they took the view that the thrower, the thrown (the coins or yarrow stalks), and the act of throwing were linked in an encompassing wholeness. They could have obtained a simple yes-or-no answer by tossing a single coin—heads, yes; tails, no. But they chose instead to make six throws of three coins (or a more complicated manipulation of yarrow stalks), establishing a pattern of lines that were also numbers (and required time to unfold), and they intuitively linked the throw of the coins with the two great world principles, Yin and Yang, both having their source in the Tao. Time was Yang, active, while space was Yin, receptive; space had to be activated, and time was the agent of activation. Using this approach, they were able to link chance and meaning, always with the assumption that whatever pattern is thrown is expressive of the wholeness of the person throwing the coins. When the person's mind was divided, change was in the air, and a changing line would be thrown, but when wholeness reigned, no change was to be expected. This correspondence between inner state and outer event belongs to the nature of the world—synchronicity is a manifestation of it. It was the principle by which the masters could transform chance into meaning.

The person posing the question becomes a representative of the Many, seeking to know what larger patterns (archetypes) she is living out and where they are likely to lead. Good fortune? Ill fortune? The questioner throws a particular number, which leads to the pattern at play in this situation. In this way, she has a hand in choosing her fate while also allowing herself to be guided by the wisdom of the old book. The I Ching reconnects her to the Tao, the original wholeness.

We, as Westerners, struggle to understand this straightforward approach, for we start from entirely different premises. The Westerner trusts what he can see or hear and believes that this is the solid ground from which to begin the search for what is ultimately real, and so align his behavior with that reality. Things are separated from each other in time and have definite locations in space. Mind and matter are separate, and our problem is to understand how the two can be brought together. The truth is to be found outside the observer—it is objectified. For the Westerner, synchronicities thus involve a "sporadic interlocking" of mind and matter which allows the unitary world to be manifested briefly.

The Eastern philosopher, on the other hand, would start his search with the world of oneness, and posit the ultimate unity of all complementarities, including mind and matter, inner and outer, subject and object. In his view, the individual is, at some profound level of the psyche, in essential unity with the world. At that level we do not see a world; we are the world. This unity, rather than dividedness, reveals the ultimate reality, which is the source of all and possesses more power, order, and intelligence than the world to which it gives rise. Mind and matter are eternally one, though their unity is only manifested to us intermittently. Our problem then becomes one of recognizing what is always present. The difference here is a fundamental one, and involves us in very different enterprises. The Eastern philosopher searches inward for truth, while the Westerner seeks truth in the outer world.

The teachings of Zen Buddhism offer a clue here when we are told that the satori experience of sudden enlightenment lies outside space and time; it appears as a total shift of consciousness that renders all previous structures irrelevant. In a way, it is the ultimate paradigm shift that takes us beyond paradigms. It has the effect of an opening, a liberation, and at the same time a catastrophe—a breakdown of long-held convictions and a breakthrough to other levels. It is the dreaded breakdown that is at once a new birth. We are told that it is not reached by thinking, for thinking keeps us always in the subject-to-object mode, separated from whatever it is that we think about. The Zen Buddhist seeks an immediate experience of reality, where self and world are not separate and a different sense of time prevails.

A Chinese Experience

According to Robert Aziz, in certain Chinese Buddhist monasteries, the abbot was chosen by lot—the whole group depending on a chance event to choose its leader.[8] In one monastery, the method worked in this way: the names of all the positions to be filled were written on small slips of paper and placed in a container. Each monk then drew a slip. The one who drew the slip with the title "abbot" written on it became the new abbot. In 1930 the one chosen had been ordained for only three months; he declined the role, feeling unready. They accordingly drew again, and this time the same monk drew the abbot slip. This time he felt obliged to accept. Five years later, on completion of his term, another drawing was held, and this time, surprisingly enough, he drew the abbot slip again. This was an example of chance, but not chance as we think of it. The process assumed that chance offers an opening through which a higher wisdom can manifest, and with which we are all in touch at unconscious levels.

Another monastery had a slightly different procedure, but again the choice of the abbot was accomplished by drawing lots. In this case, the name of each member of the group was written on a small piece of paper and placed in a metal tube. After suitable religious invocations, a senior officer would shake the tube and draw out a slip of paper, using a pair of chopsticks. The name would be recorded and the slip returned to the tube, and the tube shaken again and the drawing continued. This was repeated until the same name was drawn three times in a row. This was the name of the new abbot.

The chance of drawing the same name three times in a row from a group of more than one hundred names seems very small, but the monks testified that it always worked. Sometimes the person chosen to be the new abbot appeared to be less than adequate to the task, but once chosen he began to reveal the gifts needed by his calling.

The synchronistic point of view underlying this procedure is difficult for us to accept in such a practical matter as the choice of a leader, but it is again based on the Chinese habit of thinking in terms of the whole. Each member whose name is placed in the tube represents one facet of the whole, each one marked by the organic wholeness of the group. The one whose name is drawn is assumed to bring to the task precisely the qualities needed to complete the whole. Notice that the drawing of lots does not in itself make a synchronicity. Whether we are dealing with all the monks in the monastery or all the positions to be filled, we have a wholeness; and just as the gap in Mendeleev's chart showed precisely the nature of the element that had to be discovered to complete the matrix, so the monks agreed that the person chosen by lot had the qualities needed to complete the whole. We might call this the magic of the whole. The same situation is found in the I Ching, where, from the wholeness, the inquirer discovers the appropriate hexagram by throwing the coins.

The fact that in one monastery the same name must be drawn three times in a row is especially interesting; it represents a testing of the higher power or "arranger" that rules over the whole situation. Will it affirm and reaffirm the answer that has emerged from the "chance" drawing of the slips?

Consider the story of Gideon's dew in the Old Testament (Judges 6:36–40). Gideon, told by Yahweh to lead the Israelites in their war against the Midianites, needed a sign that Yahweh would be with him. He even prescribed a test that Yahweh must pass: let the woolen fleece that he (Gideon) would place on the ground that night be wet with dew but all the ground around be dry. The next morning, he wrung a bowl of water out of the fleece while all the ground around was dry. But Gideon was not reassured, and he asked that Yahweh submit to a further test. This time the fleece was to be dry and all the earth around it wet. And, perhaps alarmed at his own temerity, Gideon said to Yahweh, "Let not thine anger be hot against me." But Yahweh accepted the test, and in the morning the fleece was dry and the surrounding earth was wet. Yahweh passed the test. These events feel like synchronicities such as we might see today, except that the whole context is different; to the Israelites, the tribal god is the arranger of the event, and the human being is able to call on that power to meet the needs of the tribe. (Needless to say, Gideon won the battle.) Taking hold of these experiences, we are brought around again to the subject of time. We will now take up some of the many facets of time to see what light they cast on the varied aspects of synchronicity.

Time in the Classical Western View

Our understanding of time is clearly involved in all the synchronicities we have considered. It is involved in precognition when anyone gains knowledge of events that are still in the future. Both time and space are involved in telepathy and clairvoyance: a message seems to be sent by a "sender" and to be received by a "receiver," with no time elapsing between. Likewise in apparitions: a person suddenly appears in a distant place to one who has not seen him or her in many years. The movement—if movement it is—is for all practical purposes immediate. In dematerializations, a solid body, a key or a glass, is dematerialized and made to reappear instantly in another place. Can a better understanding of time and space help us to explain such arisings as part of the natural order? If so, how would this change our view of the reality in which we live?

According to legend, Galileo dropped cannonballs from the Leaning Tower of Pisa in the later part of the sixteenth century and formulated their velocity in mathematical terms.[9] Thus it was with falling bodies that the modern mathematical approach to science was born. In Galileo's equations of falling bodies, a variable represented by the letter *t* referred to the flow of time. Physicists are by no means in agreement as to the nature of time, though all would perhaps agree that time is to be approached by measurement. The habit of analyzing all phenomena by the use of measurement has deep roots in modern science, as in the equation

$$a = \frac{\Delta v}{t}$$

where Δv is change in velocity, a is average acceleration, and t is time. In this classical scientific perspective, time is limited to its measurable aspect. However, its measurable aspect can be only indirectly observed. A clock does not measure time per se; rather, it counts the oscillations of whatever mechanism is powering it. This "movement" is designed such that the rotation of the clock's hands agrees with the rotation of the earth's axis. This is what we call time, but what is being measured is the clock's movement, not time itself. Even an atomic clock operates by observing periodic fluctuations of matter. We observe time only in its effects, never in and of itself.

In equations such as the one above, every moment of time is like every other, and any moment of time can substitute for any other because time has no qualitative aspect in this framework. Time becomes a convenient measuring stick—tons of wheat grown per year, miles traveled per hour. While the ancient tradition related chance (number, cadence) to the befalling of human events in time, and led to the development of oracles to try to show what time held in store, Western science focused on that aspect of time that could be expressed in quantitative terms alone. In Galileo's legendary experiment, all cannonballs, whether large or small, fell at the same rate, no matter how many times the experiment was repeated (though this was true of only a limited range of events). The state of mind of the person dropping the balls had nothing to do with it.

Time has no particular direction in the classical equations of physics; it might as well flow backwards as forwards according to Newton's laws of motion. However, this contradicts our experience that time flows from the past to the future and never the other way around. Ilya Prigogine, a chemist by training, has argued that time is not reversible, and that the arrow of time aims in a single direction. Consider this experiment: Place a card in a beaker of water so that it divides the water in half. Add a drop of red dye to one side and blue dye to the other. Allow the colors to disperse on their respective sides of the card. Now lift the card out of the beaker and observe the colors gradually merge together. Though it is not physically impossible for all the red and blue dye to return spontaneously to their original sides, it is so unlikely that it will essentially never happen. This implies that there is a temporal order built into the universe that cannot be reversed. Irreversibility is characteristic of the vast majority of systems in our world, says Prigogine, and this is the source of new order. The future is not given and determined; it has to be discovered, while the past cannot be recovered.[10]

The time known to physics is not lived time; it is a time abstracted from a particular sequence of events in which there is no willing, planning, or purpose. Things are inert, moved only by the application of energy or pressure from some external source. If we consider the time that is actually lived by human beings, the time that carries us from childhood to maturity to old age, we have a very different kind of time. Our psychic life, our plans, hopes, and expectations, all depend upon our lifetime and its rhythms. The seasons of planet Earth are built into our very cells and tissues, as into the whole organic realm, with its birthing, growing, multiplying, and dying. For us, time is known by the days and seasons of our living and by the pulsations of our bodies, not necessarily by the measures known to physics. To properly understand synchronicity, we must take as our starting point this lived time world with its varied phases and intensities, rather than the merely quantitative aspect of time.

While clock time ticks along with unvarying regularity, subjective time seldom has this measured quality. Subjectively, it seems we are generally rushed for time; we keep calendars, consult our watches, trying to keep up with the passing of time. It carries us on from youth to adulthood to old age and the life beyond, racing along inexorably, bearing us on its shoulders. We have no choice but to go with it. Time varies according to our mood and interest. It flies when we are happily engaged, and drags when we are tired and bored. It definitely has a qualitative aspect. Consider the different attitudes toward time taken by a student preparing for an important examination, and the same student starting a long summer recess—or the woman told by her doctor that she will give birth in two weeks. Consider the Buddhist who has many lives ahead, as opposed to the Christian who has but one. Our subjective sense of time clearly makes a difference in the way we live our lives.

Time's Beginning

In Western civilization, the years are counted from the birth of the Christian Savior, revealing that even in our secular culture time still has a certain sacred quality. The coming of a great prophet marks the beginning of a new revelation of God's will; it is chosen from within the divine realm, not the human. A new era for humankind begins, and with it a new beginning of time.

Time has a mysterious and even spiritual significance. In earlier eras, the keeping of time was the work of a priestly class, and even today a quality of mystery attaches to the subject of calendars, which are kept by wise men and women who understand the celestial cycles, and can calculate their exact duration—as most of us cannot.

Objectively, we measure time by counting some regular movement, originally the cycles of the moon and the sun. We count the years by assigning a number to each peregrination of the earth about the sun. M. L. von Franz points out that taken as a rhythmic pulsation or oscillation—the one-two movement of the breath or a pendulum—the number two marks the beginning of our ability to measure and experience time, while with the number three an observing consciousness enters the scene and begins to count the succession of pulses or cycles.[11] At that point a new kind of time—sequential or linear time—is born.[12] Time becomes the arena of dramatic sequences—and of consequences. With threeness, a living world begins to take form in time and space before our very eyes. Three has always been connected to processes in time and space, perhaps because of the threefold structure of time—past, present, and future—and the three dimensions of space. But in whatever way we perceive them, time and space require each other; they are the ultimate interdependent pair.

Time, Tension, Intensity

Jean Gebser, who says that we have remained unconscious of the reality of time until very recently, proposes a new understanding of time based on our experience of it. He suggests that time manifests in a variety of modalities in accordance with our plane of consciousness, and that these varied modes do not form a logical whole.[13] In fact, to try to understand them by means of logical categories is precisely where we go wrong. For example, intensity of feeling lends time its holding or carrying power and makes it a co-constituent of our world, along with space. Events with high emotional intensity are memorable, while low-intensity events pass by leaving little impression. Temporal intensity rises either with the importance of an event, with repetition, or with trauma. Intensity has to do with memory and emotional involvement with passing events; we connect the present with the past and future by way of memory.

Tension is an expression of the polar nature of our consciousness and our subjective appreciation of time. Tension arises in opposition, such as mind versus body, or far versus near, and with something that stretches between them. A violin string and a suspension bridge are both held in tension; without it they could not be what they are. The feeling of suspense in a story is a kind of tension in the sense that the suspense connects a story's beginning to its ending. In life we choose one pole and make it our goal; we strain and stretch to reach it, for example, by training to achieve an athletic milestone. It is hard to reach such a goal because another pole, inescapably tied to it, pulls in the opposite direction. While it is possible to be stretched too tight, it is also possible to be too languid, lethargic, or lazy—to be without a goal. Life, to be lived, requires a certain tension, a stretching.

Now if time is described as tension, what are the two poles, and what stretches between them? It is our life, with our knowledge of our own mortality, that stretches between the poles of birth and death. We have a limited time here on planet Earth, and we must make what we can of it. When time is seen in this human way, we are reminded of our own limitedness, suspended as we are between a beginning and an end not of our conscious choosing, and we realize that this is what ultimately gives tone to life.

Looking beyond our own lives, we approach a mystery: what was there before there was time? The idea of a beginning of time has a certain fascination for us: Time must have had a beginning, we reason; it could not retreat forever into the shadows. That is why we need a Creator god—to get things started. Today we say that time began with the big bang, but what was there before the bang? We do not know, but we firmly believe that nothing is ever born out of nothing. For us, every beginning is in fact a transformation of something that existed before, as is every ending.

The end of time is a religious question for us as much as a scientific one, though it would seem that both the beginning and the ending are equally speculative. In Christianity, the end of time is equated with the end of the world itself: Saint John, in the Book of Revelation, says that after the Last Judgment, "There shall be Time no longer" (10:6). Time will end in cataclysmic events on earth and in heaven—earthquakes, the coming of evil spirits, giant hailstones, fires, floods, and pestilence, accompanied by the destruction of evil—for Satan will be cast into the bottomless pit for a thousand years (which suggests that someone must be keeping time after all), and all his cohorts will suffer a terrible fate. There is no reconciliation of opposites in the apocalyptic vision when time and world come to an end.

Time and Timelessness

If we stand in imagination at the edge of the universe to watch a world in its birthing into time and space, we find a possible way of looking at the mystery of time. Time emerges from timelessness or eternity, for eternity is not endless duration but simply timelessness. This involves a shift of consciousness, one which, without thinking about it, we make every day as we move from the world of dreams into waking reality and back again. This is the very rhythm of our lives. In outer reality, events move in causal sequences, but in the world of dreams they jumble together in images and plays that are somehow meaningful but not always causally related. Events do not pass by in the order we recognize in waking life. Sometimes we hear the voice of a wise and impartial observer, very much alive at the dream level. Underlying all our outer activities is a running commentary from the timeless world. We are not lacking, therefore, in the experience of timelessness.

While the present emerges from the past, time itself emerges from a timeless order. In every moment, our world is in process of creation or devolution. Recall that in the first chapter we saw how the psyche reconnoiters, explores future possibilities by way of the dream, and by way of analogy and symbol. In these activities we see the seeds of the future being born in many acts of creative unfolding as the events of our lives move out of potentiality and into experience. The timeless world, like the quantum world in Werner Heisenberg's description, is a world of possibilities and potentialities, not one of facts. The apparently separate fact or entity comes only with the birth into time. Before that, events have a certain form of existence as potentialities, as seedlings, as shadowings.

As events step out of the oneness and over the threshold into material existence, they join the world dance, and fit into the ongoing rhythms of the world. Time appears as a series of continua that hold particular configurations together in appropriate sequences. Every time phase has this dual quality; it at once arrests, captures, and holds us, even as it flees onward, giving way to its successor. Each moment of time is one phase of a moving continuum in which outer configuration and inner attitude are held together. All the contingent factors, both inner and outer, that will combine to produce the next event configuration are already in motion within the present time phase. They are the burgeoning seeds of time, experienced by an inward as well as an outward attentiveness. Each time phase, that is, constitutes a unity having both internal and external attributes.

Time, Spells, and World Possibilities

Consider the word *spell,* which is linked to time (a dry spell, a hot spell) and to a mysterious power or influence often connected to particular times (the spell of twilight, or of a moonlit night). We experience the spell of the time by a quiet absorption in it, or perhaps by exuberant participation—by a state of being, not a rational effort. It is the poet who best portrays the spell of a particular time. Feeling and mood are powerfully involved. The ancient practice of making magic spells was based on relating to time phases in this way, in the belief that human beings could influence the trends of time by magical means, that is, by intervening at the seedling stage of the development of events and by imitating nature's own spells.

A magical spell must fit the time phase. One could even say that the time itself is a spell. We speak of "Renaissance times" or "Classical times" to refer to the spirit that pervades the lives of those who live in a certain time. Bards and poets, musicians, dancers, painters—all creative persons—bring forth and embody the spirit of the time in their works, like a choir of many voices blending to create a mood of triumph, hope, or sorrow. They are favorably received by the great majority of people who share in the spirit of the time without being able to articulate it, for the time's spirit has an intensity, a gripping quality, a spell, and those caught up in it are "spellbound." Long ago, the spell of the time was thought of as a god.

By changing the tension of a musical instrument string, we change its tone. Similarly, by a change of tension, we change the quality of time—its spell. The word *tone* applies not only to music but also to expressions of feeling (such as a sarcastic tone, a loving tone). It unites an inner feeling with an outer event. The same is true of spells. When the ancient magician made conscious use of a spell, incantation, or chant, she was relying on the capacity of time, rhythm, and tone to evoke a particular world possibility, to enchant, to weave a spell. Subtle changes of the tone or spell of the moment were known to shape the possibilities that would emerge in the succeeding moment. Writers make use of this knowledge.

The word *hex,* which has become the negative side of the word *spell,* comes from the German *hexe,* meaning witch, and can be traced to the Greek *hex,* meaning six. The number six is also found in the I Ching, made up as it is of sixty-four *hexa*grams.[14] In the I Ching, the movement from one situation to the next takes place in six phases. Six is the time of manifestation. Recall that in Genesis, God created the world in six "days," and was able to rest on the seventh; we still conform to his timing. The casting of spells could be seen as an imitation of God's own creative work as it moved through the various phases from image to concrete reality. In chapter 2, we spoke of sympathetic magic as a way of imitating nature's way (or God's way) of achieving a particular purpose.

Our modern dream work has some of this same magical quality. A dream may reveal the possibilities available to the person at a particular juncture in his affairs, and sometimes suggest beneficial lines of action. A dream may remind the individual of character flaws that keep him from realizing his intentions. The dreaming psyche is not confined to the here and now as are our sense perceptions, but is more nearly related to the underground flow of the time. The ancients worked with dreams in this way and had a variety of other methods of relating to the trend of the time.

Time Has Qualities

Where the modern view sees time as an empty frame that contains events (very much as space contains objects), the ancients saw time as having definite qualities. These qualities had cosmic significance as well as important consequences that were established by the gods, and only partly conditioned by human activities. Ancient practices included the use of divination in order to discern the qualities of the time then approaching, so as to set one's affairs in accordance with time's flow. This was a religious act, often carried out in a temple. It was possible in this way to align one's own choices and activities with the universal rhythms and harmonies of nature. The life lived in this way was the ordered life, marked by high purpose. There was less concern about sin, and more interest in universal harmony. Time had a sacred quality that was related to the movements of the sun, moon, and planets, as well as to human fate. Life choices corresponding to the quality of the times would prosper, while those made in defiance of the cosmic flow would not. Through these means, people endeavored to subordinate their will to the will of the gods, revealed in the flow of time, though sometimes the higher will could not be known until the conclusion of the whole event sequence.[15]

The will of the gods could be known through other forms of synchronicity. The sensitive manor woman who acted in accord with the divine will would find many synchronicities occurring to help carry out their purposes. (In modern language, we would say that the person was carried by an archetypal pattern or "arranger" who could set all things in motion that fit the trend of the time.) We may recall that when Moses was following the will of Yahweh to lead his people out of Egypt, Yahweh arranged many signs to tell Pharaoh that it was time to let the Israelites go. "I will multiply my signs and my wonders," said Yahweh (Exodus 7:3). The ensuing miracles and plagues were believed to have been arranged directly by Yahweh for the benefit of his chosen people.

Today we would say that the future is unknowable, and the effort to align ourselves with the qualities of time is a risky business. However, we who have no guidance except for human-made moral precepts are hardly in a position to denigrate the ancient ways. We have exchanged the views of the ancients for a view that lacks the living connection to a higher will. What we hear today is that many of us have lost the sense of the meaning of life, or even that life has no meaning.

Time and Divination

Time seen in the ancient way becomes the linking factor between the higher world (such as the movements of the heavenly bodies) and the world of human needs and purposes. Moreover, the barrier that separates the past and the future is a flexible one, as shown in dreams. We know that in the dream world the psyche draws its images from the future as well as from the past. The only difference between the two is that a dream image drawn from the past is one we recognize, while one that refers to the future will very likely go unrecognized because it has not yet registered in consciousness. If the image suggests an event occurring some time in the future, we will probably have forgotten the dream when the event comes to pass, and will fail to make the connection between it and the dream. The link between inner world and outer, or between past and future, will not be seen.

The views of the ancients were more friendly toward synchronistic events and their accompanying meanings than our present views. Divination was used to insure that any undertaking—a marriage, a business deal, a pilgrimage, a military expedition—took place within the context of a favorable trend of time. In this way, the rhythms of time were never divorced from human meaning. Time clearly had a strong qualitative aspect. It was evident to everyone that certain times were favorable for particular human purposes, while others were inauspicious. (*Auspice* comes from the Latin *auspex,* a "bird seer," one whose auguries came from observing the flight of birds.) These methods were the basis of the ancient connection of time (*tempus*) and temple. Within the temple, one could learn the trend of the time through divination, and so bring one's decisions into accord with its flow. The time most favorable for a given activity was the *kairos,* the Greek term for the magically right moment.

All the arts and crafts of ancient times took account of the nature of the time phases: the farmer, the builder, the traveler, all strove to begin their activities at the most appropriate time. To the healer of ancient Egypt, who administered his medicines at the time most favorable for healing, this was sacred knowledge, closely held. The Hebrews expressed this truth as follows:

> *To every thing there is a season, and a time to every purpose*
> *under the heaven:*
> *A time to be born, and a time to die; a time to plant, and a*
> *time to pluck up that which is planted;*

> *A time to kill, and a time to heal; a time to break down, and*
> *a time to build up;*
> *A time to weep, and a time to laugh; a time to mourn, and a*
> *time to dance. . . .*[16]

Astrology and Synchronicity

Astrology can be seen as the synchronistic linkage between the physical geometry of the planets and a corresponding meaning that arises in human affairs. The development of astrology was based on the idea of establishing human decisions within the largest meaningful rhythmic configurations—the movements of the sun, moon, and planets, for the planets have their dance, which gives rise to the music of the spheres and marks off the time phases on earth. The qualities of the changing phases could be described symbolically; there was a time for coming together and a time for parting, a time for sowing and a time for reaping, a time for advance, a time for retreat. Situations were seen to "ripen" in time like all organic things; the wise person awaited the appropriate time to realize her intentions so that her own life purposes could be brought into accord with the rhythms of the world. In the Hindu tradition, the rhythmic nature of the universe is the great dance of Shiva, the god who by his dancing sustains the world.

In ancient times, the astrologer's roles included advising the local social order of impending celestial events such as the passing of the seasons as well as the arrival of comets and eclipses. The astrologer was also responsible for understanding the synchronicity between the planetary alignments and important developments within the local ecology and culture, such as famines, plagues, invasions, or the death of a king. In modern times, the only roles left for astrology are the construction of natal charts of newborns and the publishing of daily horoscopes printed in newspapers. In this modern age of the individual, astrologers have—not surprisingly—also focused themselves on the individual.

Whether charting a cultural development or creating a natal chart, the astrologer inquires as to the configuration of the planets and moon at the time in question, thereby supposing that the event is synchronistically linked to the time phase of the planets in their rhythmic dance. The astrologer's aim is to uncover the significance of the time phase by reference to the alignment of the heavens. The belief is that the individual is marked or stamped, as it were, with the imprint or patterning belonging to the time phase of one's birth. (Note that the word *template,* a device for stamping out a pattern, is related to *tempus,* time.) The planets were considered to be gods because the qualities of their alignment corresponded to a unique significance that was imprinted upon each individual. And so the planets were crucially involved in molding each individual's fate. The rhythmic interplay of all the planetary cycles converging on a particular moment and passing on to the next marked each person as they danced onto life's stage, and lived out the significance of their corresponding time phase. Their very being was acausally linked to all that unfolded from the creative possibilities of their particular birth moment.

We may understand the basis of the ancient views better by pointing out how time actually leaves its mark on things and events. A connoisseur can identify the region and vintage of a wine's origin by its color, taste, and bouquet. The particular qualities of sunlight, wind, rain, and earth that came together at a unique time brought forth a unique vintage. The wine was stamped, as it were, by the qualities of its time and place. Winds will blow again and rain will fall, but the whole configuration that shaped a particular vintage will never be repeated. Similarly, an archaeologist can tell by studying the shape and design of an ancient piece of pottery the time, place, and civilization from which it emerged. Each piece is stamped with the worldview and mythology of those who made it, and they in turn were shaped by their time and place.[17] The whole history of a tree's life, and of the times in which it lived, is contained in the concentric rings that form the trunk, a hidden part of nature's record that is made without the intervention of a conscious mind. Similar records of animal life are left in limestone, and of human life in archaeological digs, and, on a different time scale, on the human face and hands.

Time Sets Conditions

The ancient science of astrology attempted to assess, by way of the fluctuating geometry of the planets, the characteristics and the fate of an individual, social system, or other entity emerging from the unique cosmic configuration of a particular moment. All the moving patterns of the universe had coalesced to give rise to that individual moment. The ancient view attended to the single, separate person in the context of a larger conditioning background. One's lot was synchronistically related to the wheeling of the universe itself. In this way, time was seen as a shaping and formative element, not an empty arena in which events transpired.

The molding or conditioning quality of time phases is not causal, nor is there any compulsion; it is rather a kind of imprinting by which things come to "fit the picture" or blend in with the spell of the time. The term "acausal orderedness" describes this. The subtle influence that is involved is reminiscent of psychometry as we have developed the idea, in that time seems to leave its imprint on events in the same way that I imprint whatever is "mine" with my nature—indeed with my life history—while I also receive the imprints of all the things and people I have cared for. The word *imprinting* or *impressing,* leaving an impression, suggests the very physical nature of this effect. "Impressive" events linger long in the memory, pointing to a connection between imprinting and memory. We touch here on the subtle linkage—the organic, weblike quality—that characterizes the world of time and echoes the nature of the unitary world.

By an involvement of the whole being, we can enter into the ancient ways of experiencing time. The different qualities of spring and fall, of high noon or twilight, are known to us as they were known to generations before us. Or we may think of the bracing quality of a snappy winter's day, or the nostalgia and longing that grip us at harvest time with the onset of winter. These feelings are universal and quite relevant to an apprehension of time and reality. The annual recurrence of these cycles and their celebration in ritual and festival link people together in a community of shared experience.

The difference between the ancient way of experiencing time and the modern way becomes very clear: the ancient way was grounded in the experience of being human within this time world. The subjective view of time was the only view. All times had their unique qualities, some of them favorable and others unfavorable for particular human endeavors. This understanding led to divination, to attempts to understand the alignment of time and purpose that is afoot in the cosmos. We notice in the I Ching, for example, that time is a ruling factor in many hexagrams. In Hexagram 24, "The Turning Point," it is said that the transformation of the old and the introduction of the new happen easily because the movement is in accord with the time.

The Parade of Time

Time is like a parade that passes the place where you are standing. When the soldiers, horses, clowns, and elephants come and go, you know that time is passing. Those that have already gone by are the past, those still to come are the future, and those proximate to you are the ever-changing and never-changing now, the center of the present moment. Though you may say that time "itself" is not the same as the event sequences that pass "in" time, yet without these event sequences we would have no way to measure time. Measured time, that is, linear time, is evidently different from time simply experienced.

Suppose that you are yourself moving along in the parade. If you fix your eyes on those going along with you, it will be hard to tell that time is passing except by reference to the landmarks along the way. But if we take a different approach, and fly in a helicopter high above the parade, we will see that it is all moving at once; there is no past, present, future. The whole parade is on the move, now. But since we cannot be both in the parade and above it, except in imagination, it is hard for us to see both the simultaneity and the passing of time. They arise from different frames of reference.

Out of the past-present-future structure of time we find meaning, gain orientation, discover who we are, establish an identity (from the Latin *stabilis*, "firm," "stable"). In childhood, very little is stabilized; the future stretches out before us in a long arc of possibilities. In old age, more life has piled up behind us; possibilities have narrowed down to a niggardly few, and we finally ask if they were ever really possible, or only the spinning out of fantasy. Looking forward into the future we seem to see possibilities, while looking to the past we often see only inevitability.

There are many mysteries about the passing, changing structure of time. All the events of our world that have ever happened were once future to an observer located at the beginning of events; they then rolled over into the present. In becoming present, they also became "real" and added to the karmic accumulation of the person and the world. But what about all the events that did not happen but were merely intended—the poems never written, the children who died in youth, the injustices never righted, the freedom never gained? What happened to all the vast river of human desire and intention that never moved from possibility to "reality?" Did all this simply vanish, or does it, too, add to the karmic accumulation of the past, playing a subjective role, giving to that past a certain instability, an unfinished quality? For as long as these memories live in the minds and hearts of later generations, they form part of a possible future and exert a pressure on the present. A special energy attaches to them, although we think of them as "past." To the extent that this is true it is said that we are prisoners of our past—even prisoners of history. The idea of reincarnation takes form in this context.

The karmic seeds of the past may shape not only our behavior but our actual bodily nature. The Lama Govinda tells us that the human body is "materialized karma, the consciousness of past moments of existence made visible."[18] If this is true, then our very bodily form is a reservoir into which the experience of past lives has flowed. How would it affect our lives if we believed that our behavior in this life—our acts of generosity and courage as well as our mistakes and omissions—will affect our bodily nature in the next life?[19]

If we could predict the future outcome of the choices we make in the present, would we not act more wisely? It would seem so, and yet many people would say that they do not wish for knowledge of coming events, particularly if ill fortune is on the horizon, for they would not see themselves as having the power to change the course of events. Time then seems to have a relentless quality, rolling on independent of the will and wishes of the human beings caught up in its flow. What is needed is to bring our own actions and decisions into harmony with the trend of the time, not by following the fads that sweep society, but by being aware of the more profound movements that shape our lives from within.

If Time Stood Still

Let us imagine that we could hold up a cosmic stopwatch that would bring all movement to a halt for a moment of time. If we could note the position of each thing or being within that moment, we would find a certain arrangement or configuration prevailing throughout all the parts that belong to that time frame. All the parts would be interconnected aspects of a total picture.

Such a moment is pictured in the old fairy tale Sleeping Beauty, when Briar Rose, the young princess, falls into a deep sleep under the curse of a vengeful witch. Although the witch had intended for Briar Rose to fall dead, she instead falls asleep for a hundred years, thanks to another witch (one of thirteen in the kingdom) who softens the curse of death imposed by her less benevolent colleague. According to the old tale, everything in the castle goes to sleep along with the princess—the king and queen lie down in the throne room, the flies cease to crawl on the wall, the cook stops in the middle of cuffing the scullion, and the kitchen maid stops plucking the fowl. Even the fire in the hearth stops crackling and goes into a slow simmer. Only after a hundred years—the time allotted by the witch-goddess—does the castle come to life again when Briar Rose is awakened by a prince.

The sleeping castle symbolizes a world in which nothing moves in space to afford a sense of time's passing. Only the people outside the castle, faithfully marking the seasons, recognize when a hundred years have passed. Yet all things in the castle are held in timeless relationship. There is life there, a dreaming life that flickers at low intensity, like the fire simmering on the hearth, never burning out—or like the life that trembles in a seedpod, remaining in a state of dormancy for the right conditions to allow it to flower.

Our Flickering World

A very old teaching that is now being put forward in scientific circles offers a commentary on the situation in the castle. It says that all our existence has a flickering quality—that we, along with our whole world, come into being many times a second. We die and are reborn, according to one writer, fourteen times each second, retaining no memory of what we experienced when we blinked off. According to ancient Sufi wisdom, the link between the creator and his creation is renewed in every second. "Every instant one universe is annihilated and another resembling it takes its place."[20] David Peat has likened the flickering quality of the world to the formation or dissolution of a crystal in a saturated solution—now it exists in its crystalline form, and now it is gone, but when it crystallizes again it will have the same form as before, except that the transformations of ourselves and our world occur many times each second. "Unlike a single crystal of salt or quartz, the universe is in a constant process of crystallization and dissolution. At each instant the rock, the tree, the atom, the star, and the human mind die and are born anew," he says.[21]

Where, he asks, does the universe go when it blinks off? According to the story of Sleeping Beauty, everything simply goes to sleep—that is, into an alternative state of consciousness. In the story, it was a very long blink (according to our way of reckoning), but that is of no account. Doubtless the clocks in the castle stopped running. To the sleepers in the castle, it probably seemed only a short nap. When the castle flickered on again, everything resumed as before: king and queen awoke and began to reign, the flies began to crawl along the wall, the cook finished cuffing the scullion, the kitchen maid resumed plucking the fowl. Even the fire in the hearth began to crackle and pop. The patterns that had shaped the life of the castle took up where they had left off; everything went back on track.

Time and Transformation

According to modern science, the castle was in the grip of what is now called a "unitary transformation." To be sure, things changed when the prince came upon the scene, but that, too, was part of the pattern. All that followed was inherent in what had gone before. Unitary transformations involve a restructuring of patterns previously in play. Since what is to come is implicit in what already is, such transformations can in principle be predicted and sometimes controlled. These are the kinds of transformations that science has preferred to deal with. They are like the distant whistle of a freight train, far down the tracks, that tells us that very soon the train will be rumbling into town. Events are "on track" in the sense that they are already "here" if we allow "here" to be a somewhat wider space-time. The problem with such patterning is how to account for creativity, for the unexpected.

The possibility of radical novelty does exist in the world, and certainly in human affairs. That is our freedom. Not all events go on track, adhere to their given pattern. We then have non-unitary transformations, with which science is now beginning to cope. These changes have an uncanny resemblance to intelligent choice making: they seem to involve communion between systems as they fuse and transform, and a kind of feedback, or learning from past experience. The outcome of the transformation cannot be predicted simply by reference to what existed before, which might seem to preclude the possibility of precognition or of oracles foretelling the future.

But suppose that instead of merely going to sleep, the inhabitants of the castle went into a dream state where they envisioned the possibilities before them. We have discussed how the dreaming psyche reconnoiters, explores alternatives, or offers analogies from the past to help us understand events of the present. Suppose the scullion, instead of allowing himself to be cuffed, dreamed of running away; perhaps the kitchen maid dreamed of running off with him.

They might discover connections and possibilities among the varied parts of the castle that had not been suspected before. Even Briar Rose might dream of marrying some other prince! In this way, each person would be testing out the alternatives available—trying in imagination to profit from past experience, to shape the future, and to be no more a prisoner of the past.

THE KING AND THE FEMININE

The witch-goddesses in the story of Sleeping Beauty, though they are not all-powerful, are clearly the mistresses of time, descendants of the three goddesses of fate known to the Greeks. They select among the possible and cause it to enter the world of the actual, and all that they decree comes true. We may ask why it is that feminine beings govern time and fate. It is because they are the daughters of the Great Mother, who rules over all living and growing things.

You may recall that the story's difficulty begins when the king has only twelve golden plates for the great feast celebrating his daughter's birth, but there are thirteen witches in the kingdom, and so one witch is not invited. It is this thirteenth witch, coming at the eleventh hour, who places a curse of death on the princess, proclaiming that she will later, as a young maiden, prick herself on a distaff and fall down dead. Thus, jealous rage enters into the making of time in primordial days. As good fortune would have it, however, the thirteenth witch arrives just as the twelfth witch is about to bestow her blessing on the child, as the other eleven have already done before her. Although the twelfth witch cannot nullify the curse of death, she can soften it to a hundred years' sleep, and that is what comes to pass.

The trouble lies with the king's failure to take account of the transcendent world, his inability to reckon with other levels of reality. Not only does he not bestir himself to find, beg, or borrow another golden plate so that all the witches can be invited, but even after he learns what is portended, he still thinks himself superior to fate. To prevent his daughter from being wounded by the prick of a distaff, he orders that all the distaffs in the kingdom be destroyed, an expedient that is bound to fail. The distaff side, as we all know, is the feminine; it is clear that the king is not well related to the feminine. Lacking proper respect for the realm of the witches, who, like all feminine beings, are evilly disposed mainly when ignored, he stands as a symbol of those ruling ideas that would exclude the feminine nature.

By using the imagination and by resorting to symbolism, we may be able to reach out to a new frontier and come to a universal awareness in which our own minds are capable of entering into communion with the intelligence or intelligences of other levels of reality. Recall that this possibility was raised in our discussion of the philosophy of P. D. Ouspensky. We have also seen it in the work of Barbara McClintock, the scientist who "made friends" with the chromosomal level of being. This was only possible because the chromosomes, like herself, had a mental capability. She was able to tune into a kind of mind-stuff that does not operate within human categories and yet simmers in a grain of corn, giving shape to the material thing and to its life history.

The king in our story might improve his contact with the transcendent world where the witches dwell by forming a better relationship to the feminine, which in its symbolic aspect is the time ruled by the moon, the time of darkness, the sleep state. At such times, with the sun of consciousness eclipsed, premonitions and precognitions may occur. In fact, this might be the secret of precognition. Free of the constraints of time and space imposed by ordinary consciousness, the deep psyche would wander freely among events and people of earlier or later times and near or distant spaces, bringing back the knowledge it had gained. It might be able to tune into the non-unitary transformations—to things in the exercise of their freedom, to the very intentionality of things. Note that clairvoyants cannot always distinguish events that actually happen from those simply thought about, which means clairvoyants are tuning into a mental world, a world of emotion-laden imagery, rather than a physical world. To a consciousness in which past and future are alive and real, no event would be out of reach; everything would belong to an "eternal present." Perhaps that is how one might be able to predict the "unpredictable" or know the "unknowable."

What might happen is that in deep introversion the psyche would enter a state of being where all things are known (though not necessarily in the language or under the categories that we understand readily), and begin to participate in that knowledge.[22] Some dreams offer a foretaste of that state. Perhaps this is the state inhabited by shamans during their alternative states of consciousness. By an inward "trip," we would reach as far beyond our own personal realm as we now reach by outer-space travel.

The story of Sleeping Beauty tells us that, like the harvest, events will ripen in their own time. Many princes tried to break through the hedge of thorns that blanketed the castle during its hundred-year sleep, but all perished in the attempt. Time cannot be pushed or hurried; events must unfold according to their own nature and the will of the gods. Then, the time being fulfilled, entry is made without effort.

It is my considered opinion that the flickering of the world and of ourselves is a key phenomenon in thinking about synchronicities, and beyond them, of reality itself. If we think of the flickering as a pulsing, a breathing, we will bring forward its organic nature. The principle of coherence makes use of this rhythmic flickering on many planes, some of which we call "unconscious." The same flickering is central also to understanding the moment-by-moment regeneration of our world, and to explaining meditative practices that can restore and replenish our own vital energies. We have come to it through a consideration of time, and by imagining that we could stop the world at a single instant to let the holding power of the moment become real to us. Actually, of course, we are not so much stopping the world as stopping our own time awareness in order to enter a timeless state of being, the realm of eternity.

Out-of-Body Travel

Itzhak Bentov, a writer who was willing to let his imagination carry him out to distant possibilities, makes the suggestion that when we blink off, we are able to leave the body momentarily in order to take in other realms of reality by way of astral travel.[23] Although normally we have no memory of such experiences, if we could train ourselves to remember them when our consciousness comes back to the body, we would have extended the range of our perceptions to an extraordinary degree. And this would be a new way of thinking about the many recorded out-of-body experiences (OBEs), as simply more extended periods of "blinking off," in which the person, seemingly by accident, gains the ability to retain what was experienced in the OBE.

We know that in these experiences the body lies as if asleep or dead, unable to move. Meanwhile consciousness, the animating principle, roams above and looks down on the inert body or travels great distances, leaving the body behind. We may think of the Tibetan masters reported to be seen at religious festivals far from their monasteries, while at the same time present in their cells; or the "berserkers" of Germanic lore, seen in their castle while appearing as a fighting bear on some distant battlefield; or, finally, the "magic flight" of the shaman, who goes out to find the lost soul of his patient.

Bentov points out that the elementary particles of our bodies are all vibrating, merging, transforming, and separating at a rate so fast that we have no sensory way to measure their speed. Ordinarily, Bentov surmises, they would not all blink on and off in unison, but rather different particles would transform at different phases like the fireflies in a meadow on a summer evening. Were it possible, for example, through some meditative practice, to synchronize the phase of the elements of one's being, they would achieve a state of coherence. And just as coherent light can do things ordinary light cannot—it can form holograms, for example—so our consciousness might be capable of extraordinary feats in the coherent state. Very high states of consciousness might be achieved. It might be that consciousness could achieve a certain freedom from the constraints of bodily existence and new forms of creativity might arise. This would be followed, of course, by a great darkness when all blinked off together. But that darkness might be like our own dream state, filled with imagery, for in it would lie the awareness of other planes of being, other realities. And in a state of coherence the adept might have the power to enter those realms to discover their ways of being and bring back the knowledge gained. The experiencing consciousness might discover knowledge of what to ordinary consciousness is the future or the past, or, if preferred, might have telepathic knowledge of events distant in space.

Time, Telepathy, and Clairvoyance

Bentov makes use of the following thought experiment to try to explain telepathy and clairvoyance. He begins by discriminating between objective time and subjective time. Objective time is simply clock time, while subjective time—the evolution of the moment as experienced inwardly—is far more complex. It flows at different rates depending on our subjective state at the moment and on our degree of consciousness. It might slow to a crawl through the effect of "mind-expanding" drugs, or move very fast in dream or reverie where a great many things can transpire in the blink of an eye. Normally, clock time and subjective time track rather closely together, but they may draw far apart in a deep meditative state in which subjective time is almost suspended. Our level of consciousness, Bentov believes, is measured by the ratio of subjective time to objective time. In the meditative state, for example, we might have several seconds of subjective time for every one of objective time.

Bentov then posits the individual as an immaterial observer who is freed from the body many times each second by reason of the flickering of awareness, and, being incorporeal, travels unimpeded by physical constraints. As the position of an electron in an atom fluctuates probablistically in its orbit, so too may the observer fluctuate. And as an electron in certain metals may migrate from place to place, so too the observer may flit far out in space (that is, objective space) many times per second. In most of us, this observer is not trained to understand, retrieve, and record what is experienced out of the body, so there is no record of what is learned. However, in the course of traveling, the observer finds that our timelike subjective space becomes objective time. This means that while the observer is moving through what she considers space, she is actually moving through other people's (and her own) objective time and into the past or the future. This is not entirely fantastic. Recall that when we look at distant stars through a telescope we are observing their past, not their present, because of the finite speed of light. If light traveled at infinite speed, we could observe their present. This, says Bentov, may be the way clairvoyants operate. They travel into the future or the past of objective time. Or they travel to great distances in space. The observer can do this because she has left her physical body behind.[24]

This is a strange idea, certain to stretch our imagination. Our hypothetical observer may in fact be an out-of-body traveler in an out-of-body experience. If she can travel into the future of ordinary time, then the knowledge she brings back would be a prophecy or a precognition to us, since it would be a report of what she had seen on her trip into the future. The lady on Mount Macedon who experienced the terrible pain of the pilots who were to die on the mountainside may have had such a trip into the future while temporarily away from the body. In the same way, one who traveled into the past would experience a retrocognition. Note that OBEs were once called "traveling clairvoyance," a name that still invites consideration. It would say that the out-of-body traveler might see in distant places by clairvoyant vision, and return to the body with the knowledge gained.

The constant flickering of our world and ourselves is by no means a new idea. The I Ching speaks of a world-creating alternation of tension and release: the primal powers of Yin and Yang that never come to a standstill. The cycle of becoming continues uninterruptedly because a state of tension arises again and again between the two primal powers, a potential that keeps the powers in motion and causes them to unite, whereby they are constantly regenerated. Tao brings this about without ever becoming manifest. The power of Tao to maintain the world by constant renewal of the tension between the polar forces is designated as good.[25]

A central tenet of the Perennial Philosophy has always been that we are creatures with a dual citizenship: we are in but not of time, in but not of space.[26] Our life as material beings is carried out against an immaterial background that does not share the conditions and constraints to which material things are subject. As material forms, we are born into time and space, grow and mature and "in time" die, but concurrently we exist independent of a bodily structure, beyond time and space in awareness.

The timeless knowledge gained in timeless states of being can provide renewal and re-creation to ourselves and to our world. Though new evils constantly arise in the world, so too do such benefits as these. The same is true of the many technological advances that have recently come into being, not only the destructive power of the atomic bomb, but also the advances of modern telecommunications and computers. All these bring opportunities for evil in comparable measure as good. Thus, for our own sake, we urgently must achieve new levels of consciousness, so as to bring along with it new levels of ethical responsibility.

A Modern Physicist's View of Time

The modern view of time now coming into being differs greatly from all former attitudes. It owes much to the theory of relativity. David Bohm has attempted to build on Einstein's insights in ways that take account of quantum theory. He postulates the existence of a substratum of the cosmos that he calls the "implicate" or "enfolded" order, and for evidence of its existence he examines the so-called vacuum state, which, far from being a mere absence of matter is—from the point of view of quantum mechanics—a state filled with energy and potentiality. The exceedingly rapid fluctuations of the vacuum state, far beyond our ability to measure, give to empty space an energy greatly exceeding what is found in matter. The whole material world in Bohm's view becomes a set of small waves on the immense ocean of the vacuum state.

According to Bohm, the vacuum state has no physically meaningful notion of time in it. If time can be measured only by a set of ordered changes in a physical process—a pendulum's movement, for example—then the vacuum state can properly be called timeless or "beyond time" as we know it, yet it does not represent the ultimate ground of all reality. Seen in relation to still higher orders, each one unfolding creatively out of a higher level, the vacuum state becomes an "explicate" (unfolded) order.

Bohm says that where time had been regarded as a primary and universally applicable order—both in physics and in ordinary experience—it now becomes secondary, dependent on a multidimensional ground.[27] Reality cannot be comprehended fully in terms of any single time order; instead it must be understood in terms of the ever-present processes of the implicate order. Many different time orders can be derived from different sequences of movement, depending on the speed of the material system being considered. Einstein's work showed that we can no longer regard our particular space-time system as the fundamental or universal one. In the quantum domain, we cannot distinguish a "before" and an "after," a past and a future; hence history does not unfold as it does in our time nor accumulate in an ever-growing past.

Bohm adds that while relativity theory led us to conclude that there are infinitely many different systems of time and space, quantum theory goes further and says that one system of time and space may be enfolded in another, while all our common systems are enfolded in the vacuum state. Far greater systems may enfold even the vacuum state with its high-energy oscillations. Any one system has "timeless" enfoldment in another system, so that each system needs to be seen under the aspect of time and also under the aspect of the "timeless" enfolded state. The implicate state does not contain an ultimate level in which there is no time, but rather a vast range of interwoven times that enfold other times and are at once enfolded in still other times.

In Bohm's opinion, successive moments in an unfolding process (or "unfoldment") are not directly connected in the explicate order; their connection lies in the implicate order. They are creative projections of that higher order as it flashes into visibility and then retreats back into the unseen. They are neither fixed nor predetermined, but have a certain limited autonomy. Thus he makes room for a measure of freedom within the explicate order. What we have called the "flickering" of our world would be germane to his analysis.

Any system that divides reality into levels needs some method of connecting those levels if the higher is to have any influence on the lower. In Bohm's system, this is accomplished by what he calls "enfolding" and "unfolding."

Traditional language would connect the levels by such words as "emanation" or "sympathy," but the language of "unfolding" suggests the idea of opening up like an envelope or a seedpod to reveal what is hidden within; thus, as we mount the scale of being, we go to regions of deeper and deeper inwardness.

David Bohm has brought us a vision of an invisible world clothed in the language of mathematics and physics, a modern myth. Refusing to be confined by the methodological limits of physics, he describes his work with the implicate order as a form of the imagination. That order, he says, has more purpose and awareness than the explicate. He also says that there can be no ultimate theory of the physical world, any more than there can be an ultimate poem. The work of creative development of our world understanding must be done over and over in every age. What the new physics can do for us, following Bohm's example, is to expand our imagination, allowing us to develop descriptions and insights beyond anything we have attempted so far.

Time Separates and Unites

It has been said—and not wholly in jest—that the concept of time is needed so that everything does not happen at once. Time, in one of its aspects, is the separator of events, which fall into three categories: those that have not yet happened but (at least in some cases) are anticipated; those that have already happened and cannot be changed; and those that are present, but only fleetingly. Events form chains and sequences; one thing leads to another. The future is unknown, but as events move into the present they become known, then recede into the past where they leave behind decaying traceries in the physical world and in memory. The future cannot become past without passing through the infinitesimally narrow slit that is the present. In a sense, past and future have no real existence for us, so we may ask whether there is a sense in which the present, too, is not "real." The present is an ever-moving slot between an accumulating past and a future that slowly unfolds but never stops. Past and future constantly influence the present, so they must have some form of existence—apparently a subjective way of being, felt as we lay plans for the future and draw on memories of the past to interpret the meaning of the present. From this perspective, time is a separating factor.

But time is also a uniting factor. We saw a hint of this in our discussion of the qualitative aspects of time, when we said that all the events of a particular moment partake in the nature of that moment. There is something that holds them together within their moment of time. That they form a picture of the moment can be understood by thinking again about the great slumber that befell the inhabitants of the castle in Sleeping Beauty: all events in the castle blinked off when the castle went to sleep, and a hundred years later, when the castle woke up, all things resumed exactly as they had been before. A larger generalization of this belief is the astrological assumption that a person born within a particular configuration of the stars participates in the nature of that moment—not by causality, to be sure, but by synchronicity.

Before we can draw together what we know about synchronicity and time, we must face the question, precisely what events are to be included under the heading of synchronicity?

Up to this time we have regarded precognition, along with other parapsychological events, as synchronistic, but perhaps this is a questionable assumption. From a narrow stance, the two terms of a precognition—the flash of insight into a future time, and the later event in the world of history—cannot possibly constitute a "coincidence" in time, meaningful or not, because by definition a precognition occurs before the corresponding event that is foretold. By Jung's own definition, juxtaposition in time is a central criterion of a synchronicity, along with the additional criteria of meaning and acausality. The very name Jung gave to synchronistic happenings brings out their timely nature, but he seems to be untroubled by the distance in time between the events in a precognition. By his example, he encourages us to take the word *simultaneous* rather loosely. And what about OBEs? Can these "trips" be seen as synchronistic? From a narrow stance, it hardly seems so. Parapsychological phenomena must be studied one class at a time to determine whether they meet the criteria for a synchronicity.

Some psychic states reveal the transcending of ordinary time. Are these events to be classified as synchronicities? John Blofeld tells a story that illustrates this:

> A disciple of my first Lama relates that, once while traveling, the old gentleman and his followers sat down by the wayside to breakfast off some nomos (dumplings) they had bought the day before. Deciding to meditate first, the Lama plunged into samadhi. As soon as he regained his normal state of consciousness,

> he asked for some nomos, only to discover that they were stale and that the stuffing was rancid. Glancing at the awestruck faces around him, he asked how long his samadhi had lasted and was embarrassed when they told him he had sat motionless for three whole days, during which they had not broken their fast.[28]

We may imagine that the lama was in a timeless state of consciousness, while his hungry disciples were in a time-bound state. In yogic practice, two different states are recognized—samadhi "with support," and samadhi "without support." In the former, the adept depends on a point in space, an idea, or contemplation of a god to maintain his meditation, while in the latter he frees himself from all supports and attains to liberation, the supreme goal of all yogic practices.[29] He passes beyond time and space so as to make a "real descent into the very essence of the physical world," according to Mircea Eliade. In that state, he can arrest the karmic forces brought about by his past actions. Thus, he can take charge of his fate so that he is no longer condemned by past errors. For all our efforts to understand, "samadhi without support" is pervaded by the scent of eternity, and it seems to take us outside our experience of time.

However, this state of consciousness might clarify one of Jung's favorite stories, the rainmaker of Kiao-Chau, who brought a snowstorm to a drought-stricken country by moving into an alternate state of consciousness, the Tao.[30] We would imagine that the rainmaker's shift of consciousness changed not only himself but the surrounding world. Jung explains this story by reference to the "psychoid archetype," his term for that aspect of the archetype that bridges the psychic and physical realms. He likened this continuum to the spectrum of light: at one end is visible ultraviolet, which he associated with the conscious functions of the psyche; at the other end is invisible infrared, which he associated with the lower "psychoid" or quasi-psychic functions such as the sympathetic and parasympathetic nervous systems, continuing to the purely physiological on out to matter in general. This conceptualization was Jung's attempt to account for the psychophysical unity that characterizes our everyday experience, and it relates to his vision of the unitary world that lies behind and beyond psychic and physical reality, which he referred to using the alchemical term Unus Mundus. Thus,

Jung viewed the psychoid archetype as the basis for his understanding of synchronicity and parapsychology:

> The psychoid archetype . . . possesses qualities of a parapsychological nature which I have grouped together under the term "synchronicity." . . . In cases of telepathy and precognition . . . one can very frequently observe an archetypal situation . . . and since the parapsychological phenomena associated with the unconscious psyche show a peculiar tendency to relativize the categories of time and space, the collective unconscious must have a spaceless and timeless quality. . . . The psychoid archetype has a tendency to behave as though it were not localized in one person, but were active in the whole environment.[31]

A Western parallel to the account of the rainmaker is the story of Jesus at the Sea of Galilee as told in Matthew 8:23–27. Jesus was asleep in a boat when a great storm blew up, and he responded to the fearful pleas of his disciples by rising and "rebuking" the waves. Then the sea became calm. The disciples were astonished and said, "What manner of man is this, that even the winds and the sea obey him?"

Time for the Apostle

Our Western tradition contains equally striking experiences of a state that transcends the boundaries of ordinary time and space. Chapters 27–28 of the Acts of the Apostles tells the story of Paul on his final voyage to Rome to appeal his case to Caesar, under guard by a Roman centurion named Julius. The ship's officers had tarried long near Crete, hoping for good winds, and as the season waned Paul warned the crew that the voyage would now be dangerous to the ship, its cargo, and the very lives of the more than two hundred fifty aboard. They did not believe him, however, and the trip resumed. A terrible storm ensued, and after many days much cargo had been thrown overboard and hope was all but gone. Paul then told them that their lives would be saved, for the angel of the Lord had appeared to him and told him that he was to go before Caesar, and God had spared the lives of all who sailed with him. And though the ship and its cargo were lost, and those aboard had to make for shore swimming or clinging to bits of planking, all lives were saved. They reached the island of Melita, where they were treated hospitably, and Paul, by healing the father of the chief and the many others who came for healing, won the good will of the people.

Translating this into modern language (at the risk of appearing presumptuous), we may suggest that Paul the Apostle, in a precognitive experience, received knowledge of events that were to happen in the future of ordinary time. The energies that carried this knowledge took the form of an angel (from the Greek *angelos*, "messenger"). Unfortunately, our Western tradition has failed for the most part to preserve the knowledge of how to voluntarily attain the deeper timeless states where past, present, and future blend in a timeless now. We can only wonder—if, that is, we take the biblical record seriously—how Paul received such remarkable gifts from the Lord, while we do not. Our whole civilization suffers today not from the lack of faith, but from lack of knowledge of how to reach these mystical states. Such knowledge has to be won over and over in every generation, and tends to die if stored away in sacred books.

The Many Worlds of Time

As we think about lived time, the time in which we are born and mature and play out our varied roles and die, it becomes clear that time has been experienced in far different ways in civilizations of the past. If we add to that the idea of the ever-present flickering of our world and ourselves, then our world becomes far more flexible, more permeable, more subject to change than we have previously imagined. In an ever-changing world, synchronicities become more thinkable because, as Jung said, they are acts of creation in time, more likely to occur within a changing world than a fixed and immutable one. It is not that God intervenes in miraculous ways to upset the natural order, but rather that the natural order reveals itself as far richer and more mysterious than we have allowed ourselves to think.

A deeper meaning of synchronicities now emerges before our eyes, as though the world would speak to us from the perspective of its symbolic wholeness. The meaning we discover is not the effect of our own conscious willing. Nature reveals her link to us in a sudden dramatic enactment that hovers briefly before our eyes and then disappears into the larger flow. Or perhaps we should turn this around and say that our own deep link to nature is suddenly opened to ordinary consciousness. Then we may begin to free ourselves from the idea that our habitual ways of construing our reality are the only ways, and having done that we may experience a certain breakdown of the boundaries that separate us from each other in space and time. In so doing, we can ready ourselves for the "impossible" to happen.

Prefigurations

It is possible that synchronicities do not always involve a timely link between inner and outer events. They may be a shining forth of primal meaning which is omnipresent and not spatially localizable, yet which is capable of taking on form within time and space, and so revealing its presence. Some time ago, I was consulted by an older woman who had worked with me in therapy a few months before, and who had a painful personal choice to make. She wanted to discuss an experience she had had while on a trip from Los Angeles to the East Coast. Her plane was later than she realized in arriving in St. Louis, and she missed her connection to the East. She had to wait some three hours for the next flight, but on arriving at her destination she found that her luggage had gone on before and was quietly waiting for her in the carousel area.

In considering the incident from the standpoint of meaning (as if it were a dream), she recognized the theme of missing one's plane, train, boat, or bus as an archetypal one that she had seen in dreams before. The near miss is no one's fault—it just happens. It is fate, though she felt that she should have been paying better attention. However, what she noticed also was that in St. Louis she could have avoided the missed connection by taking any of three steps that were available to her had she realized that the time was short: she could have taken more care in observing the airport signs, which in her haste she had missed; she could have used the map of the airport that was provided on the plane, and so avoided getting confused in the airport; and finally, she could have asked for more help than she had ever needed before to get to the right departure area. My friend's question was, should she consider this a synchronistic event, as though the universe said to her, in dramatic language, "You have missed the boat"? Should she take comfort in the fact that her luggage was waiting at her destination?

I pointed out that the missing of the plane was an event happening in the outer world, not the inner; if it was then followed by another missed connection, that too, would occur in the outer world. Jung called such events "prefigurations" rather than synchronicities, because of his strong conviction that a synchronicity involves a connection between an inner and an outer event coming close in time. Though it did not appear to be connected meaningfully to anything then occurring in her outer life, it could well have the characteristic meaning involved in a synchronicity: you have missed the boat. However, we can seldom know this until much later. By taking it to be meaningful, she might see it as offering a form of guidance for her life. It might have the quality of ubiquity seen in archetypal patterning; that is, that the archetype is always present in some sense, but manifests only when conditions are right. And we do know that such events occur rather frequently in traveling or when people are in a transitional state, especially if the person is not "paying attention." At such times a bit of unconscious knowledge or foreknowledge that the ego would normally suppress may have the opportunity to emerge. Such experiences open us to a new—and a very old—kind of awareness, and take us beyond the narrow opening we ordinarily have on time.[32]

Nevertheless, I was struck by a different interpretation. It came to me in a sudden intuition that the flight might have become a prefiguration of another journey, the lady's approaching death, which might, of course, be many years in the future. The "luggage" would represent the life knowledge gleaned from this incarnation that she would take into the bardo, the next phase of her soul's journey. The missed plane would suggest a possible wrong turning on her journey, just as she feared, though not a disastrous one. Very tentatively, I opened this possibility for her, emphasizing that it was a speculative interpretation. The lady, though much preoccupied with immediate questions concerning her family and her living arrangements, then admitted that this same idea had come to her. We agreed that it was by no means certain, although I had seen more than enough dreams that told me that the deep psyche knows many things that the ego could also know if it could bear to listen.

Jung gives a modern example of what is meant by a prefiguration. We have mentioned how the dreaming psyche reconnoiters and explores possibilities by way of dreams; the same thing happens in the collective dreams of humanity. Jung's example concerns the papal pronouncement in 1950 of the Assumption of Mary as infallible Catholic dogma, an event which he considered the most important religious event since the Reformation.[33] According to this doctrine, the Virgin Mary was assumed into heaven at the end of her life, complete with her physical body. Although the pronouncement, issued by Pope Pius XII, left Protestants and freethinkers at a loss, Jung points to the many prefigurations that had preceded the pope's action—visionary appearances of the Virgin that had come in increasing numbers, often to children. These events, says Jung, revealed what was brewing in the deep psyche of the people—the yearning for a feminine intercessor who would stand beside God to intervene on behalf of suffering humanity. The papal decree was in part a reply to this need, and it showed the living religious process at work. By validating and defining the doctrine of the Assumption of the Virgin, Pius XII elevated the feminine to a new level in the church. The startling rise of women to positions of power and influence in the secular world appears as a later accompaniment; we dare to hope that this change will be followed by an increase of compassion in governments and other structures of power.

Jung's view would suggest that the inarticulate longing of the people and their wisdom as to what the time demands are evidence of an underlying current or archetype most likely to break through among children and simple people who have not been educated out of their own natural experience. (Although, according to Jung, even the pope himself was rumored to have had visions of the Mother of God at the time of the promulgation of the dogma.) These visionary experiences, unembroidered by a conscious ego, are the forerunners of the artistic breakthroughs coming to poets, sculptors, painters, or musicians whose training and talent enable them to expand the naive experience into a cultural product that "speaks for its time," articulating the unspoken yearnings of many. All these things show what is quietly gestating in the womb of time.

There are prefigurations that would show us, if we could put them together, that a particular archetypal pattern is being constellated. Now and then the pattern flashes into visibility, sometimes playing itself out in historical events, like the flickering of heat lightning in the summer sky that precedes an electrical storm. We have quoted Jung as saying that the psychoid archetype tends to behave as though it were not localized in one person but were active in the whole environment. This broadens the concept of the archetype considerably. As to events that may have a prophetic significance, it seems that in the Middle East in biblical times, the archetype of the Sacrifice of the Son was being constellated, and when its visible aspect played out as the Crucifixion of Christ, the whole world changed.

The idea that a prefiguration—a prophetic drama enacted in the outer world—is a synchronistic event, runs headlong into Jung's belief in a timely connection between the inner and outer aspects of the synchronicity. Probably for this reason, although he speaks of prefigurations, Jung does not call them synchronistic. But a prefiguration is simply a prophecy or a precognitive event taking place in the outer world rather than in a dream or vision. Or it appears as a dream of the world soul whose dreams become our reality. Of course no prophecy can have the character of simultaneity in time with the event to which it refers, and this is one of Jung's most important criteria for a synchronicity. A prophecy or precognition by definition comes before the event to which it refers. However, a prefiguration resembles synchronicities as it meaningfully connects these events. I am not prepared to reconcile these differing views on the temporal aspect of synchronicity, but I believe that the relationship of synchronicities to time remains an open question, and an important one.

In former times, such breakthroughs were often elaborated into living ritual for the benefit of all the people. The great dream of Black Elk, the Oglala Sioux holy man, which came as his whole culture collapsed, became a ritual dance of the entire community.[34] In ancient China, it was the custom to build altars and institute sacred rituals at places where visions or other manifestations of divine power had occurred. Duke Wen of Chin (Qin) dreamed of a great yellow serpent stretching from heaven down to earth, its mouth opened toward Mount Fu in Shanxi. He consulted a diviner about the meaning of the dream and was told, "This is a manifestation of the Lord on High. Prince, sacrifice to Him!" The duke thereupon instituted a periodic sacrifice on Mount Fu attended by throngs of his people. Regular sacrifices, held at the proper time and place, were believed to preserve the regenerative power of the serpent.[35] Through such rituals, the prince led his people in making contact with the transcendent world.

What we see here is the eternal religious process breaking through in the life of the people, compensating the imbalance of mere secularism. We also see why Jung regarded the loss of such traditions as a cultural catastrophe of the first magnitude. How to restore balance in a world without a gyroscope? When he spoke of synchronicities as "acts of creation in time," Jung meant that they represented an eruption into time of what is timeless and spaceless—eternal and ubiquitous. Such events reconnect humanity to a transcendent, timeless world, and the ensuing rituals, regularly repeated, celebrate the connection.

In the next chapter, we continue our exploration, with the emphasis more on space than on time.

CHAPTER 7

Time, Space, Synchronicity

Part 2

The collective unconscious surrounds us on all sides. . . . It is more like an atmosphere in which we live than something that is found in us.

—Jung

The favorable conditions for psi are closely similar to those involved in delicately original and creative work in the arts.

—J. B. Rhine

Just as we have reconsidered our view of time, we need to reconsider our view of space. We are daily reminded that distances on earth appear much shortened by modern methods of transportation and communication because of their speed. In fact, there is no absolute standard by which we can tell what is a "long" distance and what is a "short" one, or what is "small" and what is "large" because the concepts of distance, size, and speed of motion are relative to our frame of reference. Even location is a relative quality. An object in totally empty space (if such a space existed) could not be located, nor can the location of a point on a fractal curve be established. We know the location of anything only by reference to other things around it. Furthermore, our subjectivity colors our view of space as of time. Just as we have shown time to be an active player in the game of life, marking each person with its qualities, so we may bring forward a subjective view of space. Here our attention centers on the feel or atmosphere of particular places, and the effect this has on the human condition.

For example, a sudden sense of shock comes to us as we enter a space where a violent quarrel has just taken place. Even before our senses have had time to register the situation, we may experience a sudden clutching of the solar plexus, the beginning of psychic awareness. What is this atmosphere that we are taking in? Though not visible or audible, it has a definite presence. Does it have an aspect of materiality, since it seems to occupy a particular space? Or is it purely psychic? It seems to be both, and we feel a certain intensity, a "gripping" quality as well. In the past, this was called a "spirit," and there were good and evil spirits to be reckoned with. All places—the open countryside, a mountainous area, a seascape, a great city crowded with passersby—have their atmosphere, their indwelling spirit, and their corresponding effects on human feeling.

Sacred Spaces

In ancient times, each city had its *genius loci,* the spirit of the place. On moving to a new city, the people adopted its gods, not because the gods were taken lightly, but because people could not but be permeated by the guiding spirit of their adopted home. They breathed in its atmosphere as they took in its air and water and food, and so were indelibly marked by its ambience. The practice of naming cities after saints undoubtedly derived from these ancient beliefs, and was meant to invoke the protective powers of the saint on behalf of the locality. Stories were told, not only in ancient times, of the guiding spirit of a place rising up to save its people from attacking enemies.

In modern times, space, like time, has been desacralized, but even a brief consideration of space reveals that it has a mysterious quality. The continents of earth are dotted with places that were deemed sacred by indigenous peoples. North America has many such places, from Mount Katahdin in Maine, the home of a spiritual being who influences the local weather, to Mount Tamalpais north of San Francisco, along whose flanks the giant redwoods grow. Some holy places, like Lourdes, are still known for their healing powers; others, like Delphi, for the gift of prophecy; while still others are known for their spiritual influence on those who come there. One of the most famous sacred places in the world is Mount Kailas on the western plateau of Tibet, where four great rivers have their source, flowing in roughly the four directions. The mountain forms a giant mandala inscribed on earth that reveals the form of the sacred powers of the universe to the pilgrims who have journeyed there for uncounted generations.

The ancient science of geomancy, sometimes called sacred geography, focused on the link between human life and the landscapes of earth. Together with astrology, which connected human life with the movements of the heavenly bodies, it aimed to complete the universal harmony, relying on symbolic correspondences between human life and places on earth. Clearly if human affairs could be brought into harmony with both heaven and earth, or time and space, the universal order would be maintained. In China, where this ancient science was highly developed, the geomants were called to advise on the siting of new buildings. They studied the flow of the chi, the universal energies, and aimed at a balance of Yin and Yang energies. Traces of this ancient knowledge are found at megalithic sites in England and Normandy, and perhaps in the whole primal world. They offer clues about the state of consciousness of the people who built these sacred sites.

Our understanding of space and time has changed many times since those ancient days, and there are signs that further changes are in the air now, because our present views do not take account of the many happenings deemed "paranormal" or "anomalous." However, these events are paranormal only with respect to our theories, not to reality itself. In the previous chapter, it was the experience of precognition that pointed to a need to change our views of time. A revised view of time would take account of this phenomenon, allowing us to understand that future events may be known in some fashion in the present—that is, before they occur. In precognition, it is as though one can "remember" events of one's own future or the future of society, or as though our "memory" includes the future. Is there a part of the psyche that does not recognize our partitioning of time into past, present, and future?

But for our views of space, the primary test is either clairvoyance or telepathy, in which a distant scene or hidden knowledge becomes known to us without the use of the five senses. Ordinary space may be transcended also in the out-of-body experience (OBE), at least if we hold that in astral travel the soul actually takes leave of the body to visit distant places. At that point, our present views of space come into question—or perhaps our view of the potentialities of the human mind—or both. Other tests of our spatial understanding come in teleportation and in psychokinesis, phenomena that suggest a nonphysical force capable of moving material things through space. The force acts like a physical force, but it is not physical. The problem that has defied the best efforts of parapsychologists for a hundred years is this: How does knowledge get from a distant person or place to someone or somewhere else without traveling through the intervening space? Is this something that happens in the quantum realm, but not in the realm of the five senses?

There are many questions here, but it is important to remember that insofar as these phenomena have occurred to us even in fantasy they are legitimate subjects for our inquiry, since what we are trying to establish is a view of the deep psyche that accounts for all its contents.

Nonlocal Interactions

In recent years, physicists have developed the theory of nonlocal interactions, an idea that has been of first-rate importance for parapsychology because it promises to answer some of these long-standing questions. Formerly the locality of objects was understood to be their most important characteristic from the standpoint of movement. Each object stood independent of all others; each occupied its own space and time; and a push or pull on Object A did not affect Object B if they were independent in space. A local interaction, it was understood, involved physical dependency—direct contact of two things: A either pushes B or pushes something else that pushes B. Then B moves. The two objects are thus causally related. A nonlocal interaction, on the other hand, involves action at a distance. A, although distant from B, is somehow coordinated with B without there being any push, pull, field, or force that flashes across the distance between them. The energies of such interactions do not decrease with distance; therefore they can occur between distant objects, as well as between objects near to each other. Objects at a great distance from each other are not mutually isolated, and are never entirely separated by reason of their distance. All this is the import of Bell's Theorem, propounded by John Bell, a theoretical physicist at CERN (European Organization for Nuclear Research), who asserted that these interactions are ubiquitous and underlie all the events of daily life.

Previously physicists had thought in terms of systems whose correlation depended on their relative position in space and time. The interaction among such entities depended on physical energies that were transmitted across space. These energies typically fell off inversely as the square of the distance between the objects. Entities that were further apart were less strongly connected than those close together. But in a nonlocal interaction, distant systems are somehow connected in a way that does not depend on their locality. Interactions among quantum systems cannot be explained by any known pushes, pulls, fields, signals, or forces. It is as if they have never been separated, and so do not have to be brought together or apart. Quantum wholeness means exactly what it says—altogetherness, oneness. The seeming separateness of entities is reconciled within the wholeness of the system. No signal traveling up to and including the speed of light connects them.

But if we try to think of systems whose connection is faster than the speed of light, a new set of problems arises. Our familiar sequences in time would break down, and we could have a door opening before the key is turned.[1] Effects could happen before their causes; causality as we understand it would not be in effect. We might even be able to go backward in time to change the past. Though scientists tend to discount such possibilities, some persons interested in parapsychology have turned to this as a possible explanation for the happenings we have been discussing in these pages. With faster-than-light communication between one mind and another, one could be instantly aware of what another is thinking. The door would be opened to an array of parapsychological phenomena. Physical faster-than-light signals violate Einstein's theory of relativity, although some argue that Einstein's prohibition against faster-than-light motion applies only to material entities, not to thoughts.

Nonlocal Interactions Depend upon the Whole

How can quantum entities move in the absence of physical pushes and pulls? From a holistic perspective, such phenomena emerge from the wholeness of the system and maintain their form through constant flux. A whirlpool as it travels along a river maintains its form only through the constant flowing and eddying of the water. It quite literally "goes with the flow." The whirlpool has a precarious existence as it travels along the river, dying in every moment and being re-created, yet maintaining its form and beingness through time. It is a creature of the very flow that seems about to destroy it in every moment; it cannot be understood without reference to that larger flow.[2]

We might say poetically that the whirlpool makes a merry picture as it glides along, seeming to laugh all the way. How is it that such a nonliving thing as a whirlpool should be amenable in our imaginations to such anthropomorphic treatment? I have deliberately used this language to blur the distinction between what is living and what is nonliving. There is a tendency, as we meditate on nonlocality, to feel the presence of mind and emotion hovering at the edge of our thoughts, perhaps because the whirlpool, like other nonlocal events, shows traces of the larger entity that maintains it. Our familiar distinctions between the living and the nonliving tend to break down, and the physical world takes on the quality of a primitive mindfulness. David Bohm's suggestion of a quantum potential, which has a guiding function on quantum events, has some of the qualities of mind. We are in the boundary region between the living and the insentient. If, in some of these images, we see the beginnings of a movement that would lead to the introduction of meaning, purpose, and intentionality into the physical world, then these beginnings should receive our attention. (Psychokinesis, for example, does not depend on physical energy, and is goal oriented.)

Might the idea of nonlocality help us understand teleportation, telepathy, and other parapsychological events? In these phenomena, we are confronted by quantum particles that are instantaneously correlated with each other, but do not signal each other or exert a physical force on each other. How then do they become correlated?

As physics provides no answer, we are obliged to turn again to analogies to help us picture how a nonlocal reality might work. Imagine a couple of dozen people crowded in an elevator. When one moves, all must move. If A pushes B, it will not work if B cannot budge. For there to be movement, the whole group must move together, revealing a dependence of each part on the whole. This is a kind of nonlocal interaction. If they wish to move, the best thing they could do would be to establish an overall pattern, such as to set up a rhythmic chant or song to help them move in unison. This example applies only to physical entities, not to such nonphysical entities as ideas or opinions, which do not occupy space.

To try out another possible analogy from an entirely different realm of experience, consider a fountain, in which every drop is constantly replaced by another drop, yet the whole fountain maintains its shape in time by the patterned flowing through of all the drops together. Here the words we apply when we think of movement in space—distance, location, push and pull—do not suffice. Instead it is the overall energy pattern that gives the fountain a kind of stability based on the ceaseless movement of individual water particles. Intrinsic molecular forces and extrinsic forces that guide them create an emergent entity—the fountain.

Though we have begun to speculate how a nonlocal reality might be structured, it is still not clear how this helps us understand many parapsychological phenomena. Our further discussion will be aided by an example of telepathy.

A Case of Telepathy

In the late afternoon of June 14, 1955, Jack Sullivan was alone in a fourteen-foot trench, welding new thirty-six-inch water pipes alongside busy Washington Street in the southwest section of Boston. By 4:30 pm, the last pipe for the day had been laid in place by the power-shovel crew, who then stopped work, leaving Sullivan to finish welding the seam between the last two pipes in the trench.

Sullivan pulled the welding shield back down over his face and was about to resume welding when a calamity occurred. There was no noise, no rumble—no warning—as tons of earth, clay, and stone fell upon him from behind. The trench had caved in.

He was knocked down against the pipe in a kneeling position. His legs were doubled up under him, his head knocked against the pipe, and his nose smashed against the inside of the welding mask. At first he was conscious only of the searing pain in his right shoulder, which was jammed against the red-hot weld he had been making on the pipes. He tried to edge away from the hot pipe, but the burden of earth on top of him held him tight against it. He managed to work his left hand up along his body to the shoulder, and, wiggling his fingers, tried to get some of the dirt to fall down between the pipe and his burning shoulder. This maneuver was futile; he only burned his hand badly.

Though buried under the earth, he shouted for help, but after a few shouts he became short of breath. He thought it best to take things easily and not use up the air around the mask too quickly. With the generator running on the truck, probably no one could hear him anyhow, he realized.

Then a vivid picture of Tommy Whittaker, his best friend, came into his mind. Whittaker was a welder, too, working that day on another part of the water-main project some four or five miles away. Whittaker did not know that Sullivan was at the Washington Street job that day; Sullivan himself had not been told until noon that day. So he knew Whittaker would think he was up north of Boston, in Chelsea, working on another project. Still, Sullivan thought his friend might help him.

Farther south in Boston, Whittaker was welding more water pipes, working overtime to finish up a seam. "Welding becomes an automatic job," he later explained, "so that all sorts of irrelevant things run through your mind and you hardly know you are working." Into Whittaker's mind as he worked that afternoon came the idea that he ought to go up to Washington Street and check. It was so vague that he could hardly explain it. He felt only that something was wrong. No particular person came to mind, only the persistent idea that he should go and check.

Usually when Whittaker went home from work at this job site, he would go straight to Route 128, the superhighway around Boston. This night, however, he turned back into the heavy traffic and drove to Washington Street. He still doesn't know exactly why he did it—something seemed to be drawing him on.

Nearing the trenches on Washington Street, Tommy Whittaker saw one of his company's trucks standing there with the generator running. He drew up behind it. No one was around. He got out and walked over to the trench. At first all he saw was dirt. Then he realized there had been a cave-in. Finally he saw the hand sticking out.

Sullivan says, "When Tommy jumped into that hole, I felt the earth shake and knew that help had come. Thank God." It was 6:30 pm when he was lifted out; he had been buried over an hour.[3]

Parapsychologists would call this a need-based event or a crisis case, serving to "send" information when ordinary channels are blocked. Moreover, the information is of vital, even life-and-death import; there is a powerful motivation to communicate, but no ordinary way of doing so. Many similar cases have been recorded.

Such events are in contrast to another kind of telepathy called deficit based, in which the information seems to "leak" through to a person who lacks the filters and defenses that would ordinarily prevent it. The former type of communication appears as a strikingly creative act on the part of both participants, while the latter appears more as a lack in the receiver, though telepathic information can sometimes slip through to one who is dreaming or meditating, and this can hardly be called a "lack." A state of passivity and receptivity is required. Out of a domain that is constantly flickering with knowledge of many kinds, the receiver hears mainly what is meaningful to him or her.

Andrija Puharich, a physician and parapsychologist who relates the story given above, concludes rightly that the word *sender* in telepathy is a misnomer, in that nothing is sent. But clearly, the knowledge of Sullivan's condition must ultimately become conscious to Whittaker in such a way that he can act upon it. In this case, Sullivan is obviously identified as the "sender," while his friend Whittaker is the "receiver." But of course if there is no "sender," there can equally be no "receiver," for the two conditions are complementary. Somehow the two persons are placed in communion, but not by messages going through time and space. Puharich suggests instead that the sender becomes a kind of magnet, attracting to himself the attention of the receiver. "It is as though the sender creates a mental vacuum toward which the receiver's mind is drawn."[4] In this view, the "sender" creates a mental stage, and the "receiver" is drawn to that stage, his own mind being in correspondence with the state of the other.

Puharich attempts to explain the situation of Sullivan and Whittaker as follows: Under great stress from pain and shock, Sullivan experienced a massive adrenergic state promoted by a release of adrenalin and preparation of the body for extraordinary exertion—fight or flight, a state of high intensity. Whittaker, Puharich thinks, was very likely in a mild state of cholinergia, characterized by a release of acetylcholine and an activation of the parasympathetic nervous system. Puharich remarks that this state is accompanied by a sense of relaxation and well-being, a half-dreamy condition of receptivity, and an increase in the intuitive capacity, and he notes that sleep and hypnosis may facilitate these capacities. It is as though the mind seems to open out in widening circles toward people or situations it recognizes, as a traveler picks out the sound of his native tongue in a land of strangers. Amidst the confusion of tongues, he is alerted by what is meaningful to him. Puharich theorizes that Sullivan created a vortex of some kind toward which the vagrant attention of his friend was drawn. Thus, Puharich would explain events of a higher order (the creative telepathic act) by reference to events of a lower order (the chemical conditions in their bodies). But this still amounts to having a "sender" and "receiver," which begs the question of what constitutes the signaling system involved. However, if he does not hold that the chemical changes are the cause of the telepathic event, but rather that they form part of a total mind-body-world interaction, his theory might be more persuasive. We have already discussed some cases in which these conditions were displayed.

A notable aspect of this case is the way Whittaker is drawn into action in the outer world that he does not fully comprehend at the moment, as though acting at the will of an indescribable intentionality not his own. Equally noteworthy is the fact that Sullivan thought of his friend at all. Though in retrospect it is clear that Whittaker was the man to help him, he might as well have thought of one of the crew of fellow workers who had just left his location, or indeed of anything else. Whittaker's state of mind, then, appears to be a manifestation of a greater awareness capable of drawing him into a receptive state of consciousness. Though the telling of the story does not paint as vivid a picture of Sullivan's consciousness during his ordeal, there appears to be a kind of pattern match in the mental states of the two men that makes of them a whole—much as Yin and Yang make a whole. An elusive choreographer of wholeness seems to be at work in the happening.

Like Teaching and Learning

We might suggest that Sullivan's dangerous plight served to awaken in his friend an urgency stemming from knowledge already available to him at some deep level, but not consciously known. While in bodily appearance the two men remain separate, a state of connectedness at the deeper level is suggested in the telepathic event. Both creativity and intensity are involved, as well as the prior knowledge growing out of their friendship. Situations of desperate need do not always lead to a creative solution, but here we have an astonishing example of problem solving by which a life is saved by way of a leap to a new level of awareness. The situation is not wholly different from teaching and learning.

In teaching, nothing can be learned until an appropriate amount of preparation has been accomplished. But once that work is complete, the final insight often breaks through like a meteor in the night. The teacher showing a pupil how to do a mathematics problem is not seen as sending information through space; what she does is to bring about an integration of scattered themes, a gathering of threads of meaning in a rapid process that gains momentum and in a flash crystallizes into a new level of conscious understanding. She stimulates the pupil's own information-processing abilities to let him awaken to what he needs to know. There is purpose and excitement in that moment of attainment. Sometimes there is a mutual sparking of meaning between the two as the knowledge comes to both. The change occurs by a shift of state of being, not by a movement in space. The discovery of meaning has great power.

I think of the well-known moment when Helen Keller, blind and deaf, found her teacher spelling the name of water as the water flowed from the pump over her hand, an unforgettable instant of awakening. Flooded with excitement, she understood: not only does water have a name, but everything—everything—has a name. Every outer thing has its inner counterpart in the form of a name. The key to a world of knowledge was instantly in her hand. What power, what surprise, is contained in that awakening! This is what can happen between two people who are engaged in the creation and sharing of meaning. A new and more comprehensive level of meaning arises, energizing both. This is what Jung meant when he said that synchronicities are acts of creation in time; they are like the moment of conception. They appear as an intrusion into our reality, an intrusion of knowledge from a higher level of integration. What comes to Whittaker is only the sense of urgency—"Go to

Washington Street"—nothing more; but it arises with enough intensity and power to lead him to change his customary habits and go without knowing why. The worst thing he could do at that moment would be to try to analyze his feelings in "rational" terms, asking himself why he should go. The meaning of his going transcends conscious knowledge. Only on the completion of the action does its true significance and meaning arise in consciousness.

Factors Favoring Telepathy and Clairvoyance

Experiences of telepathy and clairvoyance have been commonly reported to occur between family members or close friends who have many shared experiences linking them together. The ties between them may be psychic and emotional, not necessarily physical, but strong, enduring, and independent of distance. Their shared memories and experiences make up a meaning field that binds them together. There are many cases in which a member of a family is injured or dies while abroad and the event is registered immediately by someone at home, showing that the family connection is not broken by distance. Jung uses the word *elastic* to describe the space that connects people in this way. The knowledge may be conveyed by a dream, telepathy, or clairvoyance, and is not dependent on the five senses. It can seemingly reach through material barriers to give rise to an awareness not mediated by the ordinary senses.

A number of researchers have recorded instances of telepathy between mother and child, and they have come to believe that this is the basic means of communication in the embryonic stage of a child's development. They have called this the "cradle of ESP." This kind of communication may continue until the child is about three and a half and drop off rapidly after that, being a continuation of the symbiosis of mother and child before birth. We have also mentioned cases of sudden intuition on the part of a mother by which she saved her infant from death. Both mother and child apparently share in this faculty. On account of such evidence, some writers have pointed to the "regressive" quality of telepathy, but this does not take account of the high quality of some telepathic communications, showing wisdom far beyond the ego's knowledge.

When students are being trained in clairvoyance, they are encouraged to take note of whatever images appear in their awareness—not to interfere by conscious judgments or imaginative embroidery, but simply to take note. This is like any creative activity in which conscious judgments can only impede the flow of the imagination. A delicate creative act of trust and openness is called for, with the whole body becoming the instrument of receptivity. The person must take note of the fragments that first appear, trusting that a whole picture will later emerge. It is sometimes said that clairvoyance is a high development of the imaginative faculty, going beyond mere fantasy to perceive an objective reality. From another perspective, it appears as a high development of the intuitive faculty.

A Psychic Speaks

Eileen Garrett, a gifted psychic who has written with great simplicity about her abilities and who makes no effort to sensationalize, says that in telepathy, whether sending or receiving, she moves into a state of untroubled emotional clarity, with a quickening of all the senses.[5] She begins by breathing deeply into the abdominal cavity, using a "detached but highly accelerated" rate of breathing. She has acquired the technique of changing her states of perception by changing her rate of breathing. Both in sending and receiving, she must be emotionally involved, very much a part of what she perceives. In receiving, she is in a state of anticipation; often there is a faint tingling and warmth of the skin, with gooseflesh forming. This is a sign to her that something needs to come through. Telepathic reception begins in the body, she says, and all the senses are alert, including smell and taste. The sensitive must be alert to her own bodily states, giving special attention to those that facilitate the telepathic process, like breathing. A state of intensity arises. Scenes begin to flash forth rapidly before her inner vision, so rapidly that she must work fast to retain them; there comes a knowledge of the feelings of those she contacts and the atmosphere in which they are immersed, which she experiences within her own body, somewhat as one might experience the feeling of entering a shady, moist forest glade from out of the sunlight. Atmospheres are perceived as carrying the very meaning of other times and places. The scenes come without her own willing or volition, as do dreams; she must learn to trust that what comes in this way is relevant and meaningful. In transmitting, all the bodily processes are quickened, and she "sends" forth her imagery on a white beam of light. In all these activities, she feels that she is allowed to enter into something that happens outside herself; she speaks of having access to a "greater reality of self," or a "superconsciousness." She feels the pain of her client in her own body. Sometimes this comes in the form of precognitive awareness, and she says she knows, a day in advance of the client's coming, what he or she will look like and what problem will be presented. From her description, telepathy seems to be a kind of empathetic resonance.

Garrett's remarks deserve attention because it is frequently said that we have no introspective knowledge of the experience of telepathy or psychometry. The knowledge simply appears in our awareness without our knowing how or why. For this reason, we cannot learn to practice these abilities by attending to the inner states that precede or accompany them. J. B. Rhine took this view, saying that it explains why it is very difficult to bring these abilities under voluntary control.[6] We don't know when we are doing them, or if we have successfully done them, how to do them again. Yet Garrett's observations suggest that this is not quite true for all persons. Perhaps it applies most clearly to beginners. Modern psychotherapists would tend to agree with her, for they find their intuitive abilities strengthened as they continue their professional work.

Spellbound

In the story of Whittaker and Sullivan, Whittaker's action brings to mind the word *spell,* which we discussed earlier in connection with time. Indeed, there is magic in the arising of a spell, as it steals like a fog over the landscapes of the mind, silent, enveloping, embracing. It overshadows the ego, leaves the will suspended. One is drawn out of the spell in which one customarily lives, and into another time, another spell. Within it one effortlessly feels what is to happen or does what is to be done. Where does it come from, and where does it go? It has no hereness, no thereness, no when- or whereness. In the old metaphysics, it was thought that spells represented an intervention in the stream of time by bringing into time what was formerly timeless and spaceless. Those who achieved this by a deliberate act were magicians. Today we would say they are in an alternate state of consciousness.

Eileen Garrett's descriptions make it appear that certain psychic abilities are simply extensions of our ordinary sensing ability. Clairvoyance, then, seems to be an extension of ordinary sight, while telepathy is an extension of hearing and speaking. Both involve relating to vibratory energies of some kind. However, precognitive and telepathic dreams, coming when all the senses are stilled in sleep, make us think that the five senses are not involved, unless we hold that the closing of the ordinary senses aids in awakening more subtle ones. Some occultists believe that these special gifts are forever unsleeping but overwhelmed by the sounds and sights that flood the waking consciousness, much as stars are hidden by daylight. Hidden from ordinary consciousness, they emerge before the dreaming psyche like creatures of the night. Individuals vary greatly in this respect, with some having ready access to veridical psychic information through their dreams, while others have very little. Just as some people are deaf to ordinary sound and must wear hearing aids, so perhaps a vast number of others are either deaf to these subtle effects, or simply have no way to translate them into conscious meaning.

Let us amplify this last point. Suppose that the emergence of an archetypal power into our world is accompanied by a certain psychic patterning or vibration of some kind. Like the sound of distant drums, such a disturbance heralds its constellation in the psyche. Now suppose we have no initial conscious awareness of its constellation. At first there would be mere vibration, which lacks conscious meaning until it is perceived by consciousness, translated into language and/or imagery. If so, we would understand why such events are known to the unconscious before they are known to consciousness. Just as the dots and dashes of a Morse code message must be translated into words to be understood, the emerging archetype requires the structures of consciousness—language and imagery—to be comprehended. To make the transition into conscious meaning, one must know the code. The same argument applies to the discovery of meaning in the DNA code: that we now can comprehend its sequence does not mean we understand its import. This may be the reason why telepathy works best between relatives or lovers—they are *familiar* with each other's psychic coding. The step over the barrier into consciousness is critical for apprehension of any kind to take place, and it would therefore be easier for those who share similar patterning of consciousness to register familiar psychic shifts in the archetypal field.

According to Phoebe Bendit, most psychics apparently do not experience their knowledge as coming through dreams. Bendit, a woman of extraordinary psychic powers, experiences her knowledge as a "purely objective perception." She experiences receiving it directly through her brain, and says it is as clear and trustworthy as any physical perception. It is in no way confused or distorted by the reactions of her own mind, and is under full conscious control.[7] From her we learn that at the level of the deep psyche, we all simply know—instantly and effortlessly—that we are connected to a universal awareness. At the deep level where we are part of that awareness, we are one with our world, and all who are in that state of awareness know as we know.

The Undeveloped Psychic

Many people have these psychic abilities in an undeveloped state. Bendit suggests that for these persons the psychic perceptions are rather like reflexes: they are experienced in the solar plexus, which she characterizes as the "brain" of the autonomic nervous system. Psychic perceptions tend toward "all-or-none" reactions, uncontrolled and undifferentiated, and are likely to be experienced suddenly and unpredictably. They arise involuntarily, and when the person tries to get hold of them they are gone. For such persons, psychic abilities are a source of disturbance rather than insight, and the individual is unable to tell whether her perceptions and her automatic responses come from some psychic source external to herself, or are a product of her own mind or imagination. Increased self-knowledge helps the individual make this distinction.

The psychics I have researched seem generally to agree that they are able to work better with some subjects than others, depending on the degree of sympathy or empathetic resonance they can establish. Such empathetic resonance then appears to be an expression of the connectedness of all human beings, a natural quality of the flickering, rhythmic nature of our selves and of all things. It is experienced by the undeveloped psyche as an expression of sympathy, empathy, love, or compassion, but the prepared mind experiences it in a more articulated and richly nuanced form.

The Poltergeist: Mind-to-Matter Connections

Where we have been considering mind to mind connections, we will now turn to mind-to-matter connections. The former occur entirely in the realm of the psyche, where distance as we know it in the sensory realm does not occur. Instead, purpose and meaning are involved, albeit at an unconscious level. There is a strong need to communicate, and no ordinary means of doing so. Now in the insignificant figure of the poltergeist we have a psychic fragment that has to do with the realm of space, as well as with a primitive meaning and purpose, often tied to the mortal fate of an individual. It seems to live between the realms of mind and matter, participating in both.

The poltergeist is a primitive invisible entity, akin to the ghosts that linger around old houses in England and elsewhere, but linked to a person rather than a place. The poltergeist, whose name means "noisy spirit" in German, mischievously creates all manner of havoc in its vicinity, such as loud footsteps, thumps, rattles, and bangs. Objects fly off tables, turn corners in mid-air, and sail down a stairway; pictures are dislodged from walls; a loud clattering is heard as dishes fall from the cupboards. The sound of a heavy rain can be heard on the roof, though no rain falls. Even thermal phenomena—sudden sensations of heat or cold—may be felt. Naturally, no one takes credit for these goings-on.

They seem to occur most frequently in the environs of pubescent youngsters, who are themselves unaware of having any connection to them. However, if the young person speaks to the poltergeist it will sometimes show that it has heard, indicating that it has some form of meaningful connection to that person. The phenomena are thought to be related to the sexual transformations of puberty, as the energies of emerging sexuality clash with childish impulses. Large but chaotic and unfocused energies are in evidence.

According to D. Scott Rogo, the youthful agent is typically marked by a great deal of repressed hostility quite unknown to himself, although a variety of other emotional conflicts may trigger the phenomena. Rogo believes that, in addition to issues of sexual maturation, the young person may have very little ability to express himself verbally, so that his anger remains unexpressed. Frustration and tension build up as the conflict remains unresolved and begins to affect others in the household. At this point, then, the psychokinetic capability of the poltergeist, a nonphysical form of energy, comes in to express what is unconscious to the young person. A transformed kind of energy possessing a primitive consciousness is born from the conflict, and candlesticks and dishes begin to fly around the house.[8]

In this we see the poltergeist psychologically as an autonomous complex, a split-off part of the agent's psyche that has escaped the domain of the ego, or possibly was never well related to the ego. It is as if the young person is "haunted" by the poltergeist in the same way that old houses can be haunted by ghosts. Unlike a ghost, the poltergeist is not visible, and is known only by the clamor it sets up. I have seen similar complexes in some of my clients, and they can be extremely difficult to get rid of. They go their own way, quite independently of the ego's authority, and usually have a repetitive, obsessive nature. Long experience over many years by priests and therapists has shown that these spirits can be a danger to the healer or exorcist, for as dependent entities they need a material object to give them form, and will attack the healer if they can.

It is worth noting the difference between the Western and Eastern interpretation of these phenomena, such as is applied in Tibet. To Rogo, a Westerner, the poltergeist belongs to the realm of psychopathology; the young agent is thought to need treatment. To the Tibetans, it is a spiritual phenomenon, practiced by monks and lamas. No hint of pathology attaches to it. Given our cultural background, it is not easy for us to see the poltergeist as a spiritual phenomenon, but if it is understood to be a spirit, then the Tibetan interpretation naturally follows. The Tibetan monk might wish to keep the noisy spirit around to do his bidding, after the manner of the shaman, who often might have a number of spirits who had consented to obey him. We, on the other hand, would believe that by transforming the spirit (now merely a "complex") into some more benign form, and by helping the agent come to more adult sexual expression, we would have dealt adequately with the poltergeist, without reference to spirits or spirituality.[9] The thermal effects sometimes generated by the poltergeist will remind some readers of the reports of *tummo,* one of many exotic practices found in the Tibetan Buddhist faith, wherein the adept learns to dry cold, wet sheets with his body heat in frigid weather. These practices are believed to occur by way of transforming sexual energy, except that they are far more evolved than the poltergeist experiences of the West, the transformation having been brought under the conscious control of the adept. Such energies can be evoked but not easily commanded. They do not begin to reveal the profundity of Tibetan Buddhist teachings.

A Teleportation

Michael Talbot tells the story of a poltergeist that accompanied him from his childhood.[10] As a boy, Talbot had made a rock collection, as boys often do. Among his rocks was a small piece of polished quartz that he had bought at a rock shop, no doubt attracted by its special shape and color. When Talbot left for college, the poltergeist went with him, but the rock collection remained at home. One day years later, noticing that the poltergeist was very active, he asked it if it could teleport objects. He had no particular object in mind that he wished to see moved, but the next morning he found the small piece of quartz lying in the middle of his desk, far from his boyhood home. The poltergeist had presumably heard his request, and this was its reply. He recognized the piece of quartz from its unique color and shape; it resembled a small lightbulb. To make certain, the next time he went home he checked, and sure enough, the stone was missing from his rock collection. According to Talbot, the poltergeist produced about a dozen such teleportations in its lifetime. It showed an ability to transcend the conditions of ordinary space and time. It even knew Talbot's address!

Reality as Information

Had Talbot's poltergeist spent a busy night traveling over a hundred miles to his new residence? Not at all, in his view. The poltergeist does not use energy to move objects through space in time; it does not belong to the sensory realm. Talbot views reality as information provided to consciousness, including information about physicality. Reality does not *have* information; reality *is* information. If the rock crystal is on some level a complex organization of information, then for the crystal to behave as he reported, its reality ceases to be its former constellation of information and its significance is transformed.

Here we are again in the marginal area where mind begins to disclose itself. It is as if the poltergeist wishes to reply to Talbot by showing what it can do. It seems to display a rudimentary comprehension, purpose, and meaning. It belongs to the psychic realm not the sensory realm. Its ability to move objects by a nonphysical power (psychokinesis) is goal-oriented and purposeful. But it does not follow the customs of our space and time, and instead makes use of the psyche to manipulate our view of reality by changing the information it contains.

Relating to the Poltergeist

Psychologically, the poltergeist can be viewed as a psychic fragment that is connected to the physical world. It can hear when we speak to it, and it can modify the significance or meaning of physical objects such as the rock crystal.

The idea of meaning recalls us to the larger subject of our study—synchronicity. Are we looking at a synchronistic event when Talbot speaks to the poltergeist and the little rock crystal appears on his desk? We seem to be seeing a meaningful event and an acausal one. A thread links Talbot's consciousness to the poltergeist. And although it is connected to his psyche, the poltergeist is not merely psychic, because it has an effective connection to the reality of the quartz crystal and gets it to move in Talbot's reality. To move the crystal consciously, Talbot would have to expend energy and move it physically through space and time, while the poltergeist operates on a different plane where different conditions evidently prevail. The reader will perhaps remember the case related in chapter 4 of the woman in the painful business of losing her religious faith, who thought that the crucifix on her bedroom wall needed to come down but could not bear to do it herself. But when she spoke—to what? to the crucifix?—it soon fell down by itself. Was this woman, unknown to herself, speaking to a poltergeist, as was Talbot? Or were both events mere coincidences? Or were they events in the imagination only?

My own leaning is to want to stop seeing the crystal as separate from the reality through which it moves, and see it instead as unfolding from the wholeness of the situation. That would include the psychic situation, both conscious and unconscious, along with the physical situation. According to Talbot, reality is information about physicality, which can materialize and dematerialize, and take on form and location in time and space. Like a whirlpool on the river, the rock crystal is a dependent entity that exists only as long as it is maintained by the enabling conditions around it (its meaning field), and it ceases to exist when those conditions change.

Talbot offers another analogy. What we know as subatomic particles, together with the objects they constitute, are "no more substantial than the panoramic images generated by the card-holding sections of stadium crowds when they create giant portraits of Lenin or Mao."[11] This image harks back to the ancient view that the world we see is a world of appearances, not of reality. What we see around us is real on its own level, just as we, too, are real on our level, but what we see with the eye of ordinary consciousness is not the ultimate reality. It is an appearance. Is there an objective reality within (or behind) the appearance? This question is open today. Quantum physics seems to say there is not, but Einstein could not swallow that. "Is the moon still there when you are not looking at it?" he asked.

The work of Suzanne Padfield and Barbara McClintock comes to mind again. These two independent observers, starting with quite different purposes, invite us to follow the ancient adage "Become what you wish to know." By first willing themselves to become very, very small and then using clairvoyance (literally, "clear seeing"), they were able to see into the life of the cells and chromosomes they studied. Padfield said that though she could not impose an alien will on the elementary units she was trying to move, she could help them choose among the alternatives already available to them. And McClintock got down and "walked" among the chromosomes to acquire information she could not have gotten in any other way. This information, she said, was always right. Perhaps the poltergeist—a trickster figure and a master of sudden changes—uses a similar method.

Transforming the Poltergeist

By observing the behavior of lightning, human beings were able to duplicate nature's ways. First we constructed lightning rods to begin to divert and defuse these energies. However, a very different process had to be discovered before we could use electricity to light our homes. We had to transform it, tame it, learn to adapt to its ways. At that point, electricity became our servant rather than our master. Similarly, we see this "taming" going on in psychotherapy when psychic energies that originally appear in dreams as threatening beasts, demons, or horrific scenes of destruction are slowly transmuted. The person must dare the seemingly indomitable power of the inner beast in order to bring healing. Without this "taming," the energies would be so powerful as to be dangerous to human life, but domesticated, they are made to serve human needs. Then, as the beast becomes friendly and trustworthy, or changes in dreams into a domesticated animal, we see a large increment of energy made available to consciousness, just as electricity brought a new energy to our society. The ox-herding story from the Zen tradition pictures this process of taming: after tracking and sighting the wild ox, the herder catches it and succeeds in taming it, ultimately riding home on its back.

We should follow the method of Padfield and McClintock, carefully observing nature and imitating her ways. In the world of the poltergeist, we observe that most cases are not cured by therapy but by nature herself. The records go far back in history. The afflicted person simply grows up. Only in cases where the natural trajectory of life does not carry the person forward would we need to intervene, freeing the person from the impediments that hinder his or her growth.

A significant principle of healing and transformation is that a movement occurring on one level will be accompanied by a similar movement on another level, provided that the patterns of the two levels are symbolically linked. This is related to the principle of sympathetic magic: we heal another by healing ourselves.

Though Talbot does not give us much background about his little quartz crystal, it seems reasonable to assume that it had belonged to him from an early age and therefore had a rich symbolic association for him with his life process. When the quartz moved from his boyhood home to the home of his mature years, we would expect a corresponding inner movement was occurring on another level, such as that certain mischievous boyish energies were now transforming into the energies of the man and folding into the flow of his adult years. This would be the psychic change necessary to the unfolding of the next phase of his life. In short, he was growing up. Relying on a symbolic correspondence or analogical connection between the energies of the poltergeist and the energies of the young man as he moved from boyhood to manhood, we see the episode as suffused with meaning, both for Talbot and the poltergeist. Both participate in the transformation. We might now expect the poltergeist to diminish or even cease, its role having been fulfilled. This seems to be what happened, from Talbot's account.

Certain persons sometimes succeed in establishing a conscious and healing connection with the poltergeist. One young man reported by A. R. G. Owen learned to control his phenomena by doing automatic writing or drawing, thus providing the mischievous energies with a substitute channel of expression.[12] In chapter 2, we saw how symptoms of a psychic illness can sometimes be controlled by way of an analogical substitute for the sacrificed activity.[13] Or the energy of the symptoms can be bent in a safe direction, much as a lightning rod rechannels the electrical charge of lightning into a safe path. In this way, the poltergeist can be linked to other paranormal phenomena such as apparitions, which reveal a latent purpose, rationality, and meaning. It would not be seen as a chaotic outpouring of wild psychic energies. Such energies could be tamed, like electricity, and made available for other purposes, such as the transformation of consciousness.

The poltergeist now takes its place among the phenomena we meet in psychotherapy. It may be viewed as a complex of repetitive meanings and responses that may appear at the adolescent phase of development and then disappear as the adult phase is consolidated. It may begin the will to individuation, the sublimation of sexual energy, or perhaps the transformation of long-simmering anger. If it is not possible therapeutically to reduce the repression and allow the expression of these energies, then some substitute activity must be found to rechannel them until such time as the triggering conditions can be metabolized by the individual. During this time, vigorous athletic participation can be recommended, to be accompanied, if possible, by some transformative work on the poltergeist.

Poltergeist, Trickster, and Savior

In Jung's view, the poltergeist belongs to the trickster archetype; it is one of the ways the trickster energies appear in our world. Jung says that the trickster is a forerunner of the savior, and this probably applies to the poltergeist as well. This means that the transformation and maturing of these primitive energies may lead to the appearance of the healer and savior, so that the work of transforming the poltergeist may have wide implications for the young subject and, indeed, for the whole of society.[14] The poltergeist can be seen as a manifestation of those energies by which mind influences matter. We presume, perhaps wrongly, that because these are primitive energies, they do not lead to higher knowledge; yet if the body is included among the material things that can be affected by this influence, then the energies of the poltergeist may well be related to the healer. Also, if the connection between body and soul occurs at the primitive level of the poltergeist, we may better understand how it is that, in the out-of-body experience, body and soul can separate. No higher power is apparently needed.

The Out-of-Body Experience

Another important phenomenon marked by extraordinary movement in space is the out-of-body experience. Suppose you wish to experiment for yourself and to have an OBE by your own willing, and you wish to be fully conscious while traveling in the astral body. Let us assume that you have had this experience many times before, but only unconsciously, in a so-called spontaneous OBE. This time it will be different, because you want to remember the happening when you return to your normal state of consciousness. You will be in an alternative state, but not an unconscious one. Of the many methods you might consider, you choose the "dream control" method, a form of wake-initiated lucid dreaming described by Sylvan Muldoon.[15] You have practiced how to retain consciousness right up to the point of going to sleep, and you have constructed a dream that will help you separate from your physical body and send you on your way. Muldoon likes to use a dream of an elevator.

Adopting his preference, you enter the elevator in your dream on the ground floor of a tall building, lie down on your back, and let yourself be carried up. Now you rise to the top floor and stand up and prepare to walk out of the elevator and around the area. Rising up, you leave your physical body and find yourself in the astral body. Your physical body is left in a cataleptic state on the floor of the elevator. As this is your first conscious trip, you may decide to turn right around and dream yourself down again, especially if the experience has been accompanied by apprehension—not to say terror. After all, you are outside your body, and you can see it lying on the floor of the elevator, unmoving. But at some point, your resolve returns, and you try again. This time you will want to dream yourself farther away, out of the range of the "silver cord" that links the astral body to the physical body, reportedly about eight to fifteen feet long. You will have programmed yourself to awaken as you come to a certain door or window. This will work like the suggestion you give yourself at night to wake up at a certain time in the morning. You find that you are fully conscious, and that you can see and hear very well, though your physical body lies motionless behind you. And you are free to go anywhere.

I have left out a number of steps here, so as not to encourage the reader to premature experimentation. Robert Monroe lays great stress on relaxation at the beginning of such an experiment, and suggests that once you have made up your mind to continue your work, you will have three categories of speed that you may choose.[16] You may walk around as you do normally, or you may travel considerably faster, so that it seems the world is coming toward you, as when you accelerate out of a train station. Or you may travel as though at unimaginable speed, covering vast distances at the speed of thought. If, for example, you wish to visit a friend at the other side of the continent, you would fix your attention on the friend you wish to see, and not on the landmarks along the way. If your friend sees you, it would mean that you are in your apparitional state when seen from her perspective, but you would be in the out-of-body state seen from your perspective. They are the same experience seen from within or without. Additionally, you would endeavor to remember the experience when you turn your thoughts homeward to rapidly return to your physical body.

Our exploration has led us to see that space and time as we know them are not universal orienting factors, and that phenomena can occur that have only a tenuous connection to our ordinary interpretations of space-time. Though our thinking tends by default to follow the well-worn pathways of the material world, we see that in the psychic world things can be very different from what we expect. Beyond that, we can posit a multiplicity of space-time worlds enfolded within each other, so that events can happen in many other time worlds than our own. Such events would present themselves as anomalies in our time world. Consider, for example, the astronauts orbiting the earth at high speed on their scientific missions, and seeing the sun rise every ninety minutes. They had to adapt to a world where a day is only one and one-half hours long. Until we learn of the many worlds enfolded in this one, such cycles may not even be thought to occur, because they do not conform to the ordinary constraints of our world.

Thinking along these lines, we have tried to enter with the poltergeist into other realms, and into the world of chromosomes and cells, or even the much smaller world of subatomic particles, and we have begun to observe a kind of intelligence in the dwellers within those worlds. That we might learn to communicate with them does not strike us now as wholly impossible. We have also seen evidence to the effect that the soul can live independently of the physical body.

An Extraordinary Psychic at Work

The difficulties with our views of the spatial realm are illustrated by the following story, told by Andrija Puharich.[17] Peter Hurkos, a well-known psychic, was given a letter sealed in a manila envelope by a man unknown to him. In the presence of Puharich, Hurkos handled the letter and then said, "This letter is from this man's wife. She seems to be in good health at the moment, but she will have trouble with her female organs." Hurkos then drew a diagram of the uterus and the fallopian tubes of this woman, showing the left fallopian tube with a large mass in the center. He went on to say that in about six months the female organs would give rise to complications that would require surgery. In this single act, Hurkos revealed the limitations of our current views of both space and time, for he "read" the sealed letter, at a distance from the woman herself, using the hand, not the eye, and took note of events that were to happen months later.

As is true in many similar experiences, there was no conscious knowledge in anyone's mind of what was to happen six months later. Therefore the knowledge that came to the psychic did not come by telepathy with another consciousness. Nor was it necessarily a case of precognition. Possibly the knowledge was already present in a deep stratum of the woman's psyche, where she was not confined to the space and time of consciousness, and it was that level that Hurkos communicated with by way of the sealed letter. Another possibility was that he was able to see anatomical features of the woman's body not consciously known to anyone, using an inanimate object, the letter, as a contact point. Possibly he was using clairvoyance to see the disturbance in the organs before it was evident to ordinary sight in the form of symptoms. His vision passed over physical barriers to reveal what was actually present and what lay in the future, but to ordinary sight was still hidden. The psychic's insights proved to be correct. Six months after the reading, the woman began to develop severe cramps, irregular bleeding, and low back pain. Her specialists eventually referred her to the Mayo Clinic, where a hysterectomy was performed. The husband was shown the medical specimen, revealing a large sealed-off mass in the left fallopian tube.

Peter Hurkos is known as an extraordinary psychic, though not alone in his abilities. He appeared able to use a variety of modalities to gain the knowledge he was looking for. Puharich says that using a photograph rather than a letter, Hurkos was able to gain knowledge not only of the physical appearance of the person shown in the photograph, but of that individual's past and, to some extent, of his future. It was found that more intelligence could be obtained from the negative than from the positive print, and none at all from a reproduction of the print. Possibly the photographic negative is read by the psychic in the same way that any other psychometrized object is read, and there is nothing special about the photograph, but in that case the person photographed has only the briefest possible contact with the negative, during the fraction of a second that the film is exposed in his direction, yet in that brief exposure a contact is made that enables the psychometrist to gain information about his past and future, an indication that something outside ordinary time is operating. "This process," says Puharich, "has absolutely no analogy in any of the known dynamics associated with matter or energy."[18] Some new principle must be found to make sense of this. This technique, were it known, might be used to diagnose approaching illness of others, and so might be helpful in healing. Thus our understanding of space and time comes into play in healing as well as in other mind-body events. Only recently have these possibilities been seriously explored.

The Role of the Body and Vibration

Our understanding of telepathy must include the role of the body. According to the psychic Eileen Garrett, telepathic reception begins in the body. It is the rhythmic nature of bodily processes that is involved, particularly the inflow and outflow of the breath. Recall that the shamanic healer chanted his story, giving to his words a rhythmic quality in order to restore the lost harmony of birthing—a rhythmic process if there ever was one. Drumming was an integral part of shamanic healing rituals. *Chant* is very near to *enchant* (from the Latin *incantare,* "in" or "against," plus *cantare,* "to sing"), which means to delight or charm, hence to act on by charm or sorcery. This is perhaps a little less mysterious if we hold to the rhythmic, bodily nature of what is happening.

We may also recall the mother who saved her child from a train wreck by attending to the trembling that overtook her after sending the child to play—one of many examples that could be brought forward to illustrate how the unconscious, in this context related to the bodily level, begins to take in the true state of affairs far in advance of consciousness. Its activity, more universal in scope, is not limited to clock time nor to the narrow window open to consciousness. Notice that the mother began to feel a trembling and apprehension (as well as a warning voice) before the train wreck had actually occurred. Therefore her dawning awareness could not have come from the outer event, but we may speculate that the knowledge was picked up by another level of the psyche where our conscious linear time does not hold. Perhaps it came from a pattern that had not yet entered the visible or audible realm, a pattern we may think of as somehow preexisting in the potential or timeless realm, perhaps having a vibratory form of existence related to sound, since it was capable of being heard. This, of course, would be precognition when seen from the point of view of the ego. (As when discussing time, I suggest that the lines separating present and past or present and future may differ with different persons or situations).

Since precognition demonstrates the perceptive abilities of the unconscious, then, in line with our earlier discussion of time and space, we might think of the unconscious as having a timeless nature that is everywhere, anywhere, and nowhere—that is, without spatial extension. Or we might suggest that the mother, with some deep aspect of herself, entered into a field of awareness that extended outside the vibratory range that the eye can see or the ear can hear, but that the body as a whole responded to.

We live in a sea of vibratory energies, but our eyes and ears can perceive only a limited range of the energies of sight and sound. Beyond the visible and audible range are other vibratory levels, reaching to unknown intensities. We could speculate that there are bodily organs capable of responding to these more subtle vibrations but not yet developed into conscious and usable conduits, still waiting to be developed in the course of our evolution. In this way, we would give to the body a potential mental ability or a kind of perception that can supplement our eyes and ears. Perhaps the ability would be represented by a function, a vibration, or a pulsing, not an organ. Some persons appear to have the capacity to respond to many of these subtle vibrations, and so are known as sensitives, while others cannot claim them and believe they do not exist. Women tend to have them more commonly than men, and we speak of "women's intuition," though some men also have excellent intuitive abilities.

So omnipresent in our life-world are these vibratory energies that we are not aware of them, but we now know that those vibrations outside the range of the five senses, like those recognized by the senses, are meaning bearers. We could not know their energies at all if they were not in some sense active within us. From ancient times, clairvoyants have said that there exists a subtle field or aura that surrounds and interpenetrates the physical body, extending out to a certain distance from it and gradually merging with the atmosphere. The human aura, they say, acts as a subtle bridging device between person and world. It resembles the "wave function" posited by some scientists when they approach this issue with the thought structures and language of modern physics. Perhaps this is the place to remember that telepathy and clairvoyance are essentially the same, according to J. B. Rhine. The former reveals the thoughts of another person, while the latter reveals objective events, like Swedenborg's famous vision in the eighteenth century of the great fire in Stockholm, which was happening at a distance of many miles. The fact that a number of prominent visitors were at Swedenborg's home and heard him describing the fire before the messenger arrived with the news made this a classic case of clairvoyance or remote viewing.

Describing her experiences in psychometry, Garrett speaks of the object she "reads"—the key or ring or book—as a living thing. Just as a tree, for example, grows in response to characteristics of its landscape, so Garrett holds that an object during its "lifetime" absorbs the atmosphere and the personality of those with whom it is associated. It then reveals its "memories" to the psychometrist who takes it in hand and reads it. Garrett says that she responds with a sense of alertness passing through her hand and a warm vibration moving through her arm as pictures, scenes, dramas, and atmospheres open before her inner vision and give way to others, as though a record sleeping in the object is awakened by the touch of her hand—or as though the record stored in the object can be opened when contact is made by someone who "tunes in" at the right frequency. Her language suggests a vibratory kind of contact.

The "atmospheres" to which Garrett alludes appear to be the subjective experience of a dynamic field of energy or intensity—a spell—apprehended by feeling and bodily attunement, and made up of images. In psychometry, these images reawaken into life in her awareness, bringing the past into the present, quivering with all the meanings the object held for those who once lived it. The psychometrist, with object in hand, seems to turn on an inner motion picture that calls up the very living presence of another person's life experience. Sometimes the future is also revealed.

It is not clear whether the object is the source of the information or is instead the means by which a psychometrist makes contact with another mind by way of clairvoyant vision. Perhaps the object alerts the psychometrist to the appropriate frequency to make contact with a particular person. Though a necessary part of the whole experience, the object can be dispensed with once the contact is made. However, it would have to be coded with the "signature," as it were, of the former owner in order to guide the psychometrist to the life story of that person. It is possible to psychometrize the possessions of a person now deceased. Recall the case mentioned in chapter 5 of the extraordinary psychic who "read" the manual of Esperanto left by a soldier killed in action. Included in the information was material that dated to a time after the soldier's death. Garrett and other mediums use an inward form of apprehension to get at these meanings, entering into a realm of shared meaning, crossing a bridge that most of us are unable to cross, to allow us a glimpse of that moment when mere vibration transforms into conscious meaning, or insight. For the psychometrist, it is a moment of awakening, when all the faculties of the psyche and body come into play.

Feeling Your Pain: Empathetic Resonance

The natural process by which human beings are connected to each other below the level of consciousness has been called "empathetic resonance" by David Lorimer.[19] The term describes a process that combines the psychic and the physical, and is a prelude to knowledge and comprehension. It appears to be linked to the older term *sympathia,* which had nearly gone out of use years before. Empathetic resonance suggests a kind of underground linkage of human beings at an involuntary, preverbal level.

By regarding this connectedness from the standpoint of consciousness, we clearly see two persons involved, but at a deeper level the two act as a unified whole. To ask which of the two initiates the telepathic communication places us in a state of division; the knowledge emerges from the wholeness of the situation. The "sending" half of the duality goes through a critical transforming experience, possibly death or near death (in the case of the welder Jack Sullivan), but he does not send a message through time and space. Similarly, no message is sent by Lord Brougham's friend dying in India; the man dies—that is all. The death itself is the "message" and becomes known throughout the psychic field that unites them. The transformation at death or near death is like an eruption of energy that disturbs the entire sensitive fabric that contains them, a fabric made up of a faint flickering of awareness that gradually becomes more clear as attention is focused on it, as the memories and shared experiences that belong to their friendship come into consciousness. Lord Brougham had to change into a state of relaxation and receptivity occasioned by the hot bath before the knowledge could break through into consciousness. The vital element is the psychic transformation, like a lightning flash, that briefly lights up the universe. In theory, everybody should "see" it, but in reality it breaks through only to the consciousness of the one person for whom that event has a special meaning, and who is in a state of readiness to receive it. Let us say it clearly: at the level of the deep psyche, we are all potentially in communication, but the actuality depends on the awakening of meaning.

Resonance itself is a universal property of the physical world. Put two violins on a table and pluck a string on one of them, and you will soon hear both of them sounding the same note. Or line up five or six grandfather clocks, and the pendulums of all of them (provided they are the same length) will soon oscillate at the same speed and rhythm. They will form a resonant system, and the more clocks in the group the more stable the system will be. Very little energy is required to maintain such a system. Add another clock having a different rhythm, and it will soon take up the rhythm of the group, though no force is applied to it and the clocks have no mechanism with which to communicate. The varied rhythms of things can be brought into harmony by way of sympathetic vibration.

Rupert Sheldrake's hypothesis of formative causation suggests that the formation and placement of the organs within the body occurs through what he terms morphic resonance.[20] This kind of resonance is not conscious, nor is it a prelude to the acquisition of consciousness, but it is creative on the physical level. It has to do with the shape and fit of the various organs of the body in time and space. Lorimer finds three kinds of empathetic resonance that are also creative in different ways: empathetic resonance with the physical states of another person, resonance with another's psychic states, and cosmic empathetic resonance in the near-death state. As to the first of these, he speaks of the sensitive who is able to diagnose the illness of a patient because she feels the pain in her own body, in the very organ that is afflicted in the sick person. Presumably her organ responds to the vibratory rate of the sick person, and she is able to transform the pain into conscious knowledge. These gifted people, often women, are known as medical intuitives. It has also been claimed that a diseased organ can be taken in and healed within the body of the healer, again by empathetic resonance. The Magus of Strovolos has made such a claim.[21] The theory is that as the diseased organ is placed in contact with a healthy body, it begins to take on the new rate by way of sympathetic vibration, and may experience a healing.

Empathetic resonance with the emotional state of another person happens very commonly in therapy. As a healing technique, it is not without danger to the therapist. It often begins at a preverbal, preconscious level without voluntary control. Other therapists have reported to me that when they experienced an awakening of insight, their patients did the same. There is also the possibility of empathetic resonance between a sick person and the intimate articles in his or her possession. Some people say that they have been made ill by handling the objects of a sick person, and the reverse process is apparently also possible. Some say they have been healed by the pills, or *ribus,* of an enlightened spiritual master who has spent months in solitary practice, and whose vibrations while in samadhi are concentrated in the *ribus*. The Lama Govinda says that these pills were eagerly sought after in Tibet. He confesses that he was once given three *ribus* by a master, but he did not need them at the time and gave two of them away, to his later regret.[22]

Jung denigrates this preconscious ability to empathize with the physical or emotional states of a sick person. Writing to an apparently inexperienced young analyst, he calls it a "well-known childhood ailment." He says that when beginning the practice of analysis, he could take no more than two patients a day, because it was too much of a strain for him.[23] It is true that psychotherapy as it is practiced today requires us to maintain appropriate boundaries simply for self-protection. The therapist cannot afford to be drawn deeply and repeatedly into the physical and emotional states of clients. But are we losing something important in this way? The ability to resonate with the emotional or physical states of another person may happen involuntarily in the beginning, but it can be trained and developed to translate the patient's pain into conscious knowledge in the form of a diagnosis or treatment plan. Such healers can return to ordinary consciousness of their own volition; they do not have to fear getting "stuck" in the strong affects of their subjects. Consciousness then takes the lead, and the healer does not simply fall into the empathetic state, as it were, "head over heels." At that point, the ability represents a higher attainment, for one has consciously mastered what was formerly involuntary. However, even when it is not yet under conscious control, the ability to heal by the use of one's own body is a very great gift, and tells us something about the connectedness of which we have spoken.

Lorimer speaks of cosmic empathetic resonance in the near-death experience, when the individual comes into a state of union with a Being of Light and suddenly feels a deep sympathy for the whole creation in its joy and agony.[24] These experiences bring profound knowledge and sympathy for the human condition, with a kind of godlike understanding on many levels. They are life changing and never forgotten. J. B. Rhine has remarked that parapsychology is religion's science, as well as the science of ethics and aesthetics. Synchronicity should also be included in this generalization. In the final chapter, we look at some of the changes that have appeared in times and places where these ideas were taken seriously.[25]

CHAPTER 8

The Synchronistic World

God produces different substances according to the different views which he has of the world, and by the intervention of God, the appropriate nature of each substance brings it about that what happens to one corresponds to what happens to all the others, without, however, their acting upon one another directly.

—Leibniz

You are not wrong, who deem
That my days have been a dream.

—Edgar Allen Poe

Life is the passage of an individual dream, a consciousness, an ego through a cosmic and collective dream.

—Frithjof Schuon

The Soul is the unity that links all individual beings. It is the indivisible continuum in which beings appear as individual conscious units.

—Alain Daniélou

Civilizations of the world seem poised for a shift of consciousness made mandatory by the contemporary challenges faced by humanity, although how this will be realized is not clear. Though the challenges we face are daunting—even to the question of our continued existence as a species—I am uplifted by the thought that this "new" consciousness will not be something never before seen in the world, but will more likely be something that has been lived by men and women of the past who were the bearers of a special prescience. What we are exploring here is whether the study of synchronicity can be the ladder by which we climb to such a new consciousness, and this precisely because synchronicities raise questions about the fundamental ordering factors that maintain our present reality—space, time, and causality.

Toward a Daylight View of the World

The story of Gustav Theodor Fechner, a German physical scientist of nineteenth-century Leipzig, points up this possibility. At the age of thirty-eight, Fechner had undergone a three-year malady so severe that his recovery was accounted a divine miracle. From that time forward, he sought to communicate to the world the knowledge that had saved him. He called his philosophy his "daylight view" of the world, after Plato, meaning that he had emerged from the darkness of the cave where he had formerly lived and where most of his contemporaries lived, into the daylight of new consciousness. Fechner interpreted his experience in terms of the beliefs of his time; today we would probably call it a near-death experience or perhaps a spiritual emergency in the sense of that term developed by Stanislav and Christina Grof.[1] We should also take note of the extraordinary healing that came to him but perhaps be less bold than he in drawing conclusions from the experience. However, it is precisely because of his attainment of new consciousness and his boldness in expressing it that he deserves our attention.

Fechner believed passionately in a world soul, as did Plato. In Fechner's view, all human consciousnesses are bound together in the consciousness of the human race, and this, together with the consciousness of the animal and vegetable kingdoms, is blended together in the world soul, which, in its turn, forms part of the larger consciousness of the solar system and so on, up to God himself. The more inclusive forms of consciousness are in part constituted by the lower forms, but they are not the mere sum of them. Our original sin, according to Fechner, both in popular and in scientific thinking, is in regarding the spiritual as the exception rather than the rule in the midst of nature. Our life is "fed at the breasts of the greater life . . . which must necessarily have more consciousness and independence than all it brings forth."[2] To that greater life Fechner owed his own ongoing life; he sought to bring others to the realization that had saved him.

As the quotation above suggests, Fechner did not hesitate to use poetic imagination in his contemplation of the living world. Here, speaking of the earth, he offers an insight that would be verified a hundred years later by the astronauts as they made their way toward the moon:

> Think of her beauty—a shining ball, sky-blue and sun-lit over one half, the other bathed in starry night, reflecting the heavens from all her waters, myriads of lights and shadows in the folds of her mountains and windings of her valleys, she would be a spectacle of rainbow glory, could one only see her from afar. . . . Green would be the dominant color, but the blue atmosphere and the clouds would enfold her as a bride is shrouded in her veil—a veil the vapory transparent folds of which the earth, through her ministers the winds, never tires of laying and folding about herself anew.[3]

Alas, the view of Fechner, whose love of the earth shines forth in his every line, did not prevail in the halls of science, where instead the universe, including the living things that walk the earth, came to be dealt with by mechanistic analogies and methods. With that choice, the living, loving connection between men and women and earth was broken, and the vision of wholeness lost. The view that sees the universe by analogy with a machine is actually a very recent one without deep roots in the cultures of the past. It has had dire effects on human life as the sense of larger meaning and purpose in life falters. We walk so lonely among the stars because we imagine that our intelligence, humor, and compassion are ours alone, not to be found anywhere in all the universe except in our tiny minds and hearts. But of course we do not know this; it is only our modern way of imagining the universe. Thus we keep ourselves in mind-forged manacles.

It was a century later, a mere moment of time in the long history of earth, as the astronauts made their way to the moon, that men and women everywhere had a chance to see the truth of Fechner's vision. The beauty and the wholeness of the earth, hanging solitary in the darkness of space, was shown forth for all to see. And the kinship of all earth's passengers, great and small, was also there to be seen. As they trained themselves to the conditions of outer space and looked back to earth, the astronauts were led to a broadened consciousness. Many came to see the earth, our home planet, as small and beautiful, and wanted to reduce the strife and contention within it and to preserve its glory for generations to come. Fechner's imaginative experience and the astronauts' outer experience—one involving an inward, the other an outward way of seeing—are very different, and yet they meet as both evoke the perception of wholeness.

Of all the ideas that arise from our study of synchronicities, the one that strikes me as most essential and at the same time most pertinent for our time is the idea of wholeness. If we are to take synchronicities seriously, we must be able to see them from a holistic standpoint—inner and outer world fused, spatial distance dissolved, time relativized—all the factors that divide the world into separately existing parts must give way and begin to lose their import. We take up this point of view not in any arbitrary fashion, but because we now see it as the way the universe works. It works as a whole; that is our reality. We are developing a language and a viewpoint that discloses the unity of all things as an antidote to the previously dominant atomistic, reductionistic point of view, and at the same time we are seeking experiences that testify to wholeness.

The idea of wholeness is more richly complicated than might be thought. Fechner in imagination saw the wholeness of the earth as if from a great distance, but he had previously realized wholeness by an inward path. He had experienced the reality that lies behind all perspectives. That experience is what brought about his miraculous healing and broadened his consciousness. Such experiences are sometimes described as "ineffable," but in truth we know a good deal about them.

Fechner's healing was a spiritual experience in which he died to the old life and was reborn to a new consciousness. Within the death experience, we may be sure that there came an interval of chaotic breakdown, beyond the ego's power to manage, followed by a reorganization of his whole being that he experienced as healing. In contrast to the astronauts, he took an inward, not an outward, path toward the realization of wholeness. This distinction is an important one for our purposes, because it is along the inward path that synchronicities occur. Notice again: if I say, "I perceive the wholeness of the universe," I place myself outside the wholeness, looking at something that lies outside myself. I am in a twoness, not a wholeness—in the dualistic consciousness. But if I place myself *within* the wholeness, what is there to be said? Unitary consciousness is not to be reached by a rational path nor described in logical terms; rather, it is demonstrated in the lives of those who, like Fechner, have realized it. Looking back over history, we see how the idea of wholeness comes to the fore in many times and places and from many sources.

Dynamic Wholeness

Published in 1926 by Jan Christiaan Smuts, *Holism and Evolution* did not receive the attention it deserved because it ran against the prevailing current of the time. Smuts was an early forerunner of many thinkers who were to advance the idea of wholeness, not as a static notion, but rather as a dynamic factor in the making of our world. He said,

> As Holism is a process of creative synthesis, the resulting wholes are not static but dynamic, evolutionary, creative. Hence Evolution has an ever-deepening inward spiritual holistic character; and the wholes of Evolution and the evolutionary process itself can only be understood in reference to this fundamental character of wholeness. This is a universe of whole-making.[4]

Not soul-making, as Keats thought, but whole-making. Perhaps both. The modern physicist David Bohm has said that "wholeness is what is real, and . . . fragmentation is the response of this whole to man's action, guided by illusory perception."[5] Both quantum theory and relativity theory imply undifferentiated wholeness. Bohm emphasizes that an experimenter, in setting up the framework of his experiment, determines the results he will get, becoming a participant-observer. The experimenter, his apparatus, and his results are not separate units, but form an undivided whole. We must give up the idea that the world is made up of separate, basic objects or "building blocks" acting autonomously, according to Bohm. Instead, the world field itself must be seen as a whole. Rather than saying, as Smuts does, that ours is a universe of whole-making, Bohm says that the various parts are creative projections unfolded from out of the whole, each one bearing the stamp of the whole within it. Thus, the whole is primary and fundamental. Wholeness is not something to be attained in the course of evolution; instead it is the Source from which the visible world emerges. The hologram, one of the many astonishing discoveries of the twentieth century, provides Bohm with an appropriate analogy for the wholeness: the whole is present in the parts, and the parts are in the whole.

Bohm's synthesis requires a very great change of consciousness and the sacrifice of many previously held notions. A similar movement, starting from an entirely different basis, is called for by Jean Gebser in his book *The Ever-Present Origin*. Gebser focuses on the nature of time rather than space. He foresees a unifying of all the earlier structures of consciousness, the magical, the mythical, and the mental, in a new structure called the integral consciousness. This form of consciousness will be far more inclusive than our present one to match the wholeness of the world. Within it, the past will come alive with new meanings rather than being relegated to "the unconscious."

Carl Jung is certainly to be numbered among the thinkers whose vision could not be contained within the ordinary mental structures of consciousness. He often used the idea of "wholeness of the personality" to describe the higher consciousness he saw developing among his patients as they struggled to find meaning in their lives. He was thinking first of all of the unique man or woman rather than the collectivity of persons, for he believed that it was only through the devoted work of single individuals that the world would be transformed. Much of his life's work consisted in helping people to move through the spiritual transformations that can lead to wholeness. Let us not forget that the verb "to heal" is related to "to make whole."

Hwa Yen: The Philosophy of Totality

In turning to the idea of wholeness, which now stands at the forefront of our sciences and our healing arts, we are reconnecting to a very old idea indeed, one explored long ago in the Chinese philosophy of Hwa Yen Buddhism, a profound strand of Buddhist teaching known as the Philosophy of Totality. The teaching dates from the sixth century CE, the time of the first of the school's five great patriarchs.[6]

Hwa Yen (or Huayen) should not be thought of as a philosophy in the Western sense. In line with the Buddhist rejection of speculative thought, it should be understood as an attempt to put into words the spiritual experiences of those whose search for ultimates went far beyond the ordinary. Hwa Yen thinking is closer to Fechner's experience of healing than to his vision of the living planet. It combines philosophy with spirituality. Rather than directly addressing our questions about synchronicity, it provides a framework within which such questions can be meaningfully addressed. The experiences and intuitions of the masters and the language they devised to describe their insights open up a wide spectrum of new life possibilities.

Hwa Yen, or the Philosophy of Totality, embraces the wholeness of the universe, from the smallest distances on planet Earth, to the immensity of interstellar space, and out to the remotest edges of the universe. It includes realms embracing other realms, from the infinitesimal to the infinite. Every great realm like the earth or the solar system is embraced by a still larger realm, and every tiny realm like a cell or a molecule contains still smaller ones. The totality of the universe is a highly ordered structure, each part taking its place within a more encompassing structure. This picture is very much in line with modern relativity theory. Size, Hwa Yen masters point out, loses its meaning as we contemplate the processes of different realms, for it depends upon the standpoint from which we measure. In this way, a very small realm can contain a large one, as my brain contains all the contents of the room I am in. Time also changes its meaning, and past, present, and future dissolve into an eternal present.

But what is a realm? A realm is an arena of meaning; it provides the context or frame of reference within which events occur. It establishes a particular order. For two people to share a common experience, they must be in the same realm. Within our planetary realm, our shared experience is that the sun rises every twenty-four hours, but there are certainly realms where this does not happen. A realm has boundaries, and the meanings that hold in one realm may not hold in another. That is why the truths we discover at one level of being turn out to be prisons at another level. Reality in its richness spills out over the containers we have built to hold it. Among the boundaries that establish our particular realm are our concepts of space and time, as well as our form of consciousness, our desires and clingings. To break through the boundaries of a particular realm to allow the truths of another to exist calls for great diligence, insight, and openness, while to be able to envision all realms in their sweep and grandeur is the Buddha Mind—it is enlightenment.

The Hwa Yen philosophers would undoubtedly accept Einstein's theory of relativity, which requires that the frame of reference of the observer be taken into account in making an observation. They would also point out that any observer, insofar as she is limited to a particular standpoint, has a limited perspective. They would definitely go along with Einstein's dictum that all frames of reference have an equal claim to validity. They would go on to point out that in all of this the observer remains in the dualistic consciousness, separated from what she observes, while the Buddha Mind goes to a higher level.

Two principles of Hwa Yen Buddhism are particularly helpful in our inquiry. The first is the principle of mutual penetration or simultaneous non-obstruction. What this means is that different realms coexist with each other and do not impede each other in their existence. Within our realm are countless other realms—that of the merchant, the chieftain, the baker, the thief, or for that matter, the dog or the sparrow. Each of these realms has its own order and its own boundaries. They mutually penetrate and do not obstruct one another, in the same way that many lamps in a room mutually penetrate the whole room and enlighten the whole. Each perspective affords a limited insight on a totality that includes all perspectives.

Within our own realm, different perspectives can be taken on the same thing, none of which impedes any other from existing. For example, concrete is at once a building material, an aggregation of molecules, and a mixture of crushed limestone, silica, alumina, and other substances, while to a philosopher it may suggest the possibility of transformation or again the idea of permanence. By shifting perspectives, we discover a very large number—perhaps an infinite number—of realms of meaning converging within the bag of concrete. These various meanings exist at the same time and do not interfere with each other. All are necessary for the concrete to be what it is. They are simultaneously arising and have a harmonious coexistence, each requiring the other. The mutual penetration of all things corresponds to the principle of "dependent arising," which says that nothing, whether physical or mental, phenomenal or noumenal, has an independent existence, but all things depend on one another for their existence and their function. They have no "own being" but exist as representatives of a larger whole, a still greater realm. Everything is at once an image and a mirror that reflects all other things.

The masters of Hwa Yen tell us that while our universe is made up of many realms, the human mind tends to lock into a single realm at a time. If we are looking at the concrete as a building material, we do not see its chemical composition, and no amount of energy spent in building concrete foundations will reveal its chemical structure. We have to start all over again with a new approach if we are to learn its chemistry. Our "boundaries" in regard to the concrete, then, are maintained by our ignorance, lack of vision, the very limitedness of our minds. This may sound as though one would have to be a chemist, a philosopher, a builder, and perhaps also a poet in order to understand a bag of concrete, but the Hwa Yen masters have something else in mind. They invite us to ponder the simultaneous non-obstruction of all realms from an inner perspective and from the standpoint of totality in order to grasp the interrelatedness of all realms. The Buddha Mind observes the greatness of our universe from an outer perspective, but even more it lays hold of the inwardness that binds all realms together. Breaking through all boundaries and integrating all the realms leads to an experiential understanding of the simultaneous non-obstruction of all realms.

Hwa Yen therefore turns to the primary insight of Buddhism, the voidness of all things. The idea of voidness or emptiness has caused much misunderstanding and requires to be understood in the proper way. Voidness is not "absence," as when we say that the cupboard is empty, meaning that though we would expect to find food in the cupboard, there is no food there. Nor is voidness or emptiness "annihilation," as in the common idea of death. Emptiness is at once nothing and the possibility of everything. It bears a certain resemblance to the physicists' description of the quantum domain as a realm of possibilities, and to David Bohm's idea of the vacuum state, a region pulsing with intense energies. The emptiness, then, pervades all realms, making them identical with each other. All things are revelations, as it were, of the emptiness. They represent the unfolding of the emptiness into all things, large and small. The emptiness evidently has a very paradoxical nature, like God. The second principle of Hwa Yen that is important to us has to do with the concept of mutual identity. This principle can be pictured by the metaphor of the waves and the ocean. The waves are a form of the water, a way that water "expresses" its nature, but they are not different from the water. Similarly, all things of dependent arising share in the identity of Sunyata, the Void.

While most men and women choose to remain within our familiar realm, those seeking higher consciousness choose all realms as their domain. To the Hwa Yen masters, that is the very meaning of higher consciousness—it embraces all realms. This leads to a paradoxical situation. The master holds to the Round View, or Round Reasoning, meaning that he can assert not only that A is A, but also that A is both A and not-A. And furthermore that A is neither A nor not-A. He always recognizes that from the standpoint of totality, where he makes his stand, the truths of one realm are not necessarily true in another. This explains the paradoxical utterances of Zen masters, often quoted in the West, where the master demands an apparently nonsensical answer to his questions. He is trying to lead his pupil away from realm-bound thinking as he skips merrily from one realm to another in mid-sentence, inviting the pupil not only to contemplate other realms, but actually to become a sojourner in those realms.

The modern physicist is forced to use some of the same paradoxical language as the philosophers have long had to use. They now tell us that the location of a subatomic particle cannot be known until a measurement is made. In a sense, then, it is the act of measuring that gives a definite location to the elusive particle. Putting it another way, we may say that it is the experimenter who establishes the frame of reference within which the particle can "take place." Thus the particle is dependent on an observer to have a very necessary aspect of the material world, namely location in space. Such dependence is hardly consistent with a separate, autonomous, independently acting entity. At this point, the physicist is obliged to admit that a particle is not really a particle. It is a momentary event. It resembles the dependent arising of the Buddhists more than a separate "thing." The Hwa Yen master generalizes this principle; he surrenders his own separateness and his own position in order to apprehend the wholeness of the world directly. What he comes back with is liberation.

It may be asked how, if all orders are equally valid, any order at all can be established as true. The reply of Hwa Yen is that it does not attempt to repudiate any order insofar as that order holds good within a specific realm, but it does relativize all orders, reminding us that there are other orders in other realms that are needed for our particular realm to exist and function as it does. We must remember that the Hwa Yen philosophy is for persons who have moved in some sense beyond the ordinary ethical problems of life so that they do not need the laws of this realm to guide their behavior; it is not for the ordinary citizen who depends on the law and is lost without it. The search for these levels of consciousness is not without danger. Doubtless some so-called psychotic episodes, particularly in the young, involve the temporary loss of the special frames of reference that all of us as earthlings depend upon. Such an event, coming spontaneously, is now sometimes called a "spiritual emergency," an apt title. The key question in valuing it is whether the person is able to take control and return to the consensual reality by her own effort.

How does Hwa Yen Buddhism help us to answer some of the questions we have raised? It does so by taking for granted the existence of other realms where our notions of time, space, and causality do not prevail. In the light of the interpenetration of all things, we see how other realms impinge on our own without impeding the existence of the things or events of this realm. It underlines the suggestion that our understanding of time is relative to our earthly situation, and that events that derive from other realms may enter our time world where they appear to be anomalies. But since our realm is interpenetrated by the events of other realms obeying different laws, this is to be expected. Space, too, is to be seen as relative to our measuring devices and our embodied status. Hwa Yen is helpful to average citizens also in that they need to have a sense that the human-made laws of our realm accord with universal principles, so that in following them they are acting in harmony with higher law. This is what the I Ching long ago attempted to do.

The issue of regarding events from different perspectives has been central to our investigation. In comparing synchronicities as experienced in depth psychology with parapsychological events as seen by the parapsychologists, we found that the great differences between the two arise from a matter of perspective. Parapsychology takes an "objective" stance, using a statistical approach, and depending on the calculus of probability to prove that parapsychological events have actually occurred. It denigrates "merely anecdotal" evidence. The study of synchronicities, by contrast, demands a case-by-case approach and an eye to the psychic state of the experiencer. Hwa Yen would comprehend these differences with ease. Every perspective we take illuminates certain aspects of the phenomenon and obscures certain other aspects, yet we must have some perspective in order to see consciously. To the Hwa Yen masters, this problem is known as the Obstruction of the Concealment and the Disclosure, which says that as any one aspect of a phenomenon is illuminated by consciousness a hidden aspect secretly establishes itself, like the dark side of the moon, necessary to the completeness of the moon—and of all things. This constitutes an inherent limitation of our form of consciousness. Only the awareness of totality allows all aspects of phenomena to be disclosed.

Our study brought us very quickly to the question of the different frames of reference from which synchronicities can be regarded. In the course of our inquiry, we considered a number of such events, all of them having the potential to open us to other realms, other domains of meaning, and in doing so to broaden our consciousness toward the totality of the universe. In considering the case of Jack Sullivan, buried by a cave-in of earth where he was welding and rescued by his friend Tommy Whittaker, we could explain it only by pointing to the fundamental unity that bound the two men together. Or in the case of some of the apparitions we considered, it was necessary to assume a state of unity between the two persons, agent and percipient, at the level of the deep psyche. This in turn suggested the basic unity of all things in our realm, present at all times but manifested to us only in synchronistic events. Hwa Yen raises this suggestion to the level of a universal principle: all things of dependent arising form a unity.

Our questions now shift their focus: we ask how we may gain knowledge of the laws or habits of these other realms so that no event that actually happens, either in the past or future, will appear anomalous to us. Clearly this involves a change of consciousness. In fact we will have to accustom ourselves not only to different ways of seeing the universe, but to different ways of being. Psychotherapists are aiding in the change of consciousness that is occurring. With our religious orientation in disarray, we are drifting toward widely varying kinds of conduct and widely disparate worldviews, so that it sometimes seems we can barely talk to each other, having no set of fundamentals on which to base our dialogue. In these circumstances, many previously forbidden perspectives are coming into view. The therapist prepares herself to deal with strange and even shocking events in the life of the patient by attempting to understand the frame of reference from which the patient operates. She preserves a nonjudgmental attitude, refusing to commit herself to a single realm. This of course does not mean that she condones reckless and lawless behavior any more than does the Hwa Yen master, but she recognizes that our society has given rise to many life-worlds, and that within those life-worlds many varying kinds of behavior will appear. A dim perception of the danger of a chaotic breakdown of affairs motivates the retreat into fundamentalism in many parts of the world, but a more open-eyed view leads us to press forward to a new mode of consciousness based on the experience of the wholeness of the universe, and it invites us to imagine how we can embody the sense of unity in our lives.

However, an openness to many perspectives is not the same as achieving an insight into all possible perspectives, or embracing reality in its wholeness. Here we see why in the Eastern religions some alternative states of consciousness are rated more highly than ordinary consciousness. It is because within these alternative states we can transcend the categories that limit consciousness to a few perspectives, disallowing all others. To us this would feel like omniscience—a glimpse of the mind of God.

Matriarchal Civilizations and Synchronicity

The great matriarchal civilizations of the past were based on the rituals and practices that flow out of a deep knowledge of synchronicity. An understanding of the organic unity of the whole cosmos was not confined to shamans or philosophers, but was the basis of the life of all men and women, and offered a way of living in harmony with the cosmos. Perhaps that is why these cultures were so long enduring and nonexploitative.

The ancients were profoundly aware of the cyclic and vibratory nature of our universe. They understood the two-thousand-year cycles of the Platonic month and recognized the changes that came on earth with the shifting of the zodiacal signs—floods, earthquakes, meteors, drought, famine, pestilence.

Were these not signs, synchronicities, messages telling of the need for a renewed spiritual orientation? Great celebrations came every thirty years when Saturn completed his majestic circuit of the sun, and the ever-changing phases of the moon were seen as carrying favorable or unfavorable meanings for affairs on earth. Human feeling and intuition and memory moved along with these cycles in sympathetic accord, changing with the movement of the seasons and the heavenly bodies—joyful, serene, hopeful, sublime, eerie, nostalgic, ecstatic. The harvest festivals that came with the fall equinox and the spring festivals at planting time brought the affairs of heaven and earth into accord through music, dance, and ritual. It was never questioned that human feeling and imagination—human subjectivity—fitted within the moving cycles of time as the lyrics of a song fit the melody, and this harmonic interdependence was the key to right living.

The larger rhythms unfolded into the yearly recurring patterns and customs of the people, while the smaller vibrations, many of them imperceptible to the senses, formed the energized substrata in which human beings also endured as vibrational forms. All this throbbing of life permeated the field of nature like the vapor on a summer night that becomes manifest as the morning dew. Birds and animals were seen to be effortlessly in tune with the whole field of nature, of which they formed a meaningful part. Their habits were observed with the greatest care as guides to the changing rhythms of human life.

As smaller cycles begin to be subsumed within larger wholes, we regain the ancient picture of a dynamically organized universe, each part dancing its dance or singing its song, enfolded in the context of a larger meaning field. It was a spiritual goal of human beings to live in harmony with that cosmic dance.

It is often said that we cannot return to the ways of the past, but of course that is not asked of us. What is asked is that we recover the ancient wisdom of wholeness and integrate it with the hard-won knowledge of today. That ancient wisdom is in truth no further away than our own depths, for it was lived by uncounted generations of human beings of the past. Within each one of us it lives in fragmentary and unrecognized form, or as a kind of yearning of the soul that rises up in moments of detached awareness. To reach it requires a profound shift of consciousness, for we now understand that the ancient knowledge was embedded in a way of life and a mode of consciousness quite unlike our own. We begin to see the truth of experiences such as are portrayed in the Old Testament and again in the New, and we realize that most of the world's sacred literature derives from types of awareness now all but lost to us.

As our awareness reaches toward the wholeness of the universe, we experience more of the total spectrum of possibilities that is reality. We awaken to other spiritual universes which correspond through synchronicity to our own physical universe. And we realize that what we experience in our present mode of consciousness is but a narrow band of the total realm of possibilities. This invites a certain questioning of the idea of the unconscious. To be sure, these other states are unconscious to us in our present mode, but the word itself has an insular connotation. Our own mode of consciousness may be equally unconscious to persons in a different mode, which we have no standing to denigrate.

Persons able to shift to this broader mode of consciousness by an act of will have mastered a human potentiality that is latent—and usually involuntary—in all of us. They have acquired the technique of the breakthrough, the "rupture of the planes," the passage through an "instability threshold" to come to other structures of consciousness. The goal of our searching, then, at least for those whose goal is more expansive consciousness, should be not only a better adjustment within our present level, but an acquaintance with more of the total spectrum. Those who achieve this will become the teachers of tomorrow.

The Pygmy Hunters

I would like to suggest how the primal cultures lived out the synchronistic worldview by two illustrations taken from different times and places, but both having a certain kinship of meaning. The first is an example of the hunting magic of a pygmy hunting tribe described by Jean Gebser, in which he shows how four hunters, three men and a woman, living in what he calls the magical structure of consciousness, evoke a particular field with their hunting magic.[7]

The hunters are seen to draw a picture of an antelope on the ground at dawn, which they strike in the neck with an arrow at the precise moment when the rising sun falls on the picture. The group then goes out on the hunt and returns with a dead antelope, struck by an arrow in the precise spot where the arrow struck the drawing. There follows the erasure of the drawing, along with an appropriate rite to divert the effects of the killing from the hunters. All this is accomplished in absolute silence. It has been suggested that since they are at the "magic" level of being, these tribal members do not quite take responsibility for their act—instead it is the sun-arrow which kills the animal, while they are merely the executors.

It seems to me that we understand this best if we see it as the evocation of a field; or alternatively, in religious terms, we might say a higher awareness (the field) is operative throughout the action, with the hunters being merely the agents who, by their magical procedures, tune into the field or evoke its powerful spell. In this way, we get a beginning sense of the world field in which both hunter and animal are enveloped, with the tribal members carefully conducting their ritual so as to avoid rending the seamless web of the field and preserve its sovereign harmony. Because we ourselves still have these magical processes moving within us, we find it possible to enter into the psychic conditions in which such a rite transpires.

The drawing of the picture is carried out intently, in semidarkness, in a state of mounting suspense and anticipation, for it is known that the rising sun will soon strike the drawing. At the instant when this happens, the leader of the group, caught up in the sudden surge of emotion and energy of the magical moment (the *kairos*), in a single unified movement of the whole being, plunges the arrow into the picture. Not through his willing but of its own volition, it seems, the arrow hits the neck. The act is accompanied by an instantaneous knowledge not localized in consciousness, but rather pervading his whole being—he is energized for the hunt, senses how it will go. The same sudden surge of anticipatory understanding instantly pervades the whole group; the sense of a favorable outcome is born in every one. Their ritual has given birth to an analogy never consciously stated: as the sun-arrow struck the picture, so their arrows will strike the animal. From then on, there is a fatedness about the unfolding of the drama. Silently they go out to complete the hunt, and silently they return with the dead animal, and their silence maintains the spell which holds throughout the world field. The concluding ritual not only diverts the effects of the killing from them, but withdraws them from that world field.

What we see here is a meaning field or pervasive atmosphere linking the inner state of the hunters and the natural world without. Together they form one world, one energy field, one unified pattern. The air is charged with high tension deriving from the age-old importance of the hunt for the very existence of the tribe, but this energy has been disciplined (channeled) by the appropriate ritual, and the hunters go out not as an unruly mob, but as a purposeful group intent on finding and stalking the game. They are "of one mind," as we say. It is as though, by their ritual, they have brought themselves into a state of complete harmony with nature in her primordial state; time and space have been set aside, and a creative drama is enacted involving humankind and nature. Or perhaps we could say that the purposes of the hunters have been conjoined to the flow of nature in a single, unified enactment. The appearance of the antelope may be seen as a synchronicity belonging to the archetypal field that has been evoked. The life dance of the antelope and the dance of the hunters meet in a fateful moment, a blending of rhythms. The whole situation reminds us of those dream instances in which a particular event is portrayed in a dream, sometimes literally, sometimes symbolically, and afterward is enacted in outer life, as though the deep psyche were already aware of and involved in the trend of the unfolding field process. The possible collaboration of hunter and prey within the field cannot be discounted.

Although it is often said that magic is worked by way of the unconscious, what stamps this magical ritual as remarkable is the hunters' *willed intention* to evoke such a field and the introduction of a counterspell to realize their own intentions. They carry out an analogical ritual proven by experience to be accompanied by the desired field effects. Even beyond this is the disciplining of the emotions to achieve the goals desired by the ego. If we take as our criterion of consciousness the manner of the ego's relating to the field intensities, the action of the hunters is not necessarily to be seen as unconscious. I do not wish to be interpreted as advocating the practice of magic, but only to point out that a knowledge of the energies involved in such a field can lead to a conscious rather than an unconscious relationship to them. The field itself, of course, may be described by the word *unconscious,* but it seems to me that we reduce its strangeness and our own confusion by speaking of a *spell,* a *meaning field,* or a *field of awareness.* We also open ourselves to the form of consciousness appropriate to a living, breathing universe as we live and breathe with it.

The Athapaskan Hunters

Another example taken from a hunting culture will show the primordial way of relating to the field, and will remind us of the vibrancy and excitement that come from being a part of nature in her dynamic wholeness. This example is reported by Hugh Brody, a modern anthropologist, who portrays the lives of the Athapaskan (or Athabascan) Indians of northeast British Columbia.[8] In the section quoted below, he describes how a hunt is proposed, but, as he says, the planning for the hunt does not resemble anything that the white man's world would understand as planning. "Between a proposal to go hunting and actual departure there is a large and perplexing divide."

> The way to understand this kind of decision-making, as also to live by and even share it, is to recognize that some of the most important variables are subtle, elusive, and extremely hard or impossible to assess with finality. The Athapaskan hunter will move in a direction and at a time that are determined by a sense of weather (to indicate a variable that is easily grasped if all too easily oversimplified by the one word) and by a sense of rightness. He will also have ideas about animal movement, his own and others' patterns of land use. But already the nature of the hunter's decision-making is being misrepresented by this kind of listing. To disconnect the variables, to compartmentalize the thinking, is to fail to acknowledge its sophistication and completeness. He considers variables as a composite, in parallel, and with the help of a blending of the metaphysical and the obviously pragmatic. To make a good, wise, sensible hunting choice is to accept the interconnection of all possible factors, and avoids the mistake of seeking rationally to focus on any one consideration that is held as primary. What is more, the decision is taken in the doing; there is no step or pause between theory and practice. As a consequence, the decision, like the action from which it is inseparable—is always alterable (and therefore may not even be termed a decision). The hunter moves in a chosen direction; but, highly sensitive to so many shifting considerations, he is always ready to change his directions.[9]

Planning, as other cultures understand the notion, is at odds with this kind of sensitivity and would confound such flexibility.

Here we see the hunter immersed in his world field, afloat in it, sensitively attuned to its every nuance, easy and relaxed, alert and flexibly flowing with its mood at some level below that of words and calculations. His course of action blends in perfect harmony with the course of nature, always open, always present to her ways, like a lover who moves in perfect accord with the arousal of the beloved, or like a musician strumming his instrument and humming the melody in gentle harmony with the mood of his listeners. Thought and action are one; inner and outer are one.

The hunters sense the secret tie that links character to event, person to life drama, tribe to the wholeness of nature. They know that the path we discover through the world is the only one we could possibly discover, being who we are and the world as it is. Or rather, they do not "know" it with their heads; they simply live as if it were true. Their relaxed alertness, their openness to the total ambience, enables them to discover the tendency of the field situation in the very process of its unfolding. For the "secret tie" is the Tao, the meaning, the way, the path we tread, whether on the hunt for game or for success, riches, love, or any of the thousand things that lead us on. And the "game" is not only the large animal, but the game of life itself.

This kind of flowing movement is very close to the dream state, and so the hunters understand it. In the old days, they explain to the author, there were great hunter-dreamers. These men could find the game in their dreams, locate the trail, and make the kill, all in the dream state. Then, when the time was right, they would take to the trail, find the animal, and make the kill in the outer world. There is power in this way of doing things, say the Athapaskans, power the white man does not understand. Even their own young people are beginning to forget the old ways, the old wisdom.

Hugh Brody gives another example of this same tribal group when they were moving into a new hunting area and needed confirmation that their choice of a place near the Bluestone River was a good one. Their method was to erect a "medicine cross" by stripping a tall pine tree of its branches and bark and attaching a crosspiece near the top with a smaller crosspiece at each end. A panel, also shaped like a cross, was attached near the base of the pole. Fastened to both the pole and the main crosspiece were clothing, medicine bundles, and drawings of animals that had appeared in the people's dreams.

The whole construction, which rose to twice the height of a man, could be taken as a symbolic linking of inner and outer worlds.

On the night the cross was completed, one of the elders had a dream. In his dream, a young cow moose came out of the Bluestone Creek area, walked around the base of the cross, and then went off in the direction from which she had come. Two days later, the hunters discovered the tracks of a young cow moose, and following these found that the animal had circled the cross and returned to Bluestone Creek. They recognized the tracks as those of the animal seen in the dream. This was an augury, a reply from nature herself to their question: yes, this was an area that would provide for the needs of the tribe.[10]

The Athapaskans' medicine cross grows out of a metaphysics at once simple and profound, as though there is a higher power or spirit pervading the entire region, setting the patterns of the life of human and animal, forest and grassland. All go through their life cycles within that wholeness, their seed time and harvest, their growth and decay, the eternal dance of life, all of them dependent upon the will of the higher power that choreographs the whole. Within the stillness everything is registered—the frightened cry of a deer, the ecstatic call of a bird—for each calls to all the rest in a language remote from words. Their paths need to intersect in ways most favorable and least disturbing to the whole fabric. Since it is the nature of human beings to be dependent upon plant and animal life for sustenance, sacrifice is part of the eternal plan. No doubt this is the origin of the sacrificial rituals of past civilizations: as plants and animals must sacrifice themselves that men and women may live, so humans must sacrifice that gods may live.

The setting up of the medicine cross is a simple act of divination, an effort to learn the will of the higher power and its tendency so as to guide the tribal life in accordance with that will. And the answer comes in the quiet ways in which nature replies—by the gift of a dream, and by the wandering journey of the young cow moose as she circles the cross. All is in correspondence, all is in harmony. The spirit of the region offers its reply to all who are attuned to her voice: yes, the place and the time are auspicious. There is a way of being in the world that rejoices in the harmonic whispering of the whole.

The Tibetan Physician

An unbroken chain connects the wisdom of the primal peoples with Eastern philosophies and spiritual practices still very much alive today. As we begin to consider certain of these practices, we will try to hold to the Eastern way of remaining interior to the phenomenon we seek to understand, or, better still, to move along with pleasurable anticipation, trying to blend our voices in an Eastern melody.

Consider, as an example, how the Dalai Lama's physician, Yeshi Dhonden, trained in traditional Tibetan healing methods, diagnosed a case of congenital heart failure after only a brief examination of a patient whose medical condition was unknown to him.[11] The Eastern physician, like the Western doctors who had invited him to visit their hospital, interpreted breathing and pulse, both of them rhythmic processes, as bearers of meaning, but from that point on his method was wholly different. The Western way is to read the pulse by counting and comparing the number with a norm established statistically. It uses conscious methods and can "know" only by differentiating one rate from another—establishing a division, a "twoness." The Tibetan physician, by contrast, took an intuitive reading of the pulse itself; what he came up with was a picture of the pathology, a symbolic reading which was mysteriously in agreement with the Western medical diagnosis. His training allowed him to hear the pulse speaking in its own language.

We might even say that Yeshi Dhonden allowed himself to dream the diagnosis. "Long, long before [the patient] was born," he said, "a wind had come and blown open a deep gate that must never be opened. Through it charge the full waters of her river. . . ." So he related the dream that rose before his inner eye as he took the wrist of the sick woman in his hand. He allowed the patient to speak to him by the pulsing of her blood, a universal language. Before the examination, he had purified himself by bathing, fasting, and prayer, ritual actions to insure that no impurity of his own would contaminate the process, thus preparing himself to be a faithful recipient of the knowledge that awaited him. He had learned through spiritual training to enter voluntarily into the dream state, and could trust himself to dream veridically. A great mystery is hidden in this quiet act of empathy, and we scarcely have a language to describe it, let alone practice it.

He understood the connection between rhythm and meaning in a way different from our own, and in accordance with that understanding had developed subtle translations of rhythm into imagery and meaning. As he meditated on the rhythm of the patient's pulse and brought himself into a like rhythm (a resonant state), he came into correspondence with the patient's condition, and the images that formed spontaneously in his mind were the pictorial or symbolic representation of that condition. In a word, clairvoyance.

The physician attends to both rhythm—pulsating energy—and meaning in a single action, which can be separated conceptually but not in the practice itself. He throbs with her throbbing, dreams with her dreaming in images that the patient might well have dreamed herself, but long forgotten. As they become one united whole, it matters little whether he dreams the dream or she relates her dream to him, for it is the same dream.

Using Jung's language, we might say that Yeshi Dhonden had tuned into the "absolute knowledge" of the unconscious, for his picture included the etiology of the condition as well as its current status. The Taoists would say that he had tuned into the eternal images in the Tao, which have a formative influence on world processes. In light of our current discussion, we might say that he was aligning himself with that deeper imagistic process, operating at a universal level in nondual attunement.

Such abilities remain dormant within us for lack of a philosophical outlook that would make them meaningful, and the modern physician surrenders his native powers to a mechanistic worldview. He lacks a *weltanschauung* that would conceive of image and symbol, rhythm and meaning as acausally linked within an organic patterning field of which he forms a vital part. He remains "outside" the illness picture, while the traditional physician moves "inside" the field of awareness.

Unfortunately the account of this diagnosis does not tell how the Tibetan physician would treat this patient. Since it was a case of congenital heart deficiency, perhaps he would feel as helpless as his Western counterparts to effect a cure. Perhaps, however, the universal nondual stance would yield an opportunity based on the wider circumstances available in the moment. John Blofeld tells of such an experience:

> While gardening in Bangkok a few months ago, I managed to get a drop of poisonous cactus juice in my eye. The pain was frightful and I was sure that my sight would be seriously affected. Strangely

> enough Bangkok's one and only Tibetan lama, who had not visited me for two years, dropped in the very next day. He uttered a mantra and blew into my eye. In a few days, the symptoms of poisoning were gone and my sight completely recovered. However, I was under daily treatment by an English doctor, and there is no way to know whether my very rapid recovery was wholly, partly, or not at all due to the lama's healing power.[12]

Whether or not Blofeld was healed by the Tibetan lama, we do see a synchronicity in the lama's appearance on that particular day. Perhaps he "saw" the need by way of clairvoyant vision and responded to it. Able to enter that deep well where all the waters of the world flow in a single stream, he was also able to come out again in an effort to bring healing. We could speak of this movement as a uniting of the inner and outer.

According to the Eastern philosopher, the problem of unifying inner and outer can be seen on two levels: to ordinary consciousness they are clearly separate, and the question is how to bring them together; but to the enlightened, they are one—eternal and inseparable—and the question of bringing them together is a pseudo-problem. It resembles the koan, the paradoxical utterance of the Zen master that cannot be rationally understood, and forces the pupil to break out of customary thought patterns.

If this is the case, then the real problem is one of developing the human soul in such a way as to achieve the enlightened condition and to be able to move between states of consciousness by way of rituals and spiritual practices. The very essence of enlightenment is the bringing together of inner and outer through spiritual disciplines. Other well-known paths to enlightenment include the practices of painting, calligraphy, archery, swordsmanship, martial arts, flower arranging, the tea ceremony, and medicine, to mention a few.

Consider the Zen painter. Wishing to paint a willow tree, she first of all cleanses herself of all impurities and agitations, then immerses himself in the ways of the willow. She lives its willowiness, flows with its flowing, dances with its dancing. She "becomes" the willow, as the artists say. Then, brush in hand, without conscious effort or contrivance, she makes a few rapid strokes on the canvas, in the unquestionable likeness of the willow. It is as if not she but something beyond herself wields the brush as it moves in her hand in the rhythm of the willow, and the strokes that appear on the canvas express its nature almost as if the willow had painted itself. Not a photographic likeness, but a revelation of the soul of the willow appears on the page. There is a conjunction of the inner and the outer by way of the spiritual discipline of the painter, her profound immersion in the living, pulsing essence of the life of the tree.

The paintings that are made in this way glow with a mysterious spiritual power; they whisper of the life rhythms that vibrate timelessly in both the tree and the painter, an awareness that breathed them both into being. Through the act of painting, the artist has brought herself into harmony not only with the tree, but with the cosmic pulse that whispers in both the willow and herself, the great heartbeat that quickens all the many forms of nature.

Is not this a synchronicity—one voluntarily produced, not by an act of will, but by consciously entering into a state where these happy conjunctions of inner and outer can occur? The painting appears as another "arrangement" of the cosmic arranger, the great pattern maker or choreographer, a single, unique act infused with the whole mystery of being—a synchronicity. In a sense, it is willed out of the devotion of the painter and her delicacy of perception, and yet can never be willed.

When the distinction between inner and outer falls away, the first step has been taken by which all other polarities are nullified—those between fullness and emptiness, time and eternity, good and evil, birth and death. We could look upon this act of unification as the reversal of God's work in creating the visible universe by a series of divisions, or perhaps as the return of the universe to its original wholeness to complete the cycle that began with "the Fall."

In such an act, the mind-body becomes completely transparent; there is a sudden awakening to the transparency of all things. They become illuminated by an inner light and seem to interfuse, all held together by the cosmic awareness. The whole objective world takes on the guise of symbol and metaphor, expressing something beyond itself and at the same time revealing its coherence with the world drama in which it participates. The Mind that is experienced at such a time, a Reality eternally aware of itself and eternally present, is yet dependent on individual minds for its recognition in the world.

All this is to suggest that, to the Eastern masters, synchronicities are not very important. Being involuntary, they are just what "befalls" in certain psychic states, when a higher spiritual power reveals its presence, and the meaning that is ever-present becomes visible even to those who would not see. The master who trains himself to participate in these powers sees nothing very special in such happenings; he would rather attend to his spiritual discipline so as to be even better able to align himself with the cosmic powers.

There are many accounts of the effects of such disciplines. One of the most engaging descriptions I know is found in the little book by Eugen Herrigel, a German professor of philosophy, in which he tells of his six years of training in Japanese archery.[13] Interestingly enough, although this book never mentions God and even puts the word *spiritual* in quotes most of the time, one cannot but see that it is discussing the way to transcendence. "If one really wishes to be master of an art," D. T. Suzuki says in his introduction to this book,

> Technical knowledge is not enough. One has to transcend technique so that the art becomes an "artless art" growing out of the Unconscious. In the case of archery, the hitter and the hit are no longer two opposing objects, but are one reality. The archer ceases to be conscious of himself as the one who is engaged in hitting the bull's eye which confronts him. This state of unconsciousness is realized only when, completely empty and rid of the self, he becomes one with the perfecting of his technical skill, though there is in it something of a quite different order which cannot be attained by any progressive study of the art.[14]

With these words, Suzuki tries to describe a state of consciousness reached in the practice of archery that points to something far beyond the sport. Like the hunters who become one with their hunting grounds or the physician who becomes one with his patient, the archer sacrifices ego claims and calculations, and arrives not at a state of confusion but at a new level of order and power, but it is no longer "his" power. He is as sure of the power that sustains him as a swimmer knows that the water will hold him up; then he can relax and allow the power to do what only it can do. In the West we might say that he achieves "self-realization," or perhaps discovers "unrealized potentialities," or even that he arrives at a level of "ego transcendence," but all these expressions fail to convey the total immersion of the human ego in a Life that stands far beyond the ego's attainments but can become conscious of Itself only through the ego. Once this is known, it is no longer a question of "my skill" or "my realization," for something of an altogether different order springs into being.

> To begin with, the pupil understands these instructions—and he can hardly do otherwise—as meaning that it is sufficient for him to refrain from observing and thinking about the behavior of his opponent. He takes this non-observation very seriously and controls himself at every step. But he fails to notice that, by concentrating his attention on himself, he inevitably sees himself as the combatant who has at all costs to avoid watching his opponent. Do what he may, he still has him secretly in mind. Only in appearance has he detached himself from him, and the more he endeavors to forget him the more tightly he binds himself to him.[15]

Herrigel describes the attitude required of the expert swordsman, who, like the archer or the physician, must purify himself of all self-serving thoughts. He must accomplish the difficult feat of clearing from his mind any thought of the opponent or of the life-and-death struggle in which he is engaged.

Only after much heartbreaking practice and an intense struggle with himself does the pupil arrive at a state of purposeless detachment or total emptiness. This is followed automatically by a change in which "It" takes over for his conscious calculation, and the fatal thrust is made even before consciousness has registered the opening. Like the painter who immerses herself in the nature of the willow tree and so makes contact with a higher life, the swordsman comes into a power far exceeding his own, and stakes his life on it. The master swordsman will avoid any contest with a man of lesser attainments, because he would not wish to kill him.

Herrigel testifies that his teacher, unlike the struggling pupil, "danced" the ceremony of hitting the target with his arrow, shooting from bright daylight into deep night with only a taper, long and thin as a knitting needle, to mark the target's location. His first arrow hit the bull's-eye, and his second splintered the shaft of the first. But this level of skill is only the outward confirmation of an inner event, an attainment that is the evidence of a "profound and far-reaching contest of the archer with himself." In what he calls the hardest schooling of his life, Herrigel learned to give up all preoccupation with himself, the bow and arrow, and the target, and to let "It" take aim, loose the arrow, and hit the target.

My guess is that the master archer would not be able to match this feat every time—if he did it would not be interesting, for he would be a mere machine. It is more likely that he was able to recognize those times when inner aptitude and outer circumstance come together to create an auspicious moment, like two wave forms that ever and again come into phase and amplify each other; feeling this as a sense of empowerment, he could then act upon it. That he could also summon those event patterns into being is also possible.

The description of the art of the Japanese swordsman, practiced at the risk of life itself and involving an overcoming of the fear of death, offers dramatic evidence of the power afforded by these disciplines. There is a transcendence of the opposites, a resolution of conflict not reached by any strictly mental effort, but by a quantum leap of the whole being that is felt as a state of emptiness, less "self-realization" than self-abandonment, a sacrifice of the ego's purposes in favor of a larger Life. The "It" that then takes over and hits the target could be described as the activation of a charged field having the attributes of life and awareness, and the archer's posture as a rhythmic attunement to the more encompassing and dynamic field, a kind of dance in which one simply cannot miss, a very convincing experience to those who know or witness it. The struggle of the swordsman or the archer to reach that state of purposelessness is the behavioral analogue of the meditator struggling with a koan, or the Western patient struggling actively with a symptom. That struggle is the "journey"; it demands the whole being. It seems not unlike Jung's descriptions of the awakening of the Self, the transcendent wholeness of the personality.

A Universal Energy

If we will allow the often insignificant "chance" occurrences we call synchronicities to open us to new understandings, we may discover new ways of being in the world. Although I have brought forward experiences from the East to light our way, I hope that these would not be seen as exotic events occurring only in remote cultures. The energies demonstrated in synchronicities are surely available to all of us.

Many synchronicities as we have come to know them relate to times of transition, when our accustomed patterns are in sudden turbulent movement and the ego's attitudes are in temporary abeyance. Things then demonstrate a capacity to express symbolic meanings, and individuals may find themselves strangely and mysteriously propelled into unaccustomed states of being. The meaning of the time, formerly to all appearances confined to our heads, now seems to envelop the entire field, and to guide all entities in purposive ways. Indeed, the meaning seems to take on a life of its own and to willfully express itself through all things. As rhythm, as symbol, as pattern, it becomes the propelling force of the whole rather than a passive aspect of the situation. The symbolic level of reality is revealed as more real and more powerful than the "real." It opens to us in the life dramas that make up the fatedness of life. To the ancients, this fatedness was the work of the gods, for how else could one interpret a shaping power with which one must contend, whether in acquiescence, resignation, or defiance?

Though the future is hidden in the recesses of time, some control could be sought through divination and rituals of evocation. To evoke (from the Latin *evocare*: *e,* or "out," plus *vocare,* "to call," from *vox* or *vocis,* "voice") is to summon forth, as from seclusion. An evocation is an act of calling forth, as from a cave or a mountain fastness—wherever the gods are known to dwell—or the summoning of a spirit by incantation. By evocation an appeal is made (or a resonance set up) to the deep generative sources in the very ground of being, both within us and in the universe as well. Note that "vocation" is a calling or summons from a higher authority to a work one is meant to do by reason of an inner bent. The inner bent or predisposition leads the individual to "resonate" to the higher calling; it represents the trace of the larger pattern within each particle of the whole. It is destiny (or destination), and in the following of it one finds the real meaning of life. But also, from another perspective, it is sound, or "calling," a summons to action that comes at once from within and from afar. Vibration, rhythm, and sound, like symbols, echo between the levels of being and so harmonize the levels.

In Greek tragedy, we see such an unfolding of destiny as the hero plays out his fated role against the backdrop of a chorus of elders or villagers, whose long, long memory reaches back into the remote past, enabling them to recognize the pattern at work. The protagonist (from the Greek *protos,* "first in order," and *agonistes,* "actor" or "struggler") carries the wholeness pattern within him and cannot escape its shaping power; the Greeks spoke of the three Fates, all feminine beings, while the Romans knew this force as fate (from the Latin *fatum,* "oracle," "what is ordained by the gods"). The gods speak to us in the fatedness of our lives. Instead of "fate," we sometimes speak of the individual's "appointed lot" (proportion, share of the whole). In this way, chance (from *cadere, cadentia*), in the sense of rhythm or cadence, enters the picture, along with the intent of a higher unifying awareness.

It is a mysterious thing to contemplate how life works out in subterranean ways to insure the particular convergence of inner disposition and outer circumstance that we know as fate, as if the deep psyche had been working all along to bring about the particular destiny that belongs to each individual. How can this be, unless there is in truth a secret linkage between the person and the world phase, such that, in the depths, the connections between inner and outer are forged, not to be broken unless by a mighty effort of the whole being? Our fate forms a synchronistic convergence of inner and outer, a mysterious uniting of chance and meaning.

When we speak of this connectedness, we are referring to something more powerful and at the same time more mysterious than a mere exchange of signals, something nearer to the "holding" power of love, a power that works by radiance, like the light of the sun, rather than by force or pressure. It is without compulsion or the application of force such as that which brings movement in a causal explanatory scheme. On the one hand it seems to be maintained as though by an interlocking of particular vibratory frequencies, but on the other hand it recalls the "natural sympathy" assumed by the Hermetic philosophers to unite the levels of being. Are we amiss to call it love? Can we allow ourselves to think that resonance and love are somehow allied? Notice how courtship, whether in birds or animals or human beings, is often seen as a dance, a reciprocal, rhythmic to-and-fro movement that reconciles the opposites and brings inner state and outer event together to complete the wholeness pattern.

Isn't this meaningful connectedness also synchronicity in its omnipresent aspect, operating behind the scenes, so subtly interwoven in the very fabric of things that we remain unaware of it? Silently working beneath the surface, it brings about all fateful encounters, all meaningful arrangements. Why do certain persons come into one's life at a particular time? Or how does a letter from a long-lost friend happen to arrive when we are thinking of her? How is it that certain paths open before us, while others remain stubbornly closed? Is it that the inner readiness is not there to bring about the fateful convergence? Or that the path we have taken is not really our own, but was imposed by convention or the pressure of elders? And how is it that when we have set our feet on a spiritual path the openings that occur generally lead to progress along the way?

Jean Gebser has a way of describing this:

> There was thought before the thinker, as there was breath before the breather, and sight before the eye. To explain this in rational terms we must suppose that the power of a possible manifestation itself creates an organ able to manifest this power. As applied to our own lives this statement shows that it is our inherent possibilities which shape the circumstances and the way we lead our lives in such a way as to allow these possibilities to become effective. In other words, the components in us which are to enter our mental awareness also create the preconditions for their own effective realization.
>
> As long as we fail to see this, we attribute our disposition and unrealized latency—which strive toward their necessary unfolding—to an intrusion of "chance" or "destiny." But chance and destiny are merely the agencies which release the intensities in ourselves which are ready for manifestation. It is these intensities that cause the decisive events to "happen by chance" or "destine" these events for us. The intensities manage the chance and destiny so that the possibilities for their own manifestation occur. In a word, we are our chances and destiny.[16]

We are the footprints we make on the shoreline of the world. Character is fate. At the deep level where fate unfolds, self and world cannot be distinguished but form an inseparable whole. Insofar as we are not consciously aware of that deep spark of ourselves that unfolds as our destiny, our "lot," our share of the whole, we are obliged to make a journey to realize it. By bringing up Eastern spiritual practices, I have tried to offer some examples of what can happen when we do at last come home.

The word *intensities* appears three times in Gebser's short quotation above. We have spoken of intensity before; in this context, it refers to a "stretching," and comes from a time when many of the metaphors that pictured forth our life were drawn from the realm of music—the right stretching of the strings brought forth precisely the right or true tone. Intensity has something to do with tension and energy, with sound and vibration, and at the same time with truth, conscience, and the inner knower who knows when we are being true to ourselves and can therefore act with genuine power. We seek the circumstances that arouse our intensity to draw forth what is merely potential in us, for we want to explore our own limits. We need to be stretched.

A great gulf separates the individual who is dragged along unconsciously by the archetypal powers (usually those in the form of the unfinished business of the parents), and the one who goes knowingly and in full awareness of her fate. If synchronicity in the sense of the meaningful connectedness of inner and outer is at work in the shaping of one's fate, we can act knowingly only if we can discover the intent of the deep psyche. Then the fatedness is transformed into a life task. This is particularly important for persons who were victimized in childhood, and who ask, "Why me? Why me?" Instead of looking backward to the wounds of the past, one deals with one's wounds and then takes on the task of the future, thus moving from the victim role to become the master of fate. In this way, life becomes a meaningful symbolic enactment, a story, a ritual, a unique answer to the summons of the higher powers.

The transformation from meaningless living—going through the motions—to meaningful living marks the single most important upward step in a life drama. No other change enables us to bear the inevitable losses and hardships of life with dignity; none offers an alternative to the bitterness, cynicism, the slow-burning resentment and violence, both mental and physical, that we see among us. In meaningful living, we lay claim to our birthright, our energy flows naturally, and we offer our measure to the world.

If I were asked how to move toward more meaningful living, I would say without hesitation: begin to appreciate the symbolic nature of things and events, and to live the symbolic life. There is nothing in this world that cannot be seen in its symbolic aspect, whatever else it may be. Symbols point beyond themselves and awaken the sleeping imagination. They point to the universal aspect of all events. While conscience prickles and logic labors, symbols leap, and delight in their leaping. They have the power to link the levels of being, connecting ordinary consciousness with a transcendent world, like the angels who went up and down Jacob's ladder a very long time ago.

In symbolic thinking, connectedness predominates over separateness. We think in this way when we speak metaphorically of animals, as when we say, "Don't badger me"; "I will ferret it out"; "He was outfoxed by his rival"; or "We must get our bearings" (from the connection of the bear to Ursa Major, the great orienting constellation of the northern sky). Every animal incarnates a rhythmic pattern (or, if you will, a morphogenetic field), an archetypal form, as in the bear, the ram, the dog, or the bull. The ancients paid tribute to this aspect of the animal when they kept it in the temple precinct and worshipped its mysterious evocation of an aspect of the larger harmony, naming it a god, or archetypal form. They saw these same forms reflected in the heavenly realms—or rather, the earthly forms mirrored those in the heavens.

Earlier in our study, we pointed out how symbols are related to symptoms, the one a "throwing together," the other a "falling together." In this way, symbols may substitute for symptoms and so bring healing. If we will open ourselves to the symbolic world, we will have fewer chronic illnesses and fewer symptoms, for we will see our struggles and conflicts giving birth to creative symbols rather than eventuating in symptoms. Though there is pain in this process, and courage is needed, we become protagonists, not victims, in the effort to cope with life's challenges.

Through symbols, we can see the world with the eyes of the magus, to whom all things are signs and signatures, and are seen as process and movement. Objects and events dance along on the stage of the world in their symbolic aspect, having the quality of transparency. Like shadows, they unite or divide, expand or contract, fade or emerge in relation to the dance of all other things. From this perspective, we may see synchronicities as analogous to the emergence of living forms out of the Void, creative events that speak of the connectedness of all things.

Sometimes, in moments of intense joy or sorrow or grief or love, we approach the powers of the gods, and energies not ordinarily known to us are evoked. At such times, material forms may be caught up in a way that is analogous to the work of the gods in creating the manifest world. An event occurs which we recognize as a synchronicity. Today these happenings take us by surprise, but if we could regain the knowledge of the initiates or reconnect to our own depths, we would recognize the action of spiritual energies that have their own intelligence.

Unimagined possibilities open to us as we try, by a great shift of consciousness, to enter more fully into a living, changing world shaped and ordered by higher intelligence, a world in which we are all branches of the same tree. Surely we would become more gentle, not out of resignation but out of trust. We might become less hurried and harried, with less need to push, coerce, demand, and manipulate our world. We would allow events to open before us, if they will, rather than trying to force them. For want of imagination, we have demeaned ourselves, have lived not only in physical poverty but even more in spiritual poverty. The word *sacrifice* would again enter our vocabulary. And the world would respond to our change of consciousness by offering new possibilities.

Once again, the ancient approach of the I Ching lights our way:

> The forces constituting the visible world are transcendent ones. Tao is taken here in the sense of an all-embracing entelechy [form-giving potential]. It transcends the spatial world, but it acts upon the visible world by means of the images, i.e., ideas inherent in it . . . and what hereby comes into being are the objects. An object is spatial, that is, defined by its corporeal limits, but it cannot be understood without knowledge of the Tao underlying it.[17]

We may take this quite literally, and assume that the form-giving potential known as the Tao is capable of bringing physical things into being, and that it acts by way of images. This becomes thinkable when we are reminded that an object is not a fixed and changeless entity, but rather an ever-changing vibratory process. By conceiving it as a process, we open it up and make possible an interpenetration between thought (or image) and object that does not seem possible in another view. Things become permeable, and mind and matter entwine creatively, as the Tao, the transcendent, formative power, is seen at work within them. They cannot be known apart from their participation in the Tao.

Having penetrated this far, we turn once more to the I Ching and read, "[The Tao is] a borderline conception lying at the extreme edge of the world of appearances." In it, the opposites "cancel out in non-discrimination," but are still potentially present:

> These seeds . . . point to something that corresponds firstly to the visible, i.e., something in the nature of an image; secondly to the audible, i.e., something in the nature of words; thirdly to extension in space, i.e., something with a form. But these three things are not clearly distinguished and definable, they are a non-spatial and non-temporal unity, having no above and below or front and back.[18]

And finally:

> In their alternation and reciprocal effect, the two fundamental forces [Yin and Yang] serve to explain all the phenomena in the world. Nonetheless, there remains something that cannot be explained in terms of the interaction of these forces, a final why. This ultimate meaning of Tao is the spirit, the divine, the unfathomable in it, that which must be revered in silence.[19]

And so, confronted by an ultimate mystery, we continue our dance, confident that from the Source that brought us into being will come new forms of guidance, new openness, new possibilities of loving participation. We will continue our exploration at the edge of the unknown because that is our nature and our fascination. We will seek out our lot, learn the many rhythms of the dance. The emotions that accompany its motions make up the color and the intensity of life. Change and movement, unfolding within the polarities that establish the contours of our lives, will alternate with stasis and stillness, as we dance and the world dances with us.

Synchronicities now become a tiny slit, a tear in the fabric of our spacetime world, peering through which we perceive the dim outlines of another, unified world order, and beyond that mystery upon mysteries. It is possible that the world orders we glimpse might turn out to be a place known to us from of old—might, indeed, open up the avenue of return to our true homeland, the half-remembered reality.

EPILOGUE

I entered the training program of the C. G. Jung Institute of Los Angeles at the age of fifty-two for what were to be eight years of training to be a Jungian analyst. Our training group was made up of a heterogeneous core of eight who would take three years of classroom work (one night a week) to be followed, after the first year, by supervised work in the clinic. All of us had received Jungian analysis for some years, and this continued while we were in the program. There were two men in the group; two of the women were the wives of analysts; nearly all of us were over forty; some were familiar with the Jungian community, while others, like myself, were strangers. We were told that the Institute would back us in our endeavors, but we understood that not all of us would make the grade. We were competitors rather than friends. As I entered the training program, I had one of those big dreams that foretell how things are to go.

> *I am on a visit to La Sierra, the hospital where I had formerly worked as a social worker. The whole place is magnificently changed. The entry has become a large two-story space enclosed in glass, the windows extending to the top and going back over part of the roof to offer a view of the sky. From the great staircase at the back, you can look down on a huge waiting area of sofas, tables, and lamps. I go around to the right to the office of Julie, our secretary, but do not find her. In a little office nearby, Dr. Bob works, and I sit and talk with him for a few minutes. Then I go out and explore the place and find it filled with the patients and their visitors, even while it is being reconstructed. I go out to the back and find a splendid high-vaulted entryway of shining brown marble, with great circular columns at the front, like a Florentine portico. As I stand looking out to the back, I see a vista of great stonework, perhaps columns and arcades. I cannot tell whether they are the ruins of an ancient city or buildings under construction. Beyond this is a vast opening in the earth like a large quarry, possibly the source of the stone for these*

building projects. The size and depth of that abyss is frightening. Back inside I try to discover the place to eat by going up and down stairways and through busy corridors crowded with people. Several people try to help me, but still I cannot discover the eating place. All the while, I marvel that Dr. Bob has so thoroughly revised and rebuilt La Sierra.

Like all great dreams, this one deserves much contemplation. What struck me from the beginning, as even in the dream, was the remarkable reconstruction of the healing center, and the way it now extended from the most modern to the very ancient forms of architecture. Its magnificence exceeded anything I could have imagined. However—and this haunted me all through my years in the program like a portent of disaster—I was confronted at the back of the hospital with a view of what may have been either a ruin or a pleroma, an overwhelming vision of the abyss of the collective unconscious. Although there was no doubt of the splendor of what had been accomplished, I was left with ambiguity.

Another worrisome aspect of the dream was the striking absence of the feminine. Julie, the department secretary, was referred to, but not seen in the dream. She was a fine secretary, on whom all the professionals depended, but a modest woman contented with her lot, while Dr. Bob, the medical director, was a great spirit and a fine physician, with much charm and humor. It was as though he had done all the work of restructuring the healing center, while Julie, representing the feminine, was absent. Moreover, I was only a spectator, unable to find any food. How to interpret this? Did it mean that my own feminine nature was relatively undeveloped as compared to the masculine? Or did it mean that the training program was not conducive to the growth and participation of the feminine? Or both? The latter was suggested by the fact that despite much searching and the help of others, I could find no food. And what was this food that was not to be found? I did not know. The dream left it to me to decide whether the effort would end in ruin or in new construction.

What the dream did not picture was the excruciating experience I had through most of the program. After the first year, which passed uneventfully, I found that every Thursday evening when I joined the class, an avalanche of something like black tar descended over my mind. No thought, no idea, could break through the thick blackness. After enduring the two hours of class, I would get in my car, shaken and frightened, but also relieved to have gotten through another meeting. I would drive the forty miles home and resume my life, with normal consciousness gradually returning, though in the latter part of the program it took longer to recover. The heavy blackness came over me too whenever I had to appear before one of the numerous evaluating committees. I did not know what the blackness was, and I did not know where to turn for help. The older analysts were withdrawing, and the younger ones were strangers to me.

Jung, of course, had written of the pain of the spiritual path, and had himself experienced a spiritual crisis of Himalayan proportions. It has been said that one's capacity for suffering is a measure of one's capacity for individuation, but none of my fellow students seemed to have suffered any such travail. The concept of spiritual emergency developed by Stanislav and Christina Grof might have helped me, but it was not published until 1989, too late for me. Jung did not help his followers distinguish between a spiritual emergency and a psychotic breakdown. In many cases, the distinction is not obvious. In the absence of a diagnosis, I called my condition "congealed terror." One of my more imaginative explanations was that in a former incarnation I had been burned at the stake as a witch, since my dreams in this life so often spoke of what were to be future events, revealing a forbidden talent long ascribed to the devil.

I had never had such an experience before in this life. In truth, I loved learning, and I was good at it. I had graduated from the University of Chicago with a Phi Beta Kappa award, and in my high school class I was the valedictorian among three hundred graduates. In graduate school I made straight As. So why was I condemned to the black terror in this situation? A sensible person would have asked why I remained in the program for eight years and accepted such suffering. The answer, of course, was in the other part of the big dream, where a great deal of growth and healing and building took place. Not only were patients being treated, but the healing center itself was going through a vast reconstruction. I was very much aware of the gains I was making with my patients, and besides I believed that I was destined to be a healer.

This conviction came out of a dream I had years before, when I began my Jungian analysis. I saw a shamaness in full regalia, a crown of antlers on her head like the headdresses of the shamans and shamanesses of the northern countries. Among the antlers were beautiful scattered roses, like lights on a Christmas tree. I drew a picture of that shamaness and found there was great power in that image—the picture came out perfectly as I drew it freehand, as though a skilled hand had taken hold of mine and guided it. The dream was all the more impressive since I knew nothing of shamanic lore at the time, but I thought that the nearest thing to being a shamaness today was to be a Jungian therapist, and that is what I wanted to do. The shamaness was an image of the Jungian self, the powerful center of the personality. One would want to cultivate the potentialities implicit in such a figure and so be true to one's deepest nature.

So, after six years of training, I went before the certifying board—and failed. My friends were encouraging; they said I would pass the next time. It was two and one-half years later that I pulled myself together and tried again, only to be turned down once more. This time it was different; people averted their eyes from me, not knowing what to say. I had no words either, though I knew in my heart that I had qualified.

I found myself plunged into a very strange situation. Many synchronicities had surrounded both my appearances before the certifying board, especially the last time. And when it was over, I had an inexplicable feeling: winning was the same as losing. I cannot forget it, and I cannot explain it; winning and losing were exactly the same! I was precipitated into a state of inner intensity, high energy, and much clarity and insight. On a trip to New York shortly after my failure, I had a number of clairvoyant experiences. Yet at the same time I knew that I was a failure, publicly and finally exposed and condemned.

Shame. If I did not know it before, I knew it now—how it writhes in the belly, confuses the mind, and contorts the body in spasms in the night. And how one needs to hide away by day so as not to avert the face and reveal one's guilt and self-loathing. The strange sense of self-sufficiency and acceptance that had come to me at the time of testing withered quickly as my whole world met me with embarrassed silence.

There was a postscript to this affair that bears on the theme of the gods. At the beginning of the second testing by the certifying board, the chairman lost the key to the building. The testing had to be delayed until a new key could be found. This synchronistic event speaks volumes to every Jungian. To lose a key is no trifling matter, whether in dreams or in life. In addition, the chairman had to miss a number of sessions because his daughter was in a scuba diving accident that involved the loss of a life. All this bespoke the presence of an archetype of loss and death. Depending on your theory of synchronicity, these incidents could be taken as the very evidence of a malevolent superordinate presence. The time of the testing was not auspicious.

When it was all over, I was told more than once that my repeat failures would not have happened if I had not been a woman. But many other women were being certified; why not this woman? A dream that came while I was still in the program told me that I was living out the myth of Saint Barbara, the legendary martyr of third-century Egypt (some say Syria), whose story was told in the well-thumbed manuscripts of medieval monasteries. Her rich father, departing on a journey, left her confined in a tower to keep her from being carried off by an admirer, but Barbara, her mind on higher things by far, had a third window cut in her tower. This symbol of the Trinity became the telltale evidence that she had converted to the Christian faith, contrary to her father's wishes. Her architectural revision was the last bit of spunk the unfortunate young lady ever showed, for her father, on returning, handed her over to the pagan authorities, who had her dragged through the streets naked as a punishment for her crime. (Public humiliation is an aspect of the archetype.) However, an angel, recognizing her steadfastness, covered her body from profane eyes. Finally, the relentless father took her up on a mountain and killed her, but he received his just reward, for God struck him down with a bolt of lightning as he walked away from the bloody deed. Barbara, meanwhile, had to go through a death-and-rebirth experience in order to come into her true calling.

The martyred Saint Barbara became the patron of architects, builders, and artillerymen. As an interesting sidelight on this archetype, my brother is an engineer and contractor, one of my sons is in construction and the other in the financing of construction, while my first husband was an artillery officer in World War II. I like to think that within this archetype is a hidden creativity; those blessed by Saint Barbara are builders, not so much bards and poets as creators of concrete forms having stability and continuity. Saint Barbara honors the material side of the spirit-matter dichotomy. The artilleryman, then, represents the polarity of the archetype, the big guns required to destroy these structures.

This mythical story presumably brought tears to the eyes of medieval readers, but it is not much to the modern taste. It speaks of the unmitigated brutality of the Terrible Father, a stand-in for the Old Testament God, and of the suffering of the feminine, whose only hope lies in the next world. That I was living out this archetype was not good news; it was certainly a role I would not have chosen, but that must have been chosen for me long ago, even before my parents named me Barbara. Our psychological assumption, of course, is that the woman caught in such a role has an "inner terrible father" whom she projects onto some outer father or group of fathers, who in this way become her oppressor. She can be healed only by withdrawing the projection and discriminating between the cosmic Father and the human beings who have come to incarnate him. To do this she must be able to discern a difference between the human Father and the godlike Great Father and, at the same time, accept her own power so that she no longer needs to project it. In the archetype of Saint Barbara, only death and rebirth can lead to liberation, an experience found in the stories of shamanic healers the world over.

In the end it was up to me to decide whether the death experience I had to endure would destroy me or bring about an effort of rebuilding. I realized that conscious awareness is not necessarily enough to deliver one from the effects of a negative archetypal pattern. More was asked of me. As I went along very quietly in the world, trying with all my might to bring something creative out of the debacle, I knew that I could not tackle this from a feminist perspective. Many women of vigorous and inquiring mind were working in that area; I had a different calling.

I took very seriously Jung's admonition that healing for anyone in the second half of life depends on the discovery of a religious standpoint. I also wanted to go back to the fundamentals to reexamine the phenomena that Jung, Freud, and the rest of the modern healers had been looking at, and to ask all over again, what were they seeing? Or, more pointedly, what is the nature of the sickness of the modern world? Do not both our sickness and our healing methods (for the two are intimately bound together) sprout out of the very roots of our common life? If it is true, as is claimed by Eastern teachers, that our Western psychotherapies seldom get beyond the higher levels of samsara and do not reach toward the higher wisdom, what does that tell us? Are we blocked in our advance by influences so embedded in our ways of being that they are invisible to our sight? "All authentic religious experience implies a desperate effort to penetrate to the root of things, to the ultimate reality," Mircea Eliade, the great student of world religions, had said. What I liked about that statement was the word desperate. I saw my own existential crisis running parallel to the existential crisis of the modern world.

I attended a seminar conducted by Joyce Goodrich based on the healing methods of Larry LeShan. As I lay on the floor surrounded by the other participants engaged in performing a healing on me, a strange thing happened. At the very edge of my mind's horizon I saw some dim lights hovering; they gradually approached me, growing larger and brighter, and became words that I could read, shining in the darkness: The Half-Remembered Reality. It was the first time I had come upon those words, and I knew instantly that this would be the name of my work. It was as though deep within me, something already knew the answers to the questions I was raising, and I must get acquainted with that inner knower. My study began to turn increasingly to an unlikely focus for a therapist, the analogy—though I had never heard of the sacred analogy and did not know of the importance of analogical thought in ancient times and in the great medieval synthesis. It proved to be one of those fascinations that kept leading me on, into a reexamination of many of the ways of seeing and believing that I had taken on as a Jungian and as a product of modern Western culture. It was as if I had laid hold of a fishing line that reached into deep waters, with many, many hooks, and as I kept pulling, one fish after another came up, many kinds, of many shapes and colors. I kept pulling with a kind of astonishment, wondering what would next appear.

In time I discovered for myself the method used by the great fifteenth-century churchman and philosopher Nicholas of Cusa, whose way of approach to God was through analogies. He delighted in setting up one analogy after another to describe God's nature—be it the eternal circulation of the waters, or the inexhaustible procreativity of the nut tree—only to break it down in favor of some other, more apt, analogy. I had to discover, too, how one can get caught in an analogy, believing it to be the final truth, only to find that a new facet of reality emerges as it breaks down. And with each opening and breaking up of analogies there came an opening of the mind to new levels of meaning. One sees this today in the crumbling of the "machine" analogy for the nature of the universe.

Although I began to think about the analogy in response to an inner fascination, I learned, after much searching, that I was being led into something more significant than I had anticipated, and that larger thing was the whole mode of thought of the "Perennial Philosophers." Theirs was a way of thinking that tended to see all things in their context—individuals in the context of their worlds, the phenomenal world in the context of the transcendent. It was an inclusive and unifying way of thinking that more and more perceived the inner connectedness of all life. As the reality of this connectedness increasingly lays hold of the mind, it leads toward a vision of the deity, not by way of logical "proofs" but out of a kind of inner necessity, for it is the divine that shines through the apparent multiplicity of phenomena to give rise to an inner relatedness.

The Perennial Philosophy reached toward a perception of the essence of things by an intuitive absorption in them. It did not try for knowledge by grasping with tooth and nail, attacking, and tearing apart—the carnivorous approach to wisdom—nor did it seek to manipulate, control, or shape things, events, and persons. Rather it sought knowledge as a lover moves toward the beloved, in gentleness and patience. Like Leonardo, it said, "Great knowledge is the daughter of profound love." And knowledge was found to enter into the recipient as her whole being enlarged to receive it. It came like the dew on a still summer night, blessing the one who melted and opened to allow it. Our whole world hungered for these two—love and knowledge—and yet was too frightened and suspicious to receive them. I could understand that very well.

I began to write again, working at the very margin of what I could understand, because that is the only way I can motivate myself to write. If I already know it, why bother to write it? I began the writing as I would begin a therapeutic process with one of my patients, in faith and hope—but without guarantees—that something creative would emerge out of our encounter. My writing became my private partner in dialogue, speaking back to me as I spoke to it, sometimes leading me into blind alleys, but having a sturdy core of purpose beyond my conscious knowing. So this is at once the story of a quest and of the reading and study I did to reestablish my life on some new foundation. I wrote while engaged in an active therapeutic practice with others who, like myself, were in search of wholeness and a firmer underpinning for their lives. I have also written impersonally, partly because my personal pain was too fiery for me to deal with, but also because I wished to move beyond merely personal concerns and enter into a larger, more universal way of being.

In addition to the analogy, I also wanted to study parapsychology. Like Jung, I was drawn to the "occult." If we wanted to understand more about the unconscious, why confine ourselves to only one method of getting in touch with it—the dream? Why not give attention to every manifestation of unconscious activity including out-of-body travel, telepathy, precognition, psychometry, and the many other ways in which the unconscious reveals itself? These phenomena have enormous theoretical value and have much to tell us about the human mind and about our reality.

A dream came as I continued my studies:

> *I have been swimming the Pacific Ocean from the Orient to Hawaii with an unknown companion. Once in Hawaii I decide to swim to the mainland of North America to get help on our "official" swim across. I run into two young men on shore, one of them riding around on his motorized scooter. The other is named Norm, and he swims with me back to Hawaii. There it seems I need to be lifted up, as if onto a ship (or perhaps a pier), and I grab a rope that is put down for me and call to those above and below to help me up. I awaken with the sense that the "official" trip will be made by boat, or at least require me to get to another level.*

What struck me most about the dream was the ease with which I made this remarkable trip. I could only marvel at it, and at the presence of the mysterious companion who swims with me and somehow gives validity to my journey. Something larger and more powerful than I must have been at work. Could my companion have been a personification of the maternal sea, the mother of all life, who bore the tiny human woman over her mighty bosom? I bow even now in respect of Her, and in respect of some powerful intentionality, mysterious as Her own depths, that must have been at work in that crossing.

I see the dream symbols as a uniting of the East and West, those opposites that have evolved for millennia in comparative isolation, and I think of my own inner opposites, so violently torn apart by my life experience, and of the nations whose opposition in the outer world has threatened the death of our planet. All these levels of opposition cry out for healing. It is a profound conviction of the Jungian way that in healing our own inner dividedness, we also help to heal our world—but only to the extent that we are guided and aided by forces beyond our own conscious knowing. Hawaii appears in the dream as the polyglot point of intersection where East meets West, and the "official" swim, I suppose, might be like the "official" record in the hundred-yard dash or the pole vault, a performance publicly recorded by which others may test their proficiency.

That the crossing is made from the Far East to the West rather than the reverse, more natural for a Westerner, suggests the idea of starting from the unknown and proceeding toward the known. It also suggests the idea of bringing back a message. The message comes from a place appropriately called the Orient, a place more profoundly steeped in a long tradition of metaphysical reality than our own.

Two young men appear in the dream, the twoness suggesting a coming to consciousness. One, whose name is unknown, rides off into the unconscious on a motorized scooter. The other young man, Norm, comes with me. His name indicates the standard, natural way things are, but also a set standard of development or achievement, an authoritative model or pattern. Like the word normal, the name comes from the Latin norma, meaning a rule, or carpenter's square, the "right angle" needed in laying the foundations of a structure. By means of the set square, the carpenter can faithfully reproduce those same square corners in buildings. Here the name begins to reveal an unexpected richness of meaning. The Latin word norma derives from the Greek gnomon, which refers to an interpreter, a discerner, or one who knows—hence Gnostic. It is also the name of the pointer on a sundial. In ancient times it was common to set up a pole perpendicular to the ground and to read the time of day by the shadow it cast. The length and angle of the shadow varied throughout the year, enabling the discerner to take note of the solstices and equinoxes and to record the annual peregrination of the sun. In simpler times, when there were far fewer tools, the norma must have seemed a marvelous instrument. Only later did I realize that the set square, in the ancient view, had to do with the measurement of both time and space, and that this dream could be seen as setting forth the direction my work would take, of which I was not aware at the time. "Norm" was surely a great gift to me. Nor did I immediately understand the meaning of the scooter, but years later, when I had retired and was living in a retirement community, I had a scooter like this of my own. This image was another flash into the future.

The extending of a rope to help me suggests the possibility of ascent, connection, uplift, and of assistance from unknown sources. Since I appear to need helpers both behind and ahead of me to climb the rope, it appears that I, the most private of persons, will have to make public what has been the most personal, even secret, of pilgrimages, as I make my lonely way immersed in the waters, trusting my life to the depths. For me that will be a critical stage of the journey, corresponding to the higher level of consciousness I need to attain.

Another interpretation of the dream, owing perhaps more to Freud than to Jung, might propose that I begin the journey in the Orient because that represents the unconscious to me, and that I proceed to Hawaii, the isle of sensuous delights, where the natives dance the hula and sing their enchanting songs while tropical breezes drift in from the sea. Since the dream does not say whether I actually get to the higher level, it will have to be decided in life, but it is evidently a difficult ascent. Possibly both interpretations are true.

To me it seems better to study the direction in which Jung was moving in his later years than to focus on what he said at any particular time. Jung's thought shifted and developed throughout his life. In his early years, he belonged to the mainstream of Western scientific thought and was concerned about maintaining his footing in that tradition—a not unworthy goal, lest he lose his way in the shadowy groves of the occultists and visionaries. His later works, however, point toward radical departures from the current Western worldview. If we build on the direction of his thought, we shall be continuing along the high road he established; to continue unimaginatively to repeat what he said will hardly enhance the prestige of the master.

The course of Jung's thought seems to lead to an exploration of both the wisdom of the East and the esoteric, mystical wing of all the world's great religions. At the same time, it leads to the roots of the human psyche, that region of great danger and sublime mystery known to the mystics of all religions, and before them to the shamans and priests of primal peoples. These men and women held to their traditional beliefs, but equally sought their own experience of the psyche; inevitably they were led to profound encounters of the inner depths. The solid core of agreement among these traditions and these experiences offers convincing evidence of the validity of spiritual teaching. For my part, I am obliged to seek out the universal truths that form the center of all the great religions, for I cannot limit myself to only one.

From another perspective, Jung's thought leads us to the study of modern science, the principles of which form the pillars of modern consciousness. In the twentieth century, the new physics began to undermine our accustomed ways of construing reality, based largely on science's own earlier conclusions. We still have not begun to integrate these new insights or to learn how the changes will affect our lives. When we finally take up this task, we will find that we are in for a restructuring of consciousness comparable to the change that came with Descartes and Newton in the seventeenth century.

In the meantime, what we are experiencing is a crumbling of long-held certainties that creates a crisis of meaning that is everywhere revealed in the lives we lead and in the social order as a whole. But as we know from ancient teachings, the crashing down of the old is accompanied by the quiet germination of the new, still in the seedling stage. One sees intimations of this new worldview in the extraordinary correlation between the insights of the new physics and those of depth psychology, suggesting that we are on the verge of a historic reunion of science with psychology and spirituality. The outcome of this unification can only be beneficial. What this means is that the search for a new and higher consciousness is not confined to the few who are called to a special work, but will fall upon each and every one of us.

I take heart from the many people who are turning to psychotherapy today; their presence testifies at once to the enormous reservoir of human suffering and spiritual poverty in the land, and at the same time to the willingness of people to take responsibility for their own distress. If they do not stop with limited goals but press on to the larger task of life exploration, they will discover the new ways of being human that lie ahead. To me, this is a creative work that summons one's most profound commitment. From my own work I have learned much about the process of human change and growth, how it can be facilitated, and how it becomes stunted. My writing is a continuation and an accompaniment of that effort; I owe a great debt of gratitude to those who have worked with me and who, out of their own struggles, have taught me so many things.

I have come to realize that a work of this kind is not finished—it is only set aside as our advancing years set their own limits. Many others are joining in the search today for a spiritual homeland. When found, it will not be simply a set of philosophical beliefs nor a "faith in the unseen"; it will be more like the soil that sustains and nurtures life and gives rise to a community of shared spiritual experience. It will, in truth, lead to a new perception of reality, born in travail, but imbued with healing power both for ourselves and our planet. It will bring a new understanding of the meaning of human life within the cosmos, that understanding which, according to Mircea Eliade, was the birthright of all those born into the traditional cultures of the past, but which we have now lost, without even knowing what it is that we have lost.

Already there are those who can see the outlines of a new vision rising up out of the mists, and are irresistibly drawn—or forced by life experience—to begin their own exploration. To all such I say, God be with you!

—Barbara Cook Loy

NOTES

PROLOGUE

1. Quoted in C. G. Jung, *Memories, Dreams, Reflections* (New York: Pantheon Books, 1963), p. 363.
2. The English edition was published three years later. See "Synchronicity: An Acausal Connecting Principle," in *The Interpretation of Nature and the Psyche* (New York: Pantheon Books, 1955).

CHAPTER 1
THE ANALOGY AS A KEY TO THE MYSTERY OF HEALING

1. *The Collected Works of C. G. Jung,* 21 vols., ed. Herbert Read, Michael Fordham, and Gerhard Adler (Princeton: Princeton University Press, 1953–1992), vol. 5, para. 203 (hereafter cited as *CW*).
2. Phyllis B. Keenan, "Eros, Logos, and Androgyny," *Psychological Perspectives* 12, no. 1 (Spring 1981).
3. *CW,* vol. 4, para. 539.
4. *CW,* vol. 4, para. 553.
5. *CW,* vol. 7, para 166ff.
6. *CW,* vol. 7, para. 171.
7. *CW,* vol. 4, para. 553.
8. *CW,* vol. 7, para. 76.
9. *CW,* vol. 7, para. 493.
10. Ibid.
11. *CW,* vol. 16, para. 353ff.
12. Ernest G. McClain, *The Myth of Invariance: The Origin of the Gods, Mathematics, and Music from the Ṛg Veda to Plato* (Boulder: Shambhala, 1978), pp. 2–3.
13. *CW,* vol. 12, para. 325–26.

CHAPTER 2
ANALOGY AND MAGIC IN HEALING

1. Claude Lévi-Strauss, *Structural Anthropology* (New York: Basic Books, 1963), p. 186ff.
2. Ibid., p. 195.
3. Ibid., p. 197.

4. Ibid., pp. 197–98.

5. Ibid., p. 200.

6. Ibid., p. 201.

7. *CW,* vol. 8, para. 314.

8. *CW,* vol. 11, para. 307.

9. *CW,* vol. 8, para. 303.

10. *CW,* vol. 8, para. 313ff.

11. Here I use the word *modern* to apply to the worldview widely believed to be revealed by science, that matter is the fundamental constituent of the universe, and that the true nature of reality is to be sought by dividing all things into their ultimate particles. Mind is believed to be dependent on matter or derived from matter. This view is now contrasted with a postmodern view, which rests on other premises.

12. P. D. Ouspensky, *Tertium Organum: The Third Canon of Thought; A Key to the Enigmas of the World* (New York: Alfred A. Knopf, 1981), p. 158.

13. *CW,* vol. 8, para. 307.

14. *CW,* vol. 8, para. 316.

15. Instead of an attempt at healing, another possible interpretation of the snake dream is that it simply repeats the patient's problem. He is wounded in the heel, in outer life by the woman's rejection, in the dream by the snake, and (in all probability) in his childhood by the mother's over-solicitous care. If anything, then, the dream equates *woman* and *snake*. What Jung is adding, of course, is that the dream links two levels of the psyche—the personal realm in which he is wounded by the girl, and the underlying (or overarching) archetypal framework of his life from which the snake image emerges.

    Or it may have occurred to the reader that the snake is none other than the serpent of the god Asklepios. The two amplifications—one connecting the serpent to Eve and the other to Asklepios—do not necessarily conflict. The serpent is a rich symbol and resonates on many levels. The one who deceived Eve was placed in paradise by the Creator himself and therefore was an attribute of the god, like the twin serpents of Asklepios. That the serpent has the dual capacity to heal or to wound is an example of the duplicity of the archetype. The symbol stands at the dynamic center where these energies meet, the point where the opposites (actually complementaries) unite.

16. *CW,* vol. 11, para. 353. Our confusion about whether the godly energies are "deeper" or "higher"—or, on the other hand, "one with us"—arises because of our need to spatialize the psyche. If the psyche has no spatial dimension, then any or all of these can be true.

17. James G. Frazer, *The Golden Bough: A Study in Magic and Religion,* abridged ed. (New York: Macmillan, 1958), chap. 3.

18. "On Psychic Energy," *CW*, vol. 8, para. 89.

19. *Symbols of Transformation*, *CW*, vol. 5, para. 214n22.

20. Marie-Louise von Franz, *Alchemical Active Imagination* (Irving, TX: Spring Publications, 1979), p. 97.

21. *CW*, vol. 8, para. 308–09.

22. *CW*, vol. 8, para. 329.

23. Lévi-Strauss, *Structural Anthropology*, p. 202

24. Ibid., p. 208.

25. *CW*, vol. 8, para. 575n.

26. *A Midsummer Night's Dream*, act 5, scene 1. The Bard understood that even "airy nothings" require a space to be when they enter our world.

27. Edward F. Edinger, *Ego and Archetype: Individuation and the Religious Function of the Psyche* (New York: G. P. Putnam's Sons, 1972), p. 240.

28. *CW*, vol. 11, para. 443.

29. Ibid.

CHAPTER 3
PROJECTION

1. *CW*, vol. 10, para. 131.

2. Marie-Louise von Franz, *Projection and Re-Collection in Jungian Psychology: Reflections of the Soul* (LaSalle, IL: Open Court, 1980), p. 8ff.

3. *CW*, vol. 8, para. 516.

4. *CW*, vol. 4, para. 662.

5. C. G. Jung, *Letters*, 2 vols., ed. Gerhard Adler, in collaboration with Aniela Jaffé (Princeton: Princeton University Press, 1973–1975), vol. 1 (1906–1950), p. 412.

6. Smith, *Forgotten Truth: The Primordial Tradition* (New York: Harper & Row, 1977), pp. 78–91.

7. Von Franz, *Projection and Re-Collection*, p. 8.

8. Raynor C. Johnson, *The Imprisoned Splendour: An Approach to Reality, Based upon the Significance of Data Drawn from the Fields of Natural Science, Psychical Research, and Mystical Experience* (Wheaton, IL: Theosophical Publishing House, 1971), p. 84.

9. Now called "remote viewing." Clairvoyance typically refers to the "transfer" of information directly from mind to mind that is contemporaneous with, and remote from, the viewer. Telepathy is the transfer of information from a physical source directly to the mind of the viewer. On the basis of experiments at Duke University, J. B. Rhine concluded that telepathy and clairvoyance are

essentially the same process. See Rhine, *The Reach of the Mind* (New York: W. Sloane Associates, 1947), p. 48.

10. Jean Gebser, *The Ever-Present Origin* (Athens, OH: Ohio University Press, 1984), p. 132.

11. Erich Neumann, "The Psyche and the Transformation of the Reality Planes," *Spring* [journal], 1956, p. 81ff.

12. Ibid., p. 85.

13. Ibid., p. 86.

14. Ibid., p. 87.

15. Ibid.

16. Jung, *Letters,* vol. 1, p. 393ff. Jung has acknowledged that "paranormal cognition" is intuitive and that the unconscious does not exist in absolute space-time.

17. Jung corrects this impression when he points out that primitives project far more than moderns. "The word projection is not really correct," he says, "for nothing has been cast out of the psyche, rather the psyche has attained its present complexity by a series of acts of introjection" (*CW,* vol. 9.1, para. 54).

18. *Letters,* vol. 1, p. 389.

19. Alfred North Whitehead considered sensory perception as a secondary form of perception, while extrasensory perception was primary. See David Ray Griffin, ed., *Archetypal Process: Self and Divine in Whitehead, Jung, and Hillman* (Evanston, IL: Northwestern University Press, 1989), p. 25.

20. Alexandra David-Neel, *Magic and Mystery in Tibet* (New York: Penguin Books, 1975), p. 235.

21. Von Franz, *Projection and Re-Collection,* p. 94.

22. "Flying Saucers: A Modern Myth of Things Seen in the Skies," *CW,* vol. 10, para. 635ff.

23. Smith, *Forgotten Truth,* p. 78.

24. Act 3, scene 2.

25. Edward Whitmont is one Jungian who has seen the need to change Jung's concept of projection. In a footnote to his valuable book *The Symbolic Quest: Basic Concepts of Analytical Psychology* (New York: Putnam's Sons, 1969), he says, "Since this book was prepared it has become apparent to me that it is important to distinguish more clearly between *projection* and *symbolic realization*. The former should refer to qualities that are capable of being integrated into one's personal structuring, while the latter involves a relation to the transpersonal symbol. Further investigation of this distinction holds great promise as a way of clearing up confusions which now exist between psychology and theology" (p. 312n1).

26. Gebser, *Ever-Present Origin,* p. 23ff.

CHAPTER 4
SYNCHRONICITY

1. Reprinted in *CW,* vol. 8 (see also prologue, n. 2, above).

2. Peat, *Synchronicity: The Bridge Between Matter and Mind* (New York: Bantam Books, 1987).

3. Evidence for the existence of psi, or paranormal abilities, in animals was found by researchers at Duke University. Among fifty-four well-authenticated cases was the story of Sugar, a cream-colored Persian cat, who in 1951 followed his owners some 1,500 miles across mountain and prairie from California to their new home in Oklahoma. When the family had attempted to take Sugar with them, he had leaped out of the car and hid, and so was regretfully left behind with neighbors. Some fourteen months later, after what must have been an arduous trip, Sugar leaped into the window of the family's new home in Oklahoma. He had a certain deformity of the left hip joint that served to identify him. Later the former neighbors in California admitted that Sugar had indeed disappeared about sixteen to eighteen days after his owners had left, but they had not had the heart to inform their friends.

4. S. K. Henniger, *Touches of Sweet Harmony: Pythagorean Cosmology and Renaissance Poetics* (San Marino, CA: Huntington Library, 1974), p. 237.

5. Roger S. Jones, *Physics as Metaphor* (New York: New American Library, 1982), p. 30.

6. *CW,* vol. 8, para. 850.

7. *CW,* vol. 8, para. 824, 967.

8. *CW,* vol. 8, para. 995.

9. *CW,* vol. 8, para. 856. By "transcendental" Jung is pointing to a god. Long ago, synchronicities were seen as acts of the tribal god. The ancients paid attention to these things. They observed the signs and portents that accompanied the start of any new venture to learn whether the gods were in favor. "I will harden Pharaoh's heart and multiply my signs and my wonders in the land of Egypt," says Yahweh (Exodus 7:3).

10. Some writers would dispute this. They would say that a cause is not a cause until it produces an effect, hence cause and effect are simultaneous. This fails to resolve the issue: how did Rhine's subjects guess the order of the cards *before* they were turned up? To explain this by causality, we would have to say that the effect *precedes* the cause, which does not make sense. However, we might imagine that the subject, by his guesses, *causes* the cards to turn up in the order he has suggested, thus reversing the causal sequence. This is a possibility worth considering. Jung does not rule it out. He speaks of the ancient belief in the "wish" as a magical action, as though one might wish the cards to fall into a particular order, or, equally, wish one's psyche to fall into the particular order of the cards (*CW,* vol. 8, para. 866n). This might help explain the fascination of gambling if a parapsychological element is involved in "runs" of good luck.

11. *CW,* vol. 8, para. 938n70.

12. *CW,* vol. 8, para. 847.

13. *CW,* vol. 8, para. 859.

14. Jung, *The Visions Seminars: From the Complete Notes of Mary Foote, 2 vols.* (Zurich: Spring Publications, 1976), vol. 2, p. 398.

15. *CW,* vol. 8, para. 823.

16. *CW,* vol. 8, para 915.

17. *CW,* vol. 8, para. 916.

18. *CW,* vol. 8, para. 917.

19. Ibid.

20. *CW,* vol. 8, para. 942.

21. Ibid., n. 71.

22. *CW,* vol. 8, para. 828.

23. *CW,* vol. 8, para. 960.

24. *CW,* vol. 8, para. 915.

25. Johnson, *Imprisoned Splendour* (see chap. 3, n. 8), p. 152.

26. Leonard Dart, personal communication.

27. Jung, *Letters,* vol. 2, p. 45.

28. *CW,* vol. 8, para. 965.

29. *CW,* vol. 8, para. 959.

30. *CW,* vol. 8, para. 965.

31. Jung goes on to point out that space and time are "elastic" in relation to the psyche, and "can apparently be reduced almost to the vanishing point, as though they were dependent on psychic conditions and did not exist in themselves, were only 'postulated' by the conscious mind. In man's original view of the world, as we find it among primitives, space and time have a very precarious existence." He adds that Kant regarded space and time as a priori categories of experience, belonging to the psyche and not to nature (*CW,* vol. 8, para. 840).

32. Ibid.

33. *CW,* vol. 8, para. 967.

34. Gebser, *Ever-Present Origin* (see chap. 3, n. 10), p. 107.

35. Johnson, *Imprisoned Splendour,* p. 239.

36. *CW,* vol. 8, para. 913.

37. *CW,* vol. 8, para. 912 and 923.

38. *CW*, vol. 8, para. 967.
39. *CW*, vol. 8, para. 866.
40. *CW*, vol. 8, para. 440.
41. *CW*, vol. 8, para. 831.
42. *CW*, vol. 8, para. 923, 912, 948.
43. *CW*, vol. 8, para. 920.
44. *CW*, vol. 8, para. 922.
45. Griffin, *Archetypal Process* (see chap. 3, n. 19), p. 25.
46. *CW*, vol. 8, para. 865.
47. *CW*, vol. 8, para. 865.
48. To take an elementary, but humorous, example, once I attempted to challenge the ancient book by asking a question a second time, as I did not like its first answer. I received Hexagram 4, "Youthful Folly." As though conscious of its age and dignity, and impersonal as well as impartial in its judgments, the wise old book seemed to be reprimanding me, the upstart questioner, and preserving its silence!
49. *CW*, vol. 8, para. 995.
50. See *CW*, vol. 8, para. 916–46.
51. Jung, *Aion: Researches into the Phenomenology of the Self* (1951), in *CW*, vol. 9.2, para. 409.
52. Jung, *Letters*, vol. 2, p. 43ff.
53. Marie-Louise von Franz, *Number and Time: Reflections Leading Toward a Unification of Depth Psychology and Physics* (Evanston, IL: Northwestern University Press, 1974), p. 247.
54. That synchronistic events are not rare at all is interestingly affirmed by Jones in *Physics as Metaphor* (see note 5 above), p. 112. He suggests that causal events may be a subclass of the far more numerous synchronistic events.

CHAPTER 5
PSYCHIC PHENOMENA: IMPLICATIONS

1. Later researchers used many of the same cases used in this early study, a circumstance that drew fire from the critics. This came about because the earlier researchers thought they had given adequate coverage to the phenomena with their 1,694 cases, and thus the research was not renewed with modern cases. As time went by, it became clear that this was a mistake.
2. Rhine, *Hidden Channels of the Mind* (New York: William Morrow, 1961).
3. All citations of Jaffé's book, originally published in Zurich, will be to the English

translation, *Apparitions: An Archetypal Approach to Death Dreams and Ghosts* (Irving, TX: Spring Publications, 1978).

4. Tyrrell's study was originally presented as a lecture in 1942, then revised and republished a decade later. See G. N. M. Tyrrell, *Apparitions,* rev. ed. (New York: Macmillan, 1953).

5. Ibid., pp. 39–40.

6. Ibid., p. 151.

7. Goethe's experiments with color might prove to be relevant to understanding these visual experiences. In *Zur Farbenlehre* (Theory of Colors), published in 1810, he showed how we create a "ghostly color," translucent and thin but unmistakable from out of our own sensory and mental apparatus. His experiments, based on a phenomenological approach to color, were not followed up, because the whole tendency of science in the later nineteenth century was in another direction.

8. Jaffé, *Apparitions,* p. 131.

9. Ibid., p. 132.

10. See, for instance, Kenneth Ring, *Heading Toward Omega: In Search of the Meaning of the Near-Death Experience* (New York: William Morrow, 1985).

11. Johnson, *Imprisoned Splendour* (see chap. 3, n. 8), p. 198.

12. Ibid., p. 225.

13. *Memories, Dreams, Reflections,* pp. 289–90.

14. Johnson, *Imprisoned Splendour,* p. 169.

15. See Rupert Sheldrake, *The Presence of the Past: Morphic Resonance and the Habits of Nature* (New York: Random House, 1988), pp. 197–222, for a discussion of the nature of memory.

16. We should not pass lightly over the idea that a place can hold a record of events that have happened there. As noted above, some believe that such records can be found in places where events of a high emotional charge have occurred, such as battlefields. Recent studies on this topic have focused on ancient sacred sites.

17. I am moved to ask whether the crime of rape is linked to an identification of the rapist with Pan. The rapist delights to create panic in his victims, and he arrogates to himself a godlike sense of power.

18. William James, *The Varieties of Religious Experience: A Study in Human Nature* (New York: New American Library, 1961), p. 25.

19. See Johnson, *Imprisoned Splendour,* p. 159, for a case in which a person "sees" a definite scene that must have occurred at Avebury Fair many years before. The perceiver was not drawn into emotional identification with the feeling content of the occasion. This would seem to involve a somewhat different faculty than that

displayed in the case of Fox—perhaps it marks the difference between the seer and the prophet.

20. Ibid., p. 177, and abridged from Eugène Osty, *Supernormal Faculties in Man: An Experimental Study* (London: Methuen, 1923).

21. *CW,* vol. 8, para. 119.

22. "Transformation Symbolism in the Mass," *CW,* vol. 11, para. 389.

23. Paper presented at the Conference on Parapsychology, Santa Barbara, California, August 1990, sponsored by the Center for Process Studies, Claremont, California. An earlier version of Suzanne Padfield's report can be found in B. D. Josephson and V. S. Ramachandran, eds., *Consciousness and the Physical World* (Oxford: Pergamon Press, 1980).

24. Jung, *Letters,* vol. 2, p. 398.

25. See Evelyn Fox Keller, *A Feeling for the Organism: The Life and Work of Barbara McClintock* (New York: W. H. Freeman, 1983).

26. "Our cells respond to our feelings (and thoughts) because we respond to their[s]. . . . Hurt my cells and you hurt me. Give my cells a healthy life, and they give me a feeling of vitality and at least minimal happiness." Charles Hartshorne, *Omnipotence and Other Theological Mistakes* (Albany: SUNY Press, 1984), p. 80.

27. One of my thoughts as I pursue these issues is that we as human beings can and do develop mental and spiritual powers to match the questions we are asking. Indeed, the progress of science demands such integration. As we come to recognize this need, we will turn increasingly to the spiritual teachers who have pioneered ways of personal growth beyond ordinary consciousness.

28. Anagarika Brahmacari Govinda, *Foundations of Tibetan Mysticism: According to the Esoteric Teachings of the Great Mantra* (New York: Samuel Weiser, 1977), p. 227.

29. John Blofeld, *The Tantric Mysticism of Tibet* (Boston: Shambhala, 1987), pp. 94–97.

CHAPTER 6
Time, Space, Synchronicity: Part I

1. Grosso, *Soulmaker: True Stories from the Far Side of the Psyche* (Norfolk, VA: Hampton Roads Publishing, 1992), p. 89.

2. Michael Loewe and Carmen Blacker, eds., *Oracles and Divination* (Boulder: Shambhala, 1981), p. 27.

3. Phoebe Bendit and Laurence Bendit, *This World and That: An Analytical Study of Psychic Communication* (Wheaton, IL: Theosophical Publishing House), p. 159.

4. David Ray Griffin, *Parapsychology, Philosophy, and Spirituality: A Postmodern Exploration* (Albany: SUNY Press, 1997), p. 35.

5. See John Briggs and F. David Peat, *Turbulent Mirror: An Illustrated Guide to Chaos Theory and the Science of Wholeness* (New York: Harper & Row, 1989).

6. Peat, *Synchronicity* (see chap. 4, n. 2), p. 91.

7. Von Franz, *Number and Time* (see chap. 4, n. 53), p. 244.

8. Robert Aziz, *C. G. Jung's Psychology of Religion and Synchronicity* (Albany: SUNY Press, 1990), p. 152ff.

9. David Ray Griffin, ed., *Physics and the Ultimate Significance of Time: Bohm, Prigogine, and Process Philosophy* (Albany: SUNY Press, 1986).

10. I. Prigogine and Isabelle Stengers, *Order Out Of Chaos: Man's New Dialogue with Nature* (Boulder: Shambhala, 1984), p. 15.

11. Von Franz, *Number and Time,* p. 94.

12. Ibid., p. 104.

13. Gebser, *Ever-Present Origin* (see chap. 3, n. 10), p. 285.

14. Each hexagram consists of six lines, either broken or solid, grouped together. There are sixty-four enumerations of such groupings, corresponding to $2^6 = 64$.

15. Jung, *Memories, Dreams, and Reflections,* p. 388. Jung expressed agreement with the ancient view. "It seems, indeed, as though time, far from being an abstraction, is a concrete continuum which contains qualities or basic conditions that manifest themselves simultaneously in different places through parallelisms that cannot be explained causally. . . ."

16. Ecclesiastes 3:1–4.

17. See Jung's foreword to the Wilhelm-Baynes translation of the I Ching, 3rd ed. (New York: Bollingen Foundation, 1950; Princeton: Princeton University Press, 1967). All citations of the I Ching and Jung's foreword are to the Princeton edition.

18. Anagarika Brahmacari Govinda, *Creative Meditation and Multi-Dimensional Consciousness* (Wheaton, IL: Theosophical Publishing House, 1976), p. 249.

19. This is confirmed by psychiatrist Ian Stevenson's work on reincarnation when he found that the person whose life ended with a gunshot wound showed the scar of the gunshot wound on the reborn body. See Stevenson, *Where Reincarnation and Biology Intersect* (Westport, CT: Praeger, 1997).

20. Seyyed Hossein Nasr, *Knowledge and the Sacred* (Albany: SUNY Press, 1989), p. 233.

21. F. David Peat, *The Philosopher's Stone: Chaos, Synchronicity, and the Hidden Order of the World* (New York: Bantam Books, 1991), p. 134.

22. See *CW,* vol. 8, para. 481, 489, and 493 for Jung's discussion of "absolute knowledge" in the unconscious.

23. Itzhak Bentov, *Stalking the Wild Pendulum: On the Mechanics of Consciousness* (New York: Bantam Books, 1979), p. 145.

24. Jung in his later writing appears sympathetic to views like Bentov's. He suggests there may be two different spaces, a physical and a psychic space, where the psyche could be understood as "unextended intensity," and not as a body moving with time. He also speaks of the possibility of faster-than-light communication. He calls his ideas speculative and says that psi phenomena "lay claim to an unusually high jump" (*Letters,* vol. 2, p. 45).

25. I Ching, p. 298.

26. See the classic book by Wilbur Marshall Urban, *The Intelligible World: Metaphysics and Value* (New York: Macmillan, 1929).

27. Griffin, *Physics and the Ultimate Significance of Time,* p. 197.

28. Blofeld, *Tantric Mysticism of Tibet* (see chap. 5, n. 29), p. 86.

29. Mircea Eliade, *Yoga: Immortality and Freedom* (New York: Pantheon Books, 1958), p. 83.

30. *CW,* vol. 14, para. 604n.

31. *CW,* vol. 10, para. 849–51

32. Many Old Testament stories have been interpreted as prefigurations of events to come in New Testament times. For example, Abraham's willingness to sacrifice his only son at God's command has been taken as a prefiguration of God's own sacrifice of the Son.

33. Jung, *Answer to Job* (1952), in *CW,* vol. 11, para. 752.

34. See John G. Neihardt, *Black Elk Speaks* (Lincoln: University of Nebraska Press, 1961).

35. *CW,* vol. 8, para. 965.

CHAPTER 7
Time, Space, Synchronicity: Part 2

1. F. David Peat, *Einstein's Moon: Bell's Theorem and the Curious Quest for Quantum Reality* (Chicago: Contemporary Books, 1990), p. 85.

2. Ibid., p. 156.

3. Andrija Puharich, *Beyond Telepathy* (Garden City, NY: Anchor / Doubleday, 1973), p. 15.

4. Ibid., p. 22.

5. Eileen J. Garrett, *Telepathy: In Search of a Lost Faculty* (New York: Garrett Publications, 1968), p. 41.

6. J. B. Rhine, *Reach of the Mind* (see chap. 3, n. 9), p. 191.

7. Phoebe Bendit and Laurence Bendit, *Our Psychic Sense: A Clairvoyant and a Psychiatrist Explain How It Develops* (Wheaton, IL: Theosophical Publishing House, 1967), p 111.

8. D. Scott Rogo, "Apparitions, Hauntings, and Poltergeists," in Edgar D. Mitchell et al., *Psychic Exploration: A Challenge for Science,* ed. John White (New York: G. P. Putnam's Sons, 1974), p. 391.

9. According to Jung, however, Professor James Hyslop of Columbia University admitted that "all things considered, all these metapsychic phenomena could be explained better by the hypothesis of spirits than by the qualities and peculiarities of the unconscious." To which Jung added: "And here, on the basis of my own experience, I am bound to concede that he is right . . ." (*Letters,* vol. 1, p. 431).

10. Michael Talbot, *Beyond the Quantum* (New York: Bantam Books, 1988), pp. 159–60.

11. Ibid., p. 163.

12. A. R. G. (Alan Robert George) Owen, "Poltergeist Phenomenon and Psychokinesis," in *The Signet Handbook of Parapsychology,* ed. Martin Ebon (New York: New American Library, 1978), p. 375.

13. In the case discussed in that chapter, the young patient's energies moved from the mother to the church as he came into maturity.

14. *CW,* vol. 9.l, para. 457.

15. Sylvan Muldoon, *The Projection of the Astral Body* (York Beach, ME: Samuel Weiser, 1973), p. 153.

16. Robert A. Monroe, *Journeys Out of the Body* (Garden City, NY: Anchor / Doubleday, 1971), p. 207.

17. Puharich, *Beyond Telepathy* (see n. 3 above), p. 42.

18. Ibid., p. 47.

19. David Lorimer, *Whole in One: The Near-Death Experience and the Ethic of Interconnectedness* (New York: Penguin, 1990).

20. Rupert Sheldrake, *A New Science of Life: The Hypothesis of Formative Causation* (Los Angeles: J. P. Tarcher, l981).

21. Kyriacos C. Markides, *The Magus of Strovolos: The Extraordinary World of a Spiritual Healer* (London: Routledge & Kegan Paul, l985), p. 197.

22. Anagarika Govinda, *The Way of the White Clouds* (Boulder: Shambhala, l970), p. 94.

23. Jung, *Letters,* vol. 1, p. 204.

24. Lorimer, *Whole in One,* p. 163.

25. Rupert Sheldrake, *A New Science of Life: The Hypothesis of Formative Causation* (Los Angeles: J. P. Tarcher, l981).

CHAPTER 8
The Synchronistic World

1. Grof and Grof, *Spiritual Emergency* (see intro., n. 1).
2. Quoted in William James, *A Pluralistic Universe* (New York: Longmans, Green & Co., 1932), p. 150. James speaks enthusiastically of Fechner.
3. Ibid., p. 162.
4. Jan Christiaan Smuts, *Holism and Evolution* (New York: Viking Press, 1926), p. 87.
5. David Bohm, *Wholeness and the Implicate Order* (London: Routledge & Kegan Paul, 1981), p. 7.
6. Garma C. C. Chang, *The Buddhist Teaching of Totality: The Philosophy of Hwa Yen Buddhism* (University Park: Pennsylvania State University Press, 1974).
7. Gebser, *Ever-Present Origin* (see chap. 3, n. 10), p. 47. The example is also found in Edward Whitmont's article "The Magic Layer of the Unconscious," *Spring*, 1956, p. 52.
8. Hugh Brody, *Maps and Dreams: Indians and the British Columbia Frontier* (Vancouver: Douglas & MacIntyre, 1988).
9. Ibid., p. 37.
10. A similar questioning of the divine plan is shown in the famous Old Testament episode of Gideon's dew, when Gideon tests God twice before going into battle against the Midianites (Judges 6:36–40).
11. Richard Selzer, *Mortal Lessons: Notes on the Art of Surgery* (New York: Simon & Schuster, 1976), pp. 33–36.
12. Blofeld, *Tantric Mysticism of Tibet* (see chap. 5, n. 29), p. 225.
13. Eugen Herrigel, *Zen in the Art of Archery* (New York: Vintage Books, 1971).
14. Ibid., p.10.
15. Ibid., p. 102.
16. Gebser, *Ever-Present Origin*, p. 250.
17. I Ching (see chap. 6, n. 17), p. 323.
18. *CW*, vol. 8, para. 921.
19. I Ching, p. 301.

INDEX

Barbara Cook Loy is a licensed California Marriage and Family Therapist (MFT), retired. Completed in the ninetieth year of her life, this book represents the culmination of her life's work as a healer and scholar of the soul. She is a graduate cum laude of the University of Chicago and a member of Phi Beta Kappa. After raising her twin boys, she trained to be a psychotherapist at the C. G. Jung Institute in Los Angeles. Upon receiving her MFT, she practiced for many decades in Claremont, California, where she still resides. She has been an active member of the Claremont Jung Club and the Claremont Religious Society of Friends.

Acknowledgments

The author wishes to thank Tracy Wilson for his friendship and support across many years, Judy Kohonen for research assistance and help organizing the manuscript, Theresa Duran for editing the manuscript, and Patrice Morris for cover design and layout. She is grateful to her family for their generous support of the writing process and assistance in publishing her work. She is also grateful for her many friends and supporters in the Claremont Jung Club and the Claremont Religious Society of Friends. Finally, she is deeply indebted to the clients of her psychotherapy practice, who, over the years, have been the best and most inspiring teachers anyone could ask for.

www.ingramcontent.com/pod-product-compliance
Lightning Source LLC
LaVergne TN
LVHW020534100826
845148LV00010B/1461

* 9 7 8 0 9 8 2 2 3 0 6 0 2 *

LES

AUTEURS LATINS

EXPLIQUÉS D'APRÈS UNE MÉTHODE NOUVELLE

PAR DEUX TRADUCTIONS FRANÇAISES

L'UNE LITTÉRALE ET JUXTALINÉAIRE PRÉSENTANT LE MOT À MOT FRANÇAIS
EN REGARD DES MOTS LATINS CORRESPONDANTS
L'AUTRE CORRECTE ET PRÉCÉDÉE DU TEXTE LATIN

avec des sommaires et des notes

PAR UNE SOCIÉTÉ DE PROFESSEURS
ET DE LATINISTES

HORACE

LES ODES ET ÉPODES

EXPLIQUÉES LITTÉRALEMENT
PAR M. SOMMER
TRADUITES EN FRANÇAIS ET ANNOTÉES
PAR M. A. DESPORTES

Tome ~~deuxième~~ 1er

L. HACHETTE ET Cie
LIBRAIRES DE L'UNIVERSITÉ ROYALE DE FRANCE

À PARIS	À ALGER
RUE PIERRE-SARRAZIN, N° 12	RUE DE LA MARINE, N° 11
(Quartier de l'École de Médecine)	(Librairie centrale de la Méditerranée)